"*The Fracture Zone* has a strong narrative voice and presents portraits of people and their land in an effort to understand the ethnic violence."

—*Milwaukee Journal Sentinel*

"His unsentimental descriptions of the area's destroyed mosques, burned houses and virulent graffiti serve as a poignant reminder that the effects of war last long after the planes are gone."

—*Publishers Weekly*

The Balkans in 1977

THE FRACTURE ZONE

A Return to the Balkans

SIMON WINCHESTER

Perennial

An Imprint of HarperCollins*Publishers*

A hardcover version of this book was published in 1999 by Harper-Collins Publishers.

THE FRACTURE ZONE. Copyright © 1999 by Simon Winchester. All rights reserved. Printed in the United States of America. No part of this book may be used or reproduced in any manner whatsoever without written permission except in the case of brief quotations embodied in critical articles and reviews. For information address HarperCollins Publishers Inc., 10 East 53rd Street, New York, NY 10022.

HarperCollins books may be purchased for educational, business, or sales promotional use. For information please write: Special Markets Department, HarperCollins Publishers Inc., 10 East 53rd Street, New York, NY 10022.

First Perennial edition published 2000.

Designed by Elliott Beard

Maps by Paul Pugliese

Library of Congress Cataloging-in-Publication has been applied for.

ISBN 0-06-095494-9

00 01 02 03 04 ❖/RRD 10 9 8 7 6 5 4 3 2 1

In memory of my friend,
Albert Meisel

The Sarajevo Sigmoid, designated on the map as the Kuci Over-thrust, is a conspicuous belt of Mesozoic flysch. It consists of thin Permian and Triassic clastics and neritic carbonates; next, of an uncomformable sequence of limestones that range from the Upper Jurassic to the Turonian, and of transgressive Dur-mitor flysch of the Senonian, whose fold fabric is characteristi-cally intricate. Going northwest, the composition of this belt becomes increasingly complex. . . . The Vardar Zone is the most complicated belt of the Balkan Peninsula. It is composed of several blocks of diverse composition, geological history, and provenance, and includes characteristic oceanic elements.

M. D. Dimitrijevic,
The Geology of Serbia and Adjoining Territories,
Republic Institute for Geological Investigations, Belgrade,
1996

But the really reckless were fetched
By an older colder voice, the oceanic whisper:
"I am the solitude that asks and promises nothing;
That is how I shall set you free. There is no love;
There are only the various envies, all of them sad."

W. H. Auden, *In Praise of Limestone,* 1948

Contents

Author's Note

THE BEWILDERING VARIETY of unfamiliar names that appear in any writing relating to the Balkans seems dramatically to inhibit any average reader's sympathetic understanding of the story. I have tried to help overcome this in three ways—by including as few personal names as possible; by omitting the confusing diacritical marks in the spelling of most of such names as I felt bound to include; and by appending a fairly full glossary of many of the terms—of people, places, concepts, and things—that have helped make the Balkans such a complicated and often confusing place. I must apply the conventional offer to admit responsibility for any errors or misjudgments to this glossary, just as I do to the main body of the story. It is difficult to keep strictly objective any Balkan word list—since it includes, as do most Balkan stories, many monstrous people and their deeds—and I hope I will be forgiven for not having tried to do so.

1

Encounters at a
Water Meadow

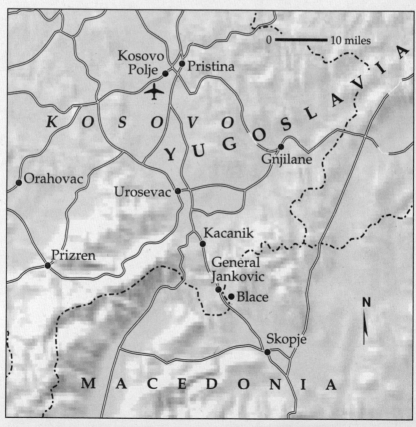

Macedonia and southern Kosovo

S INCE THE BALKAN PENINSULA has for centuries been a place of mystery, paradox, and wild confusion, it may not be too out of place to recall that this narrative properly opens—in the late summer of 1977—at a place that did not then exist, next door to a country that had at the time not been created, and among a people who, though sentient human beings in every accepted sense, had in another then not even been born.

In particular it started beside a water meadow of singular loveliness—all cypresses and lime trees, small olive groves, and cool and lush green grasses—that lies on the left bank of a prettily rushing little stream known as the Lepenec River. The river, which ultimately flows into the Aegean Sea by way of a gulf between the sacred mountains Olympus and Athos, rises in the snows of a small north-south line of hills known as the Sar Range, which themselves are a mosaic part of that formidable swath of geological wreckage—that has helped foster all the long confusion of the Balkans—the high Dinaric Alps.

This one cool alpine meadow, which first caught my eye on a sweltering afternoon in mid-August, lies at the southern end of a deeply incised and, in theory, highly strategic mountain pass, a gateway through the karst massifs of the Sar Range that is referred to by soldiers to this day (in memory of some long-forgotten hero) as the Kacanik Defile. Military maps published until very recently show that the defile and the water meadow at its lower end lie well inside the sprawling southern European entity that was known after 1929 as Yugoslavia. Since when I first went there it lay *within* the country's frontiers, it enjoyed no practical strategic role at all: it was merely a dramatic canyon, a place known only for occasional banditry and for the sighting of bears, wild birds, and at least six varieties of venomous snake.

This is no longer the case. The Lepenec water meadow and the Kacanik Defile into and from which it leads, have lately come to play a crucial and terribly symbolic part in the awful human drama that has once again engulfed the wild and refractory peoples of the Balkans. What makes it especially remarkable, in a strictly personal sense, is what I discovered when I found myself at the meadow during the first of two crucial moments during 1999: that I had been there once before, and when it was in a very different state, in more ways than one.

Twenty-two years earlier I had been en route from Oxford, in my somewhat battered old Volvo, to take up a new job in India. It had seemed to me at the time that, rather than fly to Delhi, it might be more agreeable to drive there. A look at a good map swiftly shows that the Kacanik Defile is far from being on any obvious direct route between Oxford and New Delhi: The fact that on the journey to India I eventually arrived at this particular Balkan meadow was entirely due to the liverish mood of an American friend of mine, an archivist from Washington, D.C., who had telephoned on the eve of my departure to ask if I could possibly give him a ride to Tehran.

Albert Meisel, who has since died, was to become an unwitting agent in this story because of a remark he made as we drove down a motorway in southern England. Up to that point all had been going flawlessly: As soon as I agreed to take him along he had flown across the Atlantic, made a perfectly scheduled rendezvous with us—I was traveling with my then wife and twelve-year-old son—outside the *Guardian* office in London at noon on the appointed day, and we had taken off promptly to catch the three o'clock Calais packet-boat. However, about an hour out of London, as we were speeding southeastward along the M2 in Kent, Albert suddenly glimpsed the towers of Canterbury Cathedral going past in a blur on the left, and asked, in what I thought an unnecessarily querulous tone, why we weren't stopping to have a look?

I replied, with what was probably some asperity, to the effect that I was in no mood for tourism, that I was in a hurry, and that I wanted to catch the ferry and make Mons that night—for the simple reason that I planned to make India well before the middle of September. I knew that the roads in the Punjab would be tricky with postmonsoon mud; I planned to be at the Khyber Pass in three weeks' time. Albert grunted. This was not, he muttered, going to be the pleasure trip he had imagined.

It was much the same the next day in Germany, as we sped past the twin spires of Cologne Cathedral, and then again as a succession of ever prettier Bavarian villages vanished in the rearview mirror. Albert was sulking in the backseat, his mood becoming ever blacker. But I didn't care: I now had the bit between my teeth, and though the car was going well, the roads were said to be treacherous all through Afghanistan and there might well be delays. In my view there was simply no time for standing and staring, not in this early part of the trip.

But the next day, under the emollient persuasions of my wife, I backed down. I apologized for behaving like a tyrant and, once I had looked at the maps, offered a compromise: Instead of barreling down the main trunk highway from Vienna to Belgrade and then on to Sofia—along a series of roads of insufferable tedium, jammed with long-distance trucks and littered with speed traps— I would go to Istanbul along the scenic route.

We would, if all agreed, drive through the Tauern Mountains of western Austria, go through Kitzbühel and Spittal to Villach, and thence to the Carinthian capital of Klagenfurt, reputed home to more ex-Nazis than anywhere else in the Teutonic world.

Here, I would gather later—but not back then—a careful and observant visitor could discern some vague and shrouded outlines of the coming Balkan miseries: The Austrians of Klagenfurt are said to display on occasion a deep distaste for their neighbor Slavs—for the Slovenes to their south are ethnically so—and demanded only a few years ago (in vain, as it happens) that their school system be segregated, since not a few Slav children had been osmotically seeded among them.

But in those days the subtleties of the Balkans were quite beyond me, and all I planned was that we press on and cross the Iron Curtain—for it still existed in 1977, complete with watchtowers and barbed wire, armed guards, and attack dogs, deep in the dark forests of the eastern Tyrol—and spend our first night in the northern Yugoslavian town that was the spiritual capital of the Slovenes, Ljubljana.

After that we would follow the line of the Dinaric Alps, join the Adriatic Highway at Rijeka* and then travel at a leisurely pace down to Diocletian's old retirement city of Split; on to the great fortress of Dubrovnik; turn inland around the spectacularly enchanting Gulf of Kotor up to Montenegro's old hill capital, Cetinje, and its present one, Titograd; before arriving in Skopje and eventually journeying, by way of the Vardar River valley, to a small Slavic border town called Gevgelija; after which, emerging from under the sentries' baleful stares, we would pass into the sun-baked playground (and popularly elected democracy) of Greece. We would thus make the entire one thousand miles from the Austrian frontier to the northern border of Greece within the once great country of Yugoslavia, with neither a frontier to cross nor a dinar to exchange: And what's more, I told Albert, the Dalmatian Coast Highway, as the Yugoslavs then called it and as I preferred to

---

*A city whose history even more markedly hints at the Balkan confusion to come, since it has been variously administered by the Romans, Austrians, Croatians, Venetians, Hungarians, French, British, and Italians, before being incorporated into Yugoslavia, and, since 1991, into the newly independent Croatia. It was also the city where a resident British engineer named Robert Whitehead invented the first torpedo.

think of it, was one of the most remarkably engineered and spectacular roads in the world.

That was the clincher: He agreed in a snap. So I promptly turned the car southeast for Kitzbühel, and after a fortifying break at a café in which mountains of *Schlag* (whipped cream) seemed to have been piled onto almost everything in sight, I set off with as contented a group of passengers as I can ever remember ferrying anywhere.

It took two pleasing Dalmatian days for us to reach Montenegro, after which we passed down from the wild and barren hillsides—the locals like to say that God had shaken out his last bag of rocks at the conclusion of his seven days of world-creating genesis, and where they fell, lo! there stood Montenegro—and onto a low and level plain. It was then that matters suddenly became, as I can still vividly remember from those decades past, rather more sinister, rather more strange.

It was only an aside, really. We had crossed out of Montenegro on a side road, a winding mountain switchback on which there were few other vehicles, and dozens of unanticipated donkey carts loaded with piles of late-summer hay, the early harvests from the higher fields, which swayed precariously down into the villages. Their drivers were invariably men with rather narrow, dark, pinched faces: A few of them, usually the older ones, wore white and smoothly thimble-shaped hats.

We were making first for the old town of Pec, where I had read there was a collection of stupendous Orthodox churches and monasteries, some of them six hundred years old and more, and with frescoes on their walls that dated from the fifteenth century and presented the wild pantheon of saints* and kings and godly

---

*Many of which have their eyes scratched out, and thus look even wilder and more frightening than their medieval artists had intended. The reason, however, is not so much born of sacrilege or desecration:

scenes that make the canons of Orthodoxy seem to the western mind so very strange.

The long and chessboard-flat plain that stretched shimmering for mile after scorching mile ahead, and that looked so very much like the holy flatlands of northern France near Chartres, was, by coincidence, a religious heartland as well. This was what once was called Old Serbia, and crosses were everywhere, and beards were as long and metropolitans as grand and ponderously venerable as in any sacred place. But they were not so numerous as I felt they should have been, and that was the first puzzle.

For it just seemed odd, to a stranger who had read that this plain was the holy heartland of old Orthodox Serbia, that rising from the Pec old town like a forest of needles, there were just so many minarets as well, and that there were these men, scores of them like the peasants hauling the harvests home, who were wearing the white caps of Islam, and whose women scurried beneath the modest concealments of veils and thick scarves. If this was Old Serbia, and if these surrounding wheatfields were as precious to Serbian Orthodoxy as the fields around Canterbury were precious to Anglicanism and those around Chartres to the idea of Catholicism—then why, I wondered, was this particular and holy town so self-evidently Muslim?

It was a question born out of ignorance, and one that would not be asked today—for this part of Old Serbia is Kosovo now, and the fact that so sacred an Orthodox heartland supports a vast majority of men and women for whom Mecca and the *kaaba* are the religious lodestone is one source of all the terrible mayhem to which, in twenty-odd years' time, I would return. I had more than a hint of it that summer's day, however. It came when

---

Many Serbian peasants have long held that the chalky paints used for the eyes of fresco figures are cures for blindness, if administered topically, and with permission of the local abbot.

I was filling the Volvo with gas: The attendant who was topping off the tank was a slow, genial sort of man who spoke a little English and who had asked me a few questions—where I was from, where bound? He spoke Serbian—after a number of days on the road I could recognize some of the basics—and so I remember assuming that he was indeed a Serb.

It was as he was closing the gas cap that we both noticed a group of the same darkish, thin-faced men passing along the road, two or three of the older ones in white skullcaps, the rest with long, light-brown hair. These were the people by whom this part of the world seemed to be largely populated: Though this was Serbia, according to the maps and the history books, the Serbs were clearly outnumbered by these others, these darker Muslims. The gas station owner gestured toward them, then looked at me— and suddenly spat with a twisted smirk of contempt and disdain, which he was not at all shy of demonstrating to me.

"*Albani*," he said, and then, to underline the point for me, "*Albanians!*" He spat again, and without the group being able to see him, shook his fist from behind the car with what to me was astonishingly unrestrained passion. "Absolute bastards! I hate them. Crooks, all of them. Bloody bastard *Albani!*" His venom was extraordinary, I thought—too impassioned for a languorous summer day of hay wains and the creak of wooden cartwheels and sunflowers nodding in the heat. I paid and hurried away. I never asked him to explain, and for many years, whenever I looked back at this incident that lingered powerfully in my mind, I imagined merely that the hatred was reflective of some private problem suffered by this man alone. Perhaps the men had stolen money from him or seduced his daughter. That's what it must have been: a private feud.

It was many years before I came to understand that this view— "*Albanians*—all bastards! I hate them"—was in fact the collective view of many tens of thousands of the Serbs who lived on these wide plains. I worked for the *Guardian* in those days, and I recall reading, sometime in the late eighties, reports of impassioned speeches being made in towns in this region called Kosovo, to which I reacted with interest, because I had once been there. The speeches seemed to be inflaming local tensions between such men as this, and such as those others who walked beside my car that afternoon, and whose mutual loathings had evidently been festering and fermenting for many years.

Later than evening we passed, almost unknowingly, through a town called Kosovo Polje, and drove by a bare expanse called Gazimestan. This was a place that became recognizable in the newspaper reports of a decade or so later—the infamous place where on June 28, 1989, in commemoration of a battle that had been fought (and lost) there against the Turks six hundred years before, a little-known Serbian leader named Slobodan Milosevic flew down from Belgrade to address a rally of more than a million of his Serbian brothers and sisters in which he warned of—indeed, say many historians, instigated—the violence that was then simmering and that would very soon erupt across the Balkans. His most inflammatory comment was this: "Six centuries later again we are in battles and quarrels. They are not armed battles, *though such things should not be excluded yet* [emphasis added]." I have always thought for so historically significant a piece of rhetoric, this was rather poor, banal in the extreme. Milosevic, a puffy-faced man who had hitherto been head of the national gas company, was clearly no Lincoln, no Churchill. Perhaps, to be charitable, it was simply the translation. And anyway, it clearly got results.

But no, I remember little of passing through Kosovo Polje, or the battlefield of Gazimestan, except for the name; and I remember almost nothing of the drearily utilitarian city of Pristina we came to a few miles farther on, other than it being a place of cinderblock apartments and shabby shacks and smoky factories, to which I imagined I would never return—but to which in fact I was fated to come back, more than twenty years later in very different, very much more dramatic circumstances.

I may not remember much of the place they called the Field of the Blackbirds, nor of Pristina town, nor of the four of us swinging south in the car once more onto the fast and wide road that had a European highway designation: E-65. But I do remember noticing that the these great plains were barred to the south and the west by ranges of impressive limestone mountains that shimmered blue in the afternoon heat; I do remember climbing into the southern range and passing through a spectacular gorge. I remember dark and smoky tunnels, lit only by a few fly-specked bulbs.

There was a railway track to the right, and small steam trains would chuff happily along the valley, letting off villagers at country stops that smelled of creosote and roses. Beside the tracks, kept in check by its steep banks, was the Lepenec River. It was all so very pretty—which made more shocking the sudden appearance, once we rounded a bend as we were coming out of the canyon, of a grim-looking factory, all chimneys and gushing yellow smoke. The road signs declared this to be the settlement—there was a scattering of small red-roofed houses for the workers—of General Jankovic, and I remember thinking that he could have done precious little of note in battle if he had only this obscure and smoky cement factory named for him.

I remember all that, and, most of all, I remember the water meadow that I saw quite suddenly appear in front of me, spread out invitingly, an obvious place to stop, to rest, to take in the view. This, I thought as I slowed the car, was a magnificent place.

It was quite silent, except for the soughing of the wind through the cypress trees. The grass was tall and waved invitingly in the eddies of breeze. The stream chuckled and bubbled southward, and large brown hawks whirled in the thermals above us. I spread the map out on the ground to check just where we were: I identified the river as the Lepenec, and the hills behind us on the west as the Sar Range, and the much grander mountain

chain off to the southwest—very high peaks indeed, some of
them still capped with tired and dirty-looking snow—seemed to
be the Rudoka Mountains, behind which lurked what was then
Enver Hoxha's wildly xenophobic and aberrantly Maoist state of
Albania.

When planning this trip I had very much wanted to get permission to go there: After all, I said in my letter to the nearest
embassy, it seemed that Albania's internal situation was already
changing, and there had been some softening of the Maoist line
in Tirana that very year. (The Chinese, themselves changing at the
time, and becoming more friendly with the West, were growing
exasperated with their small cheerleading section in the Balkans,
and were dropping them from their dance card. The warped
ideals of "revolutionary self-sufficiency," which the Albanians
seemed to have copied directly from Kim Il Sung's monstrous
Juche—his insanely xenophobic plan for socialist self-sufficiency—
in North Korea, were now being tried out on the Albanian
masses.)

My plea went unheard, or at least unanswered, and so the
most I could hope for was the vicarious thrill of knowing that
these hills formed the frontier, and that there must be impene-
trable fences and guard dogs lining the summits. Besides, there
were Albanians here in Old Serbia, and I could tell something
of what the people were like—if indeed they were at all similar
to those in the home country. I supposed only that the Kosovo
Albanians were different in one respect—that they at least had
the comforts of Islam: Behind those distant ranges were only
the exactions of Enver Hoxha and his unvarying strangeness. I
was not to learn for many years that the Kosovo Albanians had
exactions of their own, every bit as trying.

That day, as I scanned the horizons, it seemed that Albania was
the only foreign state in evidence: Ahead, for another two hundred miles or more, ran the vastness of Yugoslavia. Only the scattering of softly gnarled old olive trees gave a clue to the fact that

Greece lay beyond and far away. There was no marking here, no fence, no line on the road, no customs post or police checkpoint, to suggest that this mountain pass and the meadow at its end owed their significance to anything more than their being so pretty a place. We stayed for half an hour or so: I seem to recall we got out a tartan blanket and had our lunch beside the river. But my son tells me I was mistaken, and says he doesn't remember the field at all.

We pressed on: That night we spent in the southern Yugoslavian town of Skopje, and we crossed the old Turkish bridge and watched the old men smoking pensively as they gazed down into the river. We saw the ruins from the earthquake that had ruined the city in 1963. We drank sweet coffee and ate kebabs. And then we took off, emerging from behind the Iron Curtain, and headed for Thessaloníki and Alexandropolis, then for Istanbul and, by ferry in those days (the two huge suspension bridges had not then been built), we lurched across the Bosporus into Asia. After another two weeks, by way of Tabriz and Tehran, Herat and Kandahar, and the Khyber and Peshawar and the frontier at Wagah, we were in India. The troubles in India were wild and manifest, too, and for years the Balkans faded into our collective memories. No one ever said: "Remember the man who filled up the car in Pec?" or, "Remember the field by that cement factory called General Jankovic?"—because the Balkans were peaceful in those times, and we had no compelling reason to think of them.

But twenty-two years later I was to come back quite unexpectedly, and under decidedly different circumstances. Whatever vague suggestions of misery and hatred may have remained as wisps of memory from that first journey were impossibly and unimaginably compounded on the second—and never more so than when I saw that water meadow again, with a gasp of realization. It was all so terribly different a situation, the worst one could imagine, when I rounded a curve in a road and said to my companions, "My God! I've been here once before!"

It was late March 1999, and I had just been on a peculiar journey in Ireland. I had been summoned back from the United States by lawyers for the Bloody Sunday Inquiry, which had been reopened by the British government in tacit recognition that there had been shortcomings in the earlier investigation into killings by soldiers of the British army's Parachute Regiment on the streets of Londonderry in 1971. It was when I was leaving that one of lawyers with whom I walked through the Bogside on that showery spring afternoon made one of those isn't-it-a-small-world remarks, whose significance I wouldn't appreciate for a few more days: Did I realize, he asked, that the young captain who at the time of the tragedy been the adjutant of the First Battalion—and who would be, as would I, a witness at the public inquiry—was now a lieutenant general, and was in command of the NATO rapid-reaction force then waiting on the borders of Kosovo? (The Rambouillet Peace Conference on Kosovo had just ended; Milosevic and his Belgrade government had just rejected its proposals, and talk of war was in the air.) Mike Jackson, he said. Sir Michael Jackson, in fact.

I said yes, I had known Mike all those years ago: We always used to joke about his name—not least since he, unlike the pretty singer, had a most spectacularly craggy and weatherbeaten face and was in no imaginable way like his peculiar namesake. What a shame, I said; what a pity that I had no plans to go to Kosovo, and that I was going home to New York in a day or so. It would have been good to see him again.

I should have known better. The life of a foreign correspondent can be a confusion of caprices, and three days later I found myself in Mike Jackson's helicopter, scudding through the unlit nighttime skies of Macedonia a mile south of the Kosovo border.

A newspaper editor had found me in Ireland, and had wondered, in that polite and oh-so-British way, whether instead of rushing back to America, I might like to pop over to Macedonia, as he put it, just for a day or so. The NATO High Command had

just given the unprecedented order to begin bombing Slobodan
Milosevic into submission, and the warplanes had begun to attack
Belgrade. There were reports that, in part as a consequence of the
bombing, and of the Kosovo Serbs' reaction to it, uncontrollable
numbers of refugees were beginning to flood out of the province,
and in particular into Macedonia, a country I wasn't too sure even
existed. Might I like to go down, take a look, and write a piece for
the Sunday paper?

The editor was persuasive, though in truth he didn't have to
be: This was by all accounts a tremendous story, a tragedy of historic dimensions that even without a commission I would have
given my eyeteeth to see. I called a fast motorcycle taxi service*
and zoomed over to Heathrow: Six hours later (I had to fly by
way of Thessaloníki, take a taxi to the Macedonian frontier,† and
then—having penetrated the fastness of what still had a slight if
rather rusted feel of Iron Curtain about it—another taxi farther
north) I was promptly in the Macedonian capital of Skopje, and
an hour later still had telephoned Mike Jackson to ask if he
might remember me from all those years ago in Ireland. Evidently he hadn't forgotten, but he was in no-nonsense mood.
"Those bloody lawyers been onto you, too?" was the first thing
he said. "Come and have a whiskey—and then let's go for a ride."

His pilots were wearing night-vision goggles, and we were

---

*They pick you up on a motorcycle, seat you on the back, pile on your
luggage, and zoom off—scary but immense fun, if it's not snowing.

†Where by chance I ran into Jørgen Grunnet, a Dane who was now a
member of an international monitoring group that had just been
forced out of Kosovo, but with whom, when he worked for the newspaper Politiken, I had shared an office in Washington in 1972. We
hadn't seen each other for nearly thirty years: to run into him on a
remote frontier-crossing in the southern Balkans seemed yet another
example of the wayward capriciousness of this peculiar job.

talked down by ground controllers using tiny infrared needle lanterns called Fireflies. We settled down in the pitch dark of a parking lot behind a warehouse. A posse of sentries with machine guns and wearing Kevlar helmets rushed us across to a tent where, under the low glow of red lights, a clutch of colonels and majors were poring over a sheaf of large-scale maps. Whatever was going on, there was a crackling tension in the air, the feeling that something dire was happening, or was about to.

The business in the tents turned out to be—or seemed at first to be—quite unremarkably mundane. It was about chickens. How many, one colonel asked, were available? How quickly, interrupted the general, could they be brought here, to this very parking lot, a mile from the Kosovo border, to a village that, if it appeared on maps at all, was called Blace? Were the chickens whole or in parts? Were they boned or otherwise? Frozen or fresh? Were any of them *halal*?

It was that last question—an inquiry by a British army officer as to whether any of a supply of chickens had been prepared according to the rites of Islam, with the hapless birds' heads turned at least in the general direction of Mecca as the slaughtering blades bore down—that made me realize: This was a planning meeting to get food to the refugees. Refugees who, if they were the expected Albanians from Kosovo, were of course almost certainly by and large Muslim. I now remembered from twenty years ago the men in their thimble hats, the women in veils, and the minarets, the minarets. Now that I was clear about the soldiers' business I broke into the conversation: Were there that many refugees? Was it that bad a crisis?

The officers, Mike Jackson included, looked across at me silently, their leathery faces weary, grim, and set. Then the general spoke. "You've never seen anything like it, old man," he said quietly. "You get up to the border at first light. You'll never forget what you see. I guarantee it."

*   *   *

I heard them first—a huge collective murmur that rolled from somewhere up close ahead. The road from Skopje ran north along a shallow river valley, and the driver remarked that the low green hills being limned by early sunlight on my left were in Yugoslav territory, and the dark-uniformed men we could see patrolling them were MUPs, Serbs, Yugoslav Special Police, and were to be avoided at all costs. But however unpleasant the prospect of ever encountering such men—and I wasn't to know then how close I would come to them in so short a while—it was the noise that most astonished me: a deep and muffled roaring that, as we came closer to its source, separated into comprehensible constituent parts.

There were cries, some of anger, some of pain, some of utter misery. There was conversation, some urgent, some idle, some peppered with argument, with disagreement and shouting. There were barked orders, dismissive responses. There was sobbing, and wailing, and the hum of prayer, and as alto continuo, the electric wailings of thousands of unfed, unwashed children. All this vast and terrifying sound was clear from a hundred yards away, while budding trees and yellow gorse thickets and ridges of limestone kept me from seeing whoever, whatever, was making it. And then the road climbed a few more feet, the gorse thinned out, and in an instant the extent of this terrible business was at last in sight.

There was a wide field, the size of a large county cricket ground or a baseball field, lined with trees and hemmed in by a river and a railway track on the far side, and this road on its levee on the other. And on the field, cramming every square inch of its muddy grass, was what looked at first like a surreal infestation of insects, like a plague of giant locusts, a shifting, pulsating, ululating mass of the most pathetic European people I think I had ever seen.

I stood and watched, transfixed, for an hour or more, shivering in the early morning cold—though not shivering half so much as these people, who had had no benefit of sleep or warmth or food to prepare them. Macedonian police, ugly men in dark blue uniforms and with guns, reinforced after a while with Special Forces teams, their men in helmets and with clubs and gas guns, ringed the ragged edges of the mob. They were there to keep the Albanians from reaching the road and making their way down into the city. They didn't seem to mind too much when I went down into the sea of liquid mud and worse, to see firsthand some definable figures from this Bosch-like scene of mass misery.

A score of small and wretched European tragedies could be seen with any glance.

There was a young man, nineteen or so, I'd guess, clearly from his face quite mentally ill, gibbering, drooling, and he was being led by two ragged friends down a muddy slope toward a communal bucket of drinking water. He had no shoes or socks, and his feet were bleeding from the long walk of the night, and yet now his friends had mistakenly led him over a patch of wire-hard brambles, and he was crying, shrieking with the pain of the needles in his soles.

More horribly still, there was a woman, newly miscarried, who was sitting, weeping in a mess of blood, the remains of a dead infant in her arms. Other women, villagers, friends, relations—I'll never know—were trying to drag the stillborn bundle away, but she whimpered wildly, as if she was wanting to cling to one part of herself, one small token of security that she insanely believed in, through a fog, when everything else around her seemed to be going mad.

Then, the image that has remained most firmly in my mind, there was the old man, wizened, hunched, arthritic, who was being wheeled by a younger man, his son, probably, along the railway track. Each time the flat and worn iron wheel of the barrow hit a tie, so the man's insensate form was jolted, hard, and his legs and arms flailed wildly, like those of a flung corpse. But still, stubbornly, he kept his toothless jaw clenched tight, bracing his head for the next bump, the next crash, the next assault on his dignity and peace—and, no doubt, to ensure that he did not once cry out. All through it he remained mute, cringing against each battering, like a silent torture victim. He must have suffered so for hours, as his boy brought him down from Kosovo along the railway, though in a manner meant for the dead, and in a conveyance meant for dirt.

There were beautiful faces in the crowd as well. There were handsome men, it is true; but I was more drawn to some of the Albanian women, whose images might have been taken from a canvas by Modigliani or Botticelli—long intelligent faces, high cheekbones, olive skin, aquiline noses, bright eyes. I looked over the shoulder of a photographer who was sitting on the hillside and transmitting pictures—this being 1999 he had a digital camera, a small computer, a cellular telephone (there was no truck with film or developing tanks, and no wire connections)—to London. He showed me one picture of a young woman of staggering beauty, her arms around her two small fair-haired boys. Her eyes were bright and shining, despite the long night, and the longer march from whatever village had been chosen for what the Serbs had called the *cis cenje terena*—the cleansing, the ridding of the vermin, like this young family, that contaminated hallowed ground. It all seemed so monstrously wrong: that this young woman, who in other circumstances could have been a poster child for motherhood and goodness and sheer human loveliness, should in these strange and feral Balkan circumstances have been forced from her home at gunpoint, made to walk through nights and days of terror, and end up here hopeless and homeless and friendless, in an alien land, on this forlorn and infamous Golgotha, this field of bones—a place where already a dozen people, including the bloodied stillborn child I had seen, had died in the hours since it had first been settled.

I feel no shame in confessing that it was as much as anything the evident Europeanness of the thousands on this field that struck me first: for while I have in a life of wandering just like this seen many thousands of refugees and displaced and dispossessed unfortunates in Africa and Cambodia and Bengal and Java and elsewhere, and have felt properly sorry and ashamed that such calamities should befall them, my instincts on that April day at Blace Camp were very much those of a European man, looking at men and women and children who could very well, from the simple fact of their appearance, be cousins or friends or acquaintances, in a way that no one in the refugee fields in Bengal or the Congo could ever really have been.

And so my visceral reaction was simply that: That this was *Europe*, this was *now*, and here we were at the close of the most civilizing century we have known, and yet here before us was the diabolical, grotesque, bizarre sight of tens upon tens of thousands of terrified, dog-weary, ragged *European* people who were just like us, and who just a few short days before had been living out their lives more or less like us, yet who were now crammed insect-thick onto a carpet of squelching mud and litter and ordure and broken glass and dirt, while we climbed down from the kind of car in which they might have driven, after a breakfast of the kind that was customary for them to have as well, and watched and gaped and gawked down at them in uncomprehending horror and thought only, My God! This is too much. This is quite beyond belief.

Except I had one additional moment of revelation: My God! I've been here once before.

I recognized it in an instant, just at the moment when I strolled up to the Macedonian frontier post and was shooed away by policemen who were busy dealing with the endless streams still pouring past them. I had joined the incoming flood for a second or two, walking back southward, back along the way I had come, trying to make sympathetic conversation with the newcomers in the column—when suddenly, looking over at the hills where we had seen the MUP militiamen at dawn, I realized that I was on familiar ground.

There was a stream over on the right, surely. There were high and snow-lined Albanian hills ahead, surely. There should be, on the right, a water meadow of singular loveliness. And then it dawned on me: that field of wildflowers and bending grasses that had seemed so idyllic a stopping place all those years ago was the very one that was now filled with mud and dirt and misery, and peopled with this sorry infestation. My "field of dreams" was here, right here—but it had become, in twenty years, a charnel house.

And then again—why so? True, there were dreadful crimes being committed back up along the road, and there were NATO bombs dropping, and in response, even more dreadful crimes being committed. This is what the refugees were saying—telling us about slaughter and rape and burning and terror. But that didn't answer the more basic question that pushed its way into my mind, and that related to my having stood on this field before, and that was not Why this? nor Why now? but more specifically— Why here? What had changed at this water meadow that had turned it, in twenty years, into the charnel house it had become?

There was, so far as I could see, just one simple difference, one act of change that had occurred in the years since I had first been here—and it struck me in an instant that this, in simple truth, was the primary reason for what was happening here: There was, a few yards behind me now, *a border.*

Here, in the middle of what was once Yugoslavia, and through which in 1977 we had journeyed from the border of Austria to that of Greece without a single question being asked or a single fee being charged or a single policemen stepping onto the road to make demands, stood a border. Or, to be precise, two borders— the one to the north being that of the Kosovo Province of the Republic of Yugoslavia, Savezna Republika Jugoslavija, and the one to the south, where I was standing, that of a new country, since 1992 independent of its former Yugoslavian motherland, the Republika Makedonija, the Republic of Macedonia.

As was usual in border crossings between mutually hostile or less-than-friendly states, the two border stations were out of sight of each other, the flags of one being invisible to the citizenry of the other, and vice versa. Between them, through which the demarcation line was drawn, and where the white pillars that marked the frontier stood, was a no-man's land, a place of razor wire and minefields and the threatening arcs of fire from competing gun towers. This frontier, between Blace in Macedonia and Kosovo's General Jankovic—I remembered the name, and could even see from here the great man's cement factory, all now seemingly wrecked—was, without a doubt, a true, old-fashioned international frontier. It had border guards. Security police. Customs officials. Flags. Sentry towers. Searchlights. Pools of disinfectant, so that no bacillus might pass from one territory to another. Red-and-white striped poles, six inches thick and fashioned from heavy-gauge iron pipe that not even a speeding truck could breach, and which proclaimed STOP FOR INSPECTION, INTERROGATION, THE ISSUANCE OF VISA, AND PAYMENT OF ALL FEES REQUIRED and only then, PERMISSION.

A border had been made. Politicians and diplomats far away had waved their wands and had sent their surveyors and their cartographers and their global positioning devices and had created here a new frontier. (Though perhaps not too new: Many of what we think of as the new frontiers of the Balkans are only contemporary renderings of very ancient borderlines, and this, the line between Old Serbia and Macedonia, is probably, approximately, one of them.) The region had—in the purest and most classic sense of the word: "to divide a region into a number of smaller and often mutually hostile units, as was done in the Balkan Peninsula in the late 19th and early 20th centuries" (according to the *OED*'s unimpeachable authority)—been *Balkanized*. And what has happened across almost all of the world's more recently created borders—across, for examples, those frontiers thrown between the two Germanys, or the two Koreas, or the Congo and Zaire, or Namibia and in the Sahara Desert—had happened here as well.

This pathetically short and seemingly so unimportant a frontier
had suddenly, and predictably, become a fulcrum across which, in
due course, the human spirit—here of Balkan people, as had happened also to Africans and Koreans and Germans—was being savagely broken. Maybe, given the desperate history of this place,
worse would before long happen here: Maybe, as has happened
all too often before elsewhere, fights would break out across the
line, wars would be declared.

But at this moment it was simply the border as the breaker of
the human spirit that seemed most in evidence: Tens of thousands of innocent, modern European people had been driven
from the state to the north, had fled across this hitherto invisible, politically dictated line on the ground, had poured over it
past its guards and under its watchtowers, and had then collapsed, weary and wrecked, into the unfriendly and unwelcom-
ing collective arms of the state to the south, their spirits broken,
their hopes dashed from them, their dignity crushed. Why, the
question seemed so pertinent, why create borders anymore?

After all, across the rest of Europe, in the North and South and
even in much of the once Marxist East, there were everywhere the
signs that life was about becoming so very much less complicated.
Frontiers were coming down all over Europe. The passport
seemed every day less essential. The cry of "Papers!" or of "Documents, please!" became less and less frequently heard. The bor-
derless world seemed a concept well on its way to being born, and
at least in Europe itself, there was also the probability, almost a
reality now, of that elegant device to be known as the single currency.

But here in the Balkans, while elsewhere frontiers were coming
down and currencies were becoming melded and melted down
into one another, the very opposite was happening. Starting in
early summer of 1991, no less than three thousand miles of brand-
new European frontiers, *de jure* and *de facto*, had actually been
drawn, surveyed, and created. By the end of 1992 there were

whole new nation-states—Slovenia, Croatia, Bosnia, and Macedonia*—and in due course, one must imagine, there may be more: The new nations of Montenegro and possibly Kosovo may one day be created, too. New moneys were being minted as well—the brand-new central banks housed within the brand-new frontiers (one of them, in Bosnia, being run by a New Zealander) saw to it that four entirely brand-new currencies (the Croats' version named after a small and fur-covered rodent, the *kuna*) were actually spawned.

It had all been so much more stable and content—or at least had seemed so—when I was first here: When this narrative began I was at a place that did not exist, next to a country which had not then been created, among a people who, in the sense of being people with the national identity to which they now belong, had not been born. And, at least superficially, it seemed to have worked: There was a certain prosperity, a certain satisfaction among the peoples of the Yugoslavia that had been hammered together earlier in the century. But now it had all changed, and the changes that had been brought about in just the last ten years seemed to have brought nothing but woe and misery and confusion. It had brought the specter of the old Balkans back among us, to terrify those who live there and threaten those who live beyond. It seemed the most wretched of situations, even though the doomsayers and Cassandras had long said, as they do with everything connected to the Balkans, that it was bound to be so.

But once again there arose the question that seemed so eternally asked and so perpetually appropriate here: Just why? Just why is there, and seemingly always has been, this dire inevitabil-

---

*A name that the Greeks, believing they have a prior claim, still do not permit themselves to utter. "Is not Makedonia," spat my taxi driver. "Is FYROM." The latter, an acronym, stands for the Former Yugoslav Republic of M., and seems acceptable to all, except linguists.

ity about the Balkans being so fractious and unsettled a corner of the world? Just what was it that had marked out this particular peninsula, this particular gyre of mountains and plains, caves and streams, and had made it a byword, quite literally, for hostility and hate?

It was now well on in this early spring day, and it was getting dark, and some of the refugees had by now cut six-foot birch branches and stuck them in the mud, and had strung up flimsy sheets of black plastic from old garbage bags to act as windbreaks. A few of the more resourceful families now had little wood fires flickering and guttering in the chilly air, and occasionally there were blackened cooking pots sitting precariously on the logs, hissing with warming water. Here and there rusty tractors were being driven down into the morass by local Macedonian farmers, hauling a group of French aid workers who were standing on carts and tossing all they had into the crowds— small hands of green bananas, black plastic bags, bottles of Evian water—creating fierce tornadoes of stampeding, clawing, snatching, punching, spitting people. I tramped back to the car, through a shower of bitterly cold needles of rain, wondering how the refugees, in what would turn rapidly into a freezing swampy field, would be putting up with the weather that night. The border guards had said there were thirty thousand there already, and another thousand coming in every hour. How would they put up with it? How would they cope?

Mike Jackson, who had rightly promised that I would never forget what I would see at Blace, had been angry the night before, on the juddering helicopter flight back to his forward base camp at Skopje. He had been outwardly angry, mainly because the international relief agencies—not the aid workers, but their agency bosses back in the comfort of their head offices—and who were supposed to have anticipated this flood of humankind, had not done so. In consequence the world had been caught unawares by the exodus, had been unprepared for the extent and enormity of the crime that some could have foreseen would be perpetrated against these Albanians. The UN, in particular, had been caught wrong-footed, impotent, unable to bring more than a few bananas and garbage bags to the hundreds of thousands—here and elsewhere; there were massive outpourings of terrified and hungry people elsewhere in Macedonia too, as well as at the crossing points into Albania and Montenegro—who were relying on the organization for help. General Jackson was angry too that his troops were having to fill the gap, were having to deal with such mundane matters as chickens and rice, and whether they were *halal* or not, when the real business of his force, which was grandly titled NATO's Allied Rapid Reaction Corps, was fighting.

"I'm a NATO general, and I'm up here flying in the dark, in secrecy, well within the range of Yugoslav artillery, just to organize *meals* for these people," he had kept saying. "That's surely not why I'm paid to be here."

But he had been more angry still that the refugees should be here in the first place, and that made for a deeper and darker and bleaker mood. As we had stepped off the helicopter—and this was the night before I had seen the water meadow at Blace—he had muttered something about how dreadful it all was, but that he had it in his power to help. "They'll go back home, these people," he said. "They'll get their houses back, if I have anything to do with it. And we'll find the people who drove them out. A few weeks of bombing, believe me—that's all. A few weeks and the Serbs will cave in. Then we'll be taking these refugees back. By God, I hope so!"

On my way out I made a small bet with one of his staff officers as to just how long it might be before Belgrade caved in, before the refugees were in fact permitted to go home. Eighty days, someone said. It was a figure that stuck in my mind. This war, one of General Jackson's senior planners had predicted, would go on for just eighty days. It would only be an air war: No soldiers would be fighting on the ground—the Americans in particular had no stomach for the notion of losing their boys in a battle here. But the persuasive might of the combined allied air forces would be enough, the officer said. Eighty days—he was just about sure of it.

Which meant that if matters went according to plan I could be back here in Blace, standing beside the water meadow for the third time. This time, however, I would be with a force of men and machines heading north, and behind us would come the refugees again, but this time going home.

Might it work? Could it take so short a time? The officer was confident. "Trust me," he said. "These bombers are damn good."

With his words ringing in my ears I then hatched a modest plan. It came about as I was on my own ride back to Skopje through the rain the next evening, after I had seen the horror of the refugee field, and was concluding that of course I shared the general's hopes that all the homeless would be home again—but at the same time wondered whether there was much long-term wisdom and merit in the simple fact of taking all these people home and then employing international troops to guard them, for how long?—months, years, decades, maybe?—in the hope that they and the Serbs who had done all this to them might come to tolerate each another once again.

And then, as that thought duly flared and waxed and waned, so came its successor, the thought that invariably dogs anyone who is foolish enough to become interested, fascinated, or eventually obsessed with the quagmire of the Balkans. I wondered further, as the car bumped through the outskirts of the old Turkish town, the castle walls glowing warmly through the drizzle, just what it might be that was, deep down, leading these unfortunates, and all their brothers and sisters over time, to be in such a terrible situation in the first place? What forces were really at work here? I didn't mean by that the obvious ones—the forces of today's Serbian brutes with their rifles and bayonets, their cudgels and their knuckle-dusters. Nor even the equally harsh forces of their official opposition, the UCK, the Kosovo Liberation Army, the men in dark uniforms who, fighting for the idea of a Greater Albania, had already committed crimes as vile, but against the Serbs.

I meant—or thought I meant—what basal forces, what innate characteristics, what elements of competing Balkan histories and cultures and ethnicities could ever have led to such a situation as this?

For there was nothing new in this. All that had changed since the last time the Balkans erupted in horror, back in the 1940s, was that these new events were taking place under the lights of television cameras, so that all the carnage and coercion and terror and torture were being brought directly into our living rooms, live, with the newly consequent power both to shock and stun us, and yet to bore and weary and anesthetize us too. What was actually happening here at Blace's swamp camp, and all the tales we were hearing from the refugees of what had been happening up in Kosovo, were merely—as if the word *merely* could really be used in so awful a context—more manifestations of what had been going on in the Balkans for a thousand years or more. They were further excrescences of that bloodcurdling intercourse between Serbs and Croats and Bosnians and Slovenes and Macedonians and Hungarians and Rumanians and Montenegrins and Albanians and Bulgarians and Greeks and Turks and Vlachs, and who had been acting either because of pressure from great powers, or grand alliances, and who had been doing so under the various orders of, or at the behest of, or led by an endless array of sultans and emperors, grand viziers and archdukes, metropolitans and pashas, janissaries and dragomans, and whole hosts of lesser mortals whose battery of names suggests something of the bewilderment of the places where they ruled.

There were among them, to name just a very few, hosts of competing and conflicting grandees of churches and districts and parties, with titles like *aga, ajan, ban, beg* or *bey, beylerbeyi, emir, gazi, gost, imam, kapetan, kadi, khan, mameluke, mullah, pan-dur, sancàk-beg, starc, strojnik, vojnuk, voivode,* and *zupan;* or less grand but invariably more violent villains who were organized into terror bands like the White Eagles or the Black Legions, the wartime Ustashi and Chetniks, and today's Tigers. These groups were led by men like the dreaded but outwardly genial Arkan, a Serb named Zeljko Raznatovic, who once reputedly ordered all the men of one family to bite and gnaw the testicles off one another, or his compatriot and similarly steely zealot Vojislav Seselj, a Serb paramilitary who boasted publicly of scooping out the eyeballs of his Croatian captives using only a rusty shoehorn.

And in thinking about all this I suddenly realized that I, like a score of wanderers and wonderers before me, had all of a sudden become fascinated—enraptured even—by the savage mysteries of this wretched peninsula. I had no standing in these parts at all; from centuries back, I realized as I scanned the bibliographies of the books I had, clever men and women had come to these parts in an effort to learn. And now, driven by the same strange compulsion that had brought them here before, I very much wanted as well to try and learn a little more, to see a little more, to begin to understand a little more.

After all, I was here. I had some time on my hands. I had enough to survive on for a few weeks. And this war, by all accounts, would end in eighty days. Might I not stay in the Balkans for some or all of this time, looking the place over, looking at a place that was being convulsed by a war that I could hear as distant thunder all the while but in which I could not play a part?

It seemed a beguiling idea. It was now the beginning of April. If all went as the planners believed—and I had this curious faith that it well might—then the engagement between the West and Belgrade ought to be over, and some definable event—the retaking of Kosovo by the western forces, for example—should have taken place by the middle of June. So why not stay, and contrive some way to understand something of the context behind all that was happening?

Why not use the time, I then said to myself, to make a journey, to visit as much of the Balkans as it was possible to see, in the hope of completing a mosaic picture of the complexities of the place, one out of which might emerge something that, however blurred and fuzzy it might at first appear, did paint an approximate portrait that gave, at least to me, a context to what was happening in Kosovo?

I decided there and then. I telephoned a friend of mine, a clever and congenial traveling companion, and splendid linguist, called Rose. I had met her five years before, in an Internet discussion group about Ireland. She had been a modern linguist at Oxford—her degree was one of those very rare Congratulatory Firsts, in which the papers she wrote were so brilliant that the dons assembling for the *viva voce* part of the final examination stood up and applauded her work and asked not a single further question. When we met she was a graduate student at the University of Pennsylvania in Philadelphia, then went on to work at *The Nation* in New York City, and finally became the senior writer at *Colors*, the original and highly inventive Venice-based magazine. Six months before I telephoned she had embarked on the risky adventure of being a full-time freelance writer: When I tracked her down she was in Rajasthan.

She agreed readily, scenting a fascinating plan, as I knew she would. I told her that my approximate idea was to make a scimitar-shaped journey between Vienna and Istanbul,* the two cities whose competing empires had done so much to create the frictions and complications of the regions between. I hoped very

---

*A city whose vast lexicon of names also hints at the bewilderments of its history: *Constantinople* is well known, of course, as is *Byzantium*; and readers of Graham Greene and Agatha Christie will recognize the

much, I said, that we would reach the town from where I was tele-
phoning, Skopje, in time to see the ending of the war that I had
already seen begun.

So might we meet, in a week's time, say, in Vienna, at Frau
Demel's fussy and mirrored old *Konditorei*, behind the Hofburg? I
needed to go to Vienna first, I added, because there was the possibility that I might win permission there to see one appropriately
gruesome symbol of the landscape that lay beyond. I wanted to go
to Vienna to see something that had not been seen publicly for a
quarter of a century, and that had more than a little relevance to
what was going on in the Balkans—the severed head of a long-
dead Turk.

---

names *Stamboul, Estamboul,* and *Czarigrad.* But there are also refer-
ences aplenty to the city as *Kushta, Gosdantnubolis, Rumiyya-al-Kubra,
New Rome, New Jerusalem,* and the *City of Pilgrimage,* as well as, more simply, *Polis,* or just plainly the *City.* More than anything, Istanbul is a city
of a dynasty, and that Ottoman dynasty was to do much, both for good
and evil, to shape the destiny of the vast and complex mountain lands
that lay between the Golden Horn and the faraway city that so very
nearly fell into the sultan's hands, Vienna.

2

A Meeting
with a Turkish Gentleman

The Siege of Vienna, 1683

H APPY IS THE COUNTRY, wrote George Bernard Shaw, that has no history." And, by extension, unhappy are the Balkans, that have too much of it. To comprehend just *why* so much unhappiness, to begin any sort of understanding of the travails of this benighted place, one needs to do more than simply make a journey through its geography: It is essential also to make some kind of foray into its daunting chronology. And given that the story of the Balkans is, in essence, the story of the ebbing and flowing of the two great empires, Hapsburg and Ottoman, that vied for sovereignty over the lands between them, so it seemed to me at the start of this journey that our tour of Balkan history, as well as our venture into the Balkan landscape, should most properly begin in the Hapsburg's once-great capital city, Vienna.

So we began in the old coffeehouse in the Kohlmarkt (the city's onetime cauliflower market), with a *Kaffee brauner* and a bright pink box of those silky-smooth chocolates known by the vaguely macabre—but when you see them oh-so-apposite—name of *Katzenzungen* or *langues du chat* (cats' tongues). The scene could hardly have been more comfortably Viennese: The bustlingly starched waitresses were dealing with flotillas of sturdy, haughty, and obviously respectable matrons (most from Vienna, though some no doubt from Nebraska or New York). If I looked carefully I could see them glancing surreptitiously at themselves in the rococo-gilded mirrors, adjusting their hats, patting the buttons on their tightish brown tweed jackets to make sure that there was room for the anticipated mountain of whipped cream that would be served with the *Kaffee mélange*, or perhaps, if it was not too indecently early, for the iced *mazagran*, the coffee with its gill-and-a-half of cherry liqueur, and the ever-so-tiny slice of Demel's infamously good *Nusstorte*.

Coffee seemed the appropriate metaphor with which to start. The first coffeehouse had opened in Vienna in 1685, two years after the Ottoman armies had failed in their attempt to capture and sack the city. It has long been an element of Viennese folklore that among the extraordinary bounties left behind by the fleeing armies,* there were sacks of coffee beans, from which a local pleasure industry was promptly born. Everywhere today there are posters for one particular brand, Julius Meinl: the trademark is a young lad, wearing an absurdly elongated fez, and the company says it opened its first coffee shop on the very spot where the sacks of Turkish bounty were discovered. Moreover, the crescent-shaped pastry, the croissant, which in Vienna is known as the *Kipferl*, was created, all schoolchildren learn, by a long-forgotten Viennese *Hausfrau*, in celebration of the defeat of the would-be invaders and the banishing of their crescent flags. The connection between Turk and Austrian, between Istanbul and Vienna, is never far from the surface.

Not entirely by chance I had with me that morning, for deliberately light *Kaffeehaus* reading, several very old copies of *National Geographic* that underlined that very point, since each one contained an essay concerning the Balkans. In one of them, the February 1921 issue, there was a lengthy piece by one George Higgins Moses, a now-long-forgotten U.S. senator from New Hampshire and an American minister to—when it was an independent state—the Kingdom of Montenegro. It was all very

---

*Among the array of creatures found in the abandoned tents was the Ottoman grand vizier's pet ostrich, which he had ordered beheaded to prevent it falling into the hands of the infidel Catholics who had broken his siege.

dated, a pompous and orotund essay titled *The Whirlpool of the
Balkans*. But it did have some rather good lines, lines that were
amply relevant to what was happening a thousand miles to the
south of where we sat. The ones I thought most appropriate
came in a paragraph toward the essay's end, and I pointed them
out to Rose:

> It is at Constantinople that the problems of the Near East have
> always centered in their acutest form. There, where teeming
> thousands throng the Bridge of Galata; where twenty races meet
> and clash with differences of blood and faith never yet cloaked
> beneath even a pretense of friendliness; where fanaticism and
> intrigue play constantly beneath the surface of oriental phleg-
> matism and sporadically break forth in eddies of barbaric reac-
> tion; where all the Great Powers of Europe have for generations
> practiced the art of a devious diplomacy—there, I say, has
> always been found the real storm-center of the danger zone of
> Europe. There it is that the currents which cause the whirlpool
> of the Balkans have both their origin and their end. This Impe-
> rial city, for nearly two thousand years a seat of power, still
> clutches at the key . . .

Oh, the pleasure—to sit in a Viennese *Kaffeehaus* and to read of
Constantinople! Once they read and thought of little else. Even
these days the Viennese still cast an occasional backward glance at
Turkey, to see what it's up to, to see if it is still roiling the waters.
Considering how close they came to being subjugated by the
Ottomans, the Viennese have good cause to do so—though less
these days than once.

In 1921, when Senator Moses was writing, a sultan was still on
the throne in the newly built palace on the Bosporus, the
Dolmabahce Serai, and there was some modestly forlorn hope
among political innocents like the senator—and the vaguest of
fears among the more sensitive Austrians—that the Ottoman

Empire, Sick Man of Europe though it may have been, might yet contrive to carry on.

It was not to be, of course. For a hundred years or more the cynical leaders of the Great Powers, East and West—the Bismarcks, Wellingtons, Castlereaghs, Metternichs—had all endeavored to keep the old tottering empire alive—for fear that it might be replaced by something far, far worse. But by the twenties the fate of the Porte—the Sublime Porte, as the empire was generally known (named for a gate into the vizier's offices)— had already been firmly sealed. At the end of World War I, Constantinople was a city under foreign occupation; only a few years before it had suffered the indignity of being occupied by the Bulgarians, who went so far as to temporarily depose the sultan.

The sultan at the time of the senator's essay, Mehmet VI, had but a year to live and reign, and his own successor, a cousin, though he had a further two years in the palace, was reduced by international agreement from sultan to the mere status of caliph. He eventually abdicated from that lowly post as well, going away by Orient Express to Paris. And then Kemal Atatürk came and finished off the Ottomans once and for all, made Turkey into a modern secular state, turned Topkapi and Dolmabahce into museums and Hagia Sofia into a third, and renamed the city "Istanbul." With a wave of a republican wand, one more of the earth's proud empires suddenly faded away, and all that was Ottoman was washed up and done with. Such threat as the Viennese might have imagined was gone for all time.

Except that even at the empire's very end, and for a long, long while after, there was a good deal of truth to the senator's words—that Constantinople was "where the currents that cause the whirlpool . . . have their origin and their end." Flashes of the Ottomans' refulgent but meretricious presence still haunt the Balkans today, more than a century after the pashas and the beys were forced out of the region, and seventy years after they were forced to vanish altogether. There were stories aplenty in the Austrian papers that morning to illustrate the point—stories from refugees who were by now fanning across Macedonia, Albania, and Montenegro, recounting the terrible things that had befallen them and their families.

The happenings—some too dreadful to believe, stories of women being raped and hurled down wells, of men eviscerated, of children butchered on bayonets—were to no small extent a legacy of the old Ottoman times. The Kosovo Serbs, Orthodox Christian almost to a man and woman, had chosen to pit themselves so savagely against Albanians, seeing them as descendants of people who had been converted to Islam by "the Turk," as the Serbs always insultingly referred to the Ottoman invaders.

There are students of the Near East today—scholars who still dabble in "the Eastern Question," as it once was called—who will airily remark that "ancient ethnic hatreds" have precious little to do with today's struggles in the Balkans. They argue, persuasively and knowingly, that what is happening in the region now has much more to do with struggles for territory, with economic disputes between landlord and tenant, with the cynical manipulations of contemporary politics and the Machiavellian involvements of outside powers. And they are probably technically right in saying so. But ask a Serbian Christian—as I was to do more than once in the ensuing weeks—just why is it that he, like the man in the gas station in Pec, loathes his Albanian neighbors so. Why he loathes them enough to rape Albanian women and toss them down wells. Or to eviscerate Albanians, or flay them and leave them skinless and drying in the sun.

Ask him, and he will be sure to say, in one of his breathless sentences of explanation, that he hates them deepest down of all because they are Turks, Muslims, Asians, godless fiends who have no business being in Europe in the first place.

Serbs like to remind us even today that the Battle of Kosovo Polje, back in 1389, had been a desperate attempt by Christian Europeans like themselves to halt the onrushing armies of the

Asian Turk. They failed, but the nobility of their attempt goes some way to explain why Kosovo is so important in the Serbian mind. They remain bitter—or some of their more vicious leaders do—that so little in the Balkan history that then followed, or in the human geography it created—the cities, the buildings, the bridges, educational systems, houses of worship, systems of bureaucracy—managed to escape the influence, sometimes benign but more often malign, of those majestically corrupt Ottomans.

At the height of its powers the Ottoman Empire extended from the Caspian Sea almost to the gates of Vienna. Its power and influence ebbed and flowed with the fortunes of war and sultanly whim, but for more than five hundred years, from before the Battle of Kosovo until well after the Treaty of Berlin in 1878, the Ottomans presided over vast tracts of territory—and, as the sultans liked to put it, seventy-two and a half races*—with magnificent and perfumed equanimity.

Ottoman dominion over the Balkans had actually been in place a full sixty years before 1453, the year when Mehmet the Conqueror overran Constantinople and, standing his horse on a pile of broken bodies, had formally turned the Hagia Sofia from the Byzantine Cathedral of Divine Wisdom† into his empire's central mosque. But once the city had been successfully wrested away from the Greeks, the new rulers of so much of the Balkans and the Lower Danube Valley—and much else besides—always looked back east to the Topkapi Serai and the Sublime Porte as the spiritual and temporal centers of their authority. The Ottomans were the center of the whirlpool, and Constantinople was where the whirlpool gained its power.

---

*The half referring to the Gypsies.

†Which is what *Sancta Sophia* means in Latin: The structure was never named after any saint, Sophia or otherwise.

And from 1453 onward it was from Topkapi that the orders went out for the steady expansion of the sultan's domains. By 1521 the crescent battle flags had reached as far north as Belgrade and Bucharest, and as far south as Alexandria and Cairo, Jerusalem, Damascus, and Beirut. A century later the territories ruled by beys and *beylerbeis* and pashas had expanded outward in all directions, like the ripples on a pond, to include the cities of Baghdad and Benghazi. By then the shores of the Black Sea were entirely Ottoman-run. Rome was the sultans' early primary goal—the so-called Red Apple of Ottoman desire.

A red apple—an odd choice for the symbol of imperial hopes and dreams. It had a long history: It went back even to before the attack of 1453, when the apple was said to be the orb held in the right hand of the statue of Justinian that stood in front of the Hagia Sofia—a symbol, in other words, of Constantinople itself. Then, once the Ottomans had won that city and gathered Hagia Sofia and the ancient statue (which was later torn down) into their territory, so a new apple had to be found—and Süleyman I the Magnificent, the greatest Ottoman sultan of them all, decreed that it should be Rome.

"To Rome! To Rome!" was said to be a constant cry in Süleyman's court. He had made one vain attempt on the city in 1529, trying to besiege Vienna on the way. But he failed after a mere eighteen days. Like Napoleon in Moscow, he was defeated at least in part by the unfamiliar and atrocious winter weather.

It was a century and a half later, under the Sultan Mehmet IV, that the cry was for a new red apple—the city of Vienna itself, the seat of the Hapsburgs' Holy Roman Empire. Once captured, it would be a bridgehead to the soft underbelly of Central Europe. This time the Turks were so numerous, their armies so well organized, and their self-confidence so unparalleled that they imagined it could be done. In the summer of 1683 their invading army reached the southern gates of the great city and prepared to lay siege. The city cathedral and the Hofburg were squarely in the sights of the Ottoman harquebuses and within the range of their siege mortars.

In any event, it was to be a close-run thing. Had the Turks prepared a little more certainly and fought a little more aggressively, Vienna might well have gone the way of Belgrade and Budapest, Sofia and Sarajevo, Thessaloníki, Athens, Alexandria, and Cairo, and become a place of souks and mosques and dreamy Levantine administrators. But the city escaped capture, and the only memorials to just how close it came to surrender and having to endure the jeweled Ottoman heel are the croissant (baker-heroes working deep in the Viennese basements supposedly heard the Ottoman tunnelers laying mines), and places like Demel here, which owes its existence to the finding of those Turkish coffee beans. Which is why stuffy old Senator Moses made more than worthwhile reading that April day, among the ladies who lunched within the salon's walls of ancient but reassuring mirrors.

Most of the ladies who were lunching alone seemed to be reading local popular magazines like *Profil* and serious local newspapers like *Die Presse*, papers with front pages—this was April, and the bombing campaign was still only a few weeks old—covered with images of war and carnage from a thousand miles away. There were black headlines about the questionable actions of NATO and the sturdy defiance of the tyrants in Belgrade. Vienna is a prosperous city, and the Viennese can, if they care to, project an aloof and comfortable air. But those I talked to in the coffee shop that day seemed very well aware what was going on—and aware, too, of the extraordinary role that their city and their former Hapsburg rulers, as well as the sultans who nearly fell upon them, had played in bringing about this particular aspect of modern European history.

Each nodded assuredly when I asked if there was a connection to be made between what was happening in Kosovo today and what had happened in Vienna three hundred years before. "Of course, of course," one old lady said. "There can be no doubt.

"Not for nothing had Metternich—oh, my, was it Mr. Metternich?" she asked the waitress, who shook her head "—said that the Balkans began at the Ringstrasse. Or was it *Asia* that begins at the Ring? Or the Orient? I can't quite remember."

She was a venerable and genteel lady, and she looked briefly stymied. "But anyway, it is so true what they say—that we are on the edge of things just here. Poised between East and West. Just look at our eagle—the head that points both ways, indeed! And then, we were very nearly over the edge, you know, in 1683. We all know that from school. Like the story of the *Kipferl*. We all know that. We remember the Turks every day. The posters in the stores, and the bus stops. And then again things were bad for us in 1908, when we annexed Bosnia. Remember that? And once more in 1914, of course, when that Serb shot our archduke, in Sarajevo. And now here we are again today. All of it, everything going on down there, has something to do with the Viennese and the Ottomans. Or rather the Hapsburgs and the Ottomans. That's why this is, for us, so very interesting." And she smiled proudly at her eloquence, and puffed out her chest and looked most importantly Viennese as she asked the waitress for her bill.

So the Ottomans very nearly won the city in 1683—but they didn't, and that is what brings a satisfied smile to the lips of most Viennese. One grisly and rarely seen trophy symbolizes the fact that they didn't, and that the Viennese triumphed during that long hot summer three centuries ago. I had come to Vienna to try and see it. It was the severed head of the grand vizier of the court of the Sultan Mehmet IV, a greedy, violent, and xenophobic Turk with a fire-damaged face named Kara Mustafa Pasha.

His was the siege—a siege that had all taken place so very close to here. It had begun in the middle of July, in a 1683 when elsewhere William Penn was innocently settling Pennsylvania and Newton was gently explaining his new theory that linked the running of tides to the phases of the moon. Kara Mustafa's first cannonades—one of which hit the spires of St. Stephen's Cathedral, the ball remaining there to this day—came on either the fourteenth or the fifteenth, and to the terrified Viennese within the fortifications, it looked as though all was lost.

The Ottoman armies were camped all around the city, below the great walls and the moat that, two centuries later, were torn down and filled in, respectively, to make today's magnificently noble beltway, the Ringstrasse. The invading force was said by some to comprise about one hundred thousand men, most of them massed just outside the southern gates of the city, immediately beneath the towers of the Hofburg. So impressive was their encampment, and so huge, that Viennese remarked that it looked like another city, well able to rival Vienna itself—the Vienna that had taken a millennium to mature was almost eclipsed by a tent city that had sprung up in two days. (The remainder of the two hundred thousand Turks who had marched up from the Balkans were in reserve or engaged, with Tartars who had come up to join them from Crimea, in other actions in nearby towns.)

The greater part of the force were massed just a few hundred feet from where we sat that April lunchtime: A siege gun's shell could easily reach the Kohlmarkt, and doubtless many did. By chance the city was on one level well-defended, surrounded by a newly built stone girdle of embrasures, barbicans, ravelins, and bulwarks; but on another it was frighteningly vulnerable, since there were only two thousand soldiers in the garrison. Emperor Leopold I, fearing "that the whole might of Turkey is pressing upon me and this good city," decided two weeks beforehand to run away with his family, for what he assured his citizens would be only "a few hours." He was to sneak away undetected between the Tatar campfires, and would not return for another sixty-nine days.

The eight weeks of the siege itself caused privation and misery for thousands of the Viennese who remained. Shellfire, sniping, exploding mines, and fires caused untold damage. There was an epidemic of dysentery. Food ran out—with the result that the

Viennese, normally fastidious diners, had to fall upon horses, mules, and occasionally the local cats: These they called "roof rabbits," claiming that when larded with smoked bacon and taken with a glass or two of muscatel, they tasted quite acceptable.

The siege did, however, come to a satisfactory end. It was raised in mid-September, when, quite unexpectedly, two armies of friendly foreign troops—Germans under Charles V, duke of Lorraine, and Poles under the man who was to become a Viennese folk hero, King John III Sobieski—stormed down from the north and routed the Turks in what was to be called the Battle of Kahlenberg on the twelfth of the month. The Turks had a mighty force—their encampment, wrote Sobieski to his wife back home, was every bit as big as Warsaw. But their soldiery had no stomach for the kind of battle that the Germans and Poles could wage, and Kahlenberg was quickly over.

From the Turks' perspective the action, both battle and siege, was a humiliating failure. The first failure, some would say, of many. The Ottoman equivalent of the Battle of Midway. The first stage of the long and unyielding Ottoman decline, a decline that would only end two and a half centuries years later when the final sultan, demoted now to caliph, stood homeless and humiliated on the arrival platform of the Gare de Lyon.

There are many reasons for the Turks' defeat at Vienna—the principal one, from a strictly military perspective, being the combined strength of the force that was eventually sent against them. But there was more to it than that: Underlying the Turks' inability to fight back as properly as their huge numbers suggested they should was their studied indolence, their posturing and misbehavior, and the decadent luxury of their army's leadership, most especially that of the drunken and demented Kara Mustafa himself.

The grand vizier's force was prodigious—a hundred thousand infantrymen who were lodged in twenty-five thousand tents, with a tremendous array of camp followers, who included, besides a sizable army of prostitutes, any number of jugglers, clowns, and singers to keep the soldiers more politely amused. There were flocks of sheep, buffaloes, mules, camels, and cattle. Food caravans swept in from Hungary at regular intervals, bringing honey and corn, sugar and fat—and coffee. The Armenian cooks kept up the army's grand traditions of corruption, however, by baking bread and selling it to the besieged Viennese, or swapping it for favors.

In the middle of the great crescent-shaped arrangement of his troops—the shape owing more to practical coincidence rather artful arrangement, students of war believe—stood the tent of Kara Mustafa himself. It was a structure of almost impossible beauty with, as one Austrian observer noted, "the appearance of a magnificent palace, surrounded by several country houses, the tents being of different colors, all of which made for a very agreeable diversity."

Parts of the camp are still on display in the Historical Museum of the City of Vienna, and they look fine enough for the sultan's prime minister,* with delicate embroidery and a patchwork of gaily colored fabrics. The Ottomans were prodigious users and makers of tents—the influence, no doubt, of their past as nomads. Topkapi Serai, the palace on the Bosporus from which all orders came and all demands emanated, and from which all imperial Turks drew power and sustenance, was regarded by all within and without as no more or less than a tent fashioned from stone—and down the subtle gradations of the Ottoman bureaucracy, everyone else in the empire was due a tent appropriate to his station. The grand vizier's was by custom purple, the interiors tricked out in gold-embroidered silk.

What cannot be seen today, but is only known from contemporary accounts, are the Turkish encampments, with their

---

*Although the word *vizier* translates into "the sultan's foot," which is where the official sat, on the raised platform known as the *sofa*.

enclosed gardens, mechanical fountains, the streams of perfumed water, the priceless carpets, the chandeliers, and the
menageries with their exotic animals and birds (the soon-to-be
decapitated ostrich among them) from which the old vizier was
to take pleasure and relief.

Both of these last were provided also by the vast personal traveling harem that Kara Mustafa brought to Vienna with him. Fifteen hundred compliant Turkish women, guarded by the usual
elite corps of black eunuchs, were there to serve him day and
night—their numbers topped up frequently with fresh supplies of
captured Christian girls (who, according to the siege historian
Thomas Barker, much preferred to stay with their captor than be
returned to the miseries of the besieged city). When it was apparent that he had been defeated, and had to flee south and west
back to friendlier lands, the vizier was said to be troubled by the
possible fate of the woman he regarded as the harem's most beautiful. To prevent her falling into the hands of the infidels he
meted out the same fate as for his beloved ostrich, and had her
head cut off as well.

When the Germans and then the Poles bore down on his
troops at Kahlenberg, Kara Mustafa took off, heading fast down
the Danube Valley for Belgrade, which had been more or less
safely in Ottoman hands for a century and a half. He hoped to be
able to see his sultan, to explain the reasons for the debacle—not
that too many of them were explicable. But Mehmet had himself
moved on, and was in Edirne, en route back to the Porte, when
the message came that his vizier had wanted to see him.

What comes next has all the dignified inevitability of classical
Turkish kismet. Kara Mustafa Pasha, more widely loathed than
any grand vizier in memory, was to die by the bowstring—that
was a certainty for any military leader who had allowed the
defeat of the sultan's armies. A series of pleading messages were
sent from Belgrade to Constantinople throughout the rest of

that Balkan autumn, but to no purpose. The sultanate had no option but to bring the affair to its proper conclusion.

It was while the infidels were celebrating Christmas Day that the high chamberlain and the court-martial arrived from Topkapi at Belgrade's imperial palace, and demanded the return of the three most important signs of Kara Mustafa's tokens of office— the imperial seal, the holy banner, and the key to the Kaaba, the building containing the black stone at the Great Mosque in Mecca. The emissaries then delivered their sentence to the vizier, who was beginning midday prayers. The formula is archaic, and rather charming: "Whereas for the Defeat of Our Armies at the City of Vienna Thou deservest to Die, it is Our Pleasure that Thou entrust Thy Soul to the Ever Merciful Lord, and that Thou allow to be Delivered Thy Head to these our Messengers."

"Then I must die?" asked the ghastly old man. "So be it." He lifted his beard and allowed the court strangler to fasten the bowstring around his neck. Such throttling had been practiced many times, and was all over in three minutes. The executioner then sliced the head from the body, skinned it, and stuffed it, and then—well, then the trail runs a little cold. Some say the head was placed in a velvet bag and sent down to the Porte for the sultan to see. Others say it was buried in the grounds of the Belgrade palace. Still others say the sultan saw it and then ordered it to be reunited with the body—presumably back in Belgrade. Yet others claim that by then the body had been buried in Kara Mustafa's home village in Anatolia. It is an unsatisfactory puzzlement with which to end the vizier's otherwise well-chronicled if decidedly unlovely life.

Whatever did happen to the head in the immediate aftermath of his execution, it is long supposed to have been eventually brought back to Vienna. This happened because the Austrians, who were suddenly energized by having lifted the siege of their capital, raced down the Danube in pursuit of the fleeing Ottoman armies. They fought them several times, winning each time: they took Buda (which was to merge with its sister city across the river to become Pest-Buda, and only later Budapest) in 1686, kicking the Turks out of the *hammam* they had created from the local hot springs, and they were in Belgrade by 1688.

And it was there that the local Society of Jesus dug up the grand vizier's head, placed it in a vitrine, and presented it to the Government of the City of Vienna. It was brought back to the city in triumph, given first into the custody of the Catholic cardinal-archbishop of Vienna, and then placed on permanent display for the delight of the people, at the Historisches Museum der Stadt Wien. Or at least that's what was supposed to happen. In fact, sometime in the 1970s, during a fit of self-examination and political correctness—a symptom of what one writer called "our lily-livered age"—the museum curators ordered the head to be removed and locked away in a basement.

The Turks seemed to have had a global sense-of-humor failure: they had just complained to the Japanese about a certain type of brothel being named *Toruku*—for "Turkish bath"—and demanded that it be renamed, as it is today, "soapland," *Soperanda*. Having scored that small victory in the East, the Turkish government then turned its attention to the gruesome relic held in Vienna. Diplomats asked either that it be returned to Turkey or given a decent burial. To have it on public display, they said, was undignified and, moreover, potentially damaging to relations between two sovereign states that were now otherwise filled with mutual amity.

That final veiled threat was enough. The Austrian government sent out a warning to the Vienna city fathers, and the head of Kara Mustafa promptly vanished from public view. Disappointed visitors were told it had been removed to a warehouse. It was still very much in Austrian custody—that would not change under any circumstances—but where it had stood in the museum, there was a picture of the vizier, and that would have to do. It now hasn't been seen for a quarter of a century. Even at the great exhibition staged in 1983 to mark the three-hundredth anniversary of the siege, Kara Mustafa remained locked away, invisible.

But I was curious. The vizier's head was not only powerfully symbolic of the long and troubled relationship between Hapsburg and Ottoman, which had for so long dominated the Balkans; it was also, it seemed to me without unduly stretching the point, symbolic of the whole process of violence and separation that lay at the heart of the Balkans' eternal problem. And actual decapitation is still a feature of Balkan violence: Scores of severed heads seemed always to stand at the gateways of palaces and on the buttresses of bridges; and in reports from Bosnia and Croatia, and now from Kosovo too, the act of taking a sword to a man's neck seemed almost a casual matter. Besides, keeping so important a relic out of public view but yet hanging on to it seemed rather absurd. I thought I might try to see it.

The curator of armaments at the museum turned out to be scholarly woman, *Frau Doktor* Sylvie Mattl, who, when I first approached her, said it would be utterly out of the question to see the vizier's head. She happily showed me around her other charges—all manner of large Turkish tents, horsehair-trimmed spears and staves, cannons, rifles, flags, and a massive chart of the action around the beleaguered city, painted in extraordinary detail at the beginning of the eighteenth century. There was the painting of the grand vizier, too, which showed him bearded and turbaned, but it was not the ugly, fire-ravaged face of the drunken bully that he was known to be. And it was not, more to the point, his head. Might it not be possible to see him, just this once?

The *Frau Doktor* suggested that I get in touch with the museum's eminent *Direktor*, Dr. Günter Düriegl, stating just why I wanted to see the relic. I duly did this and received a reply a day or so later saying, to my surprise, that yes, in this one particular case an exception to the general rule could be made, and Kara Mustafa would be brought out of his faraway warehouse and

shown to me, shortly after breakfast a couple of days later. I was—
though more than a little squeamish, and well aware of the mor-
bid nature of the object—delighted.

It was pouring with rain when we arrived on the appointed Friday, and I was not altogether surprised to find that there was a
problem. Dr. Mattl, who met us as she was shaking out her
umbrella in the hall, looked grim. The *Direktor*, she explained, had
had some communication—she could not say whether it was
diplomatic, Turkish, academic—and had apparently changed his
mind. He was waiting in his office and would see me immediately,
to explain.

Dr. Düriegl inhabited the kind of comfortably untidy book-
lined room that I remember from Oxford. Indeed, with his
tweeds and his pipe and his air of studied calm, he looked just
like a professor, wearily receiving a student to whose essay he
would shortly be forced to listen. He was courtesy itself, explaining that it was with great regret that because a certain approach
had lately been made, it would not be altogether—how to
say?—*prudent* to show the grand vizier's head at this time.

I must have looked more than expectedly crestfallen. The
Direktor looked at me over his half-glasses, put his hands
together as though in prayer, and asked me simply: "Why don't
you tell me exactly why it is you want to see the object."

At this point I must have looked even more crestfallen,
because he said, with measured amusement, "Don't worry—this is
not Oxford. This is not a tutorial. Just a brief explanation will do."

And so I spluttered my way through what I felt was the sym-
bolism of the article, that it was a powerful reminder of the kind
of appalling carnage that was going on even at this moment,
that my interest in it was not, as he might suspect, purely
voyeuristic, and that seeing the head was a historically appropriate way to start a geographic progress through the Balkans,
especially if I could find out where in Turkey his body might be
buried—and then in an instant, like a weathervane in a squall,

Dr. Düriegl changed his mind and agreed. "Very well, very well," he said, with a sudden genial display of impatience. "Dr. Mattl? Will you take this gentleman down to meet—the other gentleman?"

Dr. Mattl took Rose and me down in the museum elevator. "As a precaution, and because I thought the *Direktor* might well eventually agree," she whispered, "I took the decision to bring the grand vizier here from the warehouse last night. So he is downstairs. I'll take you to him directly."

And a moment later we were standing inside a locked room filled with the detritus—bottles, paints, knives, brushes, frames—of restoration and picture cleaning, looking down at a small cardboard box decorated with the logo of a furniture removal company, sealed with plastic tape. Marked in ballpoint pen on its lid, and in a handwriting that was more casual than perhaps the chief minister of the Ottoman court might have deserved, were the words *Herr K. Mustafa*. A large and gloomy assistant who had been on sentry duty outside the door, and who had followed us in to ensure that proper security procedures were observed, took an Exacto blade and carefully slit the tape. Dr. Mattl opened the box, took out some wrapping paper, then reached in, and gently lifted out into the light the vitrine that contained one of the most famous skulls in all Balkan history.

He had probably not been a handsome man. His skull was brown and mottled. The eye and nose sockets were large and deep, the eyes compressed into what must have been a permanent frown. There were five long teeth in the upper jaw, yellowed and rotten and widely spaced. The entire lower jaw was missing. A length of finely made burgundy cord had been wrapped tight around his neck, or the post upon which his skull was mounted. It had a tassel on one end. Might this have been the cord with which the court strangler choked the life out of him?

Sylvie Mattl grinned and shook her head. "They are not even a hundred percent sure this is his head," she said. "*Ach!* There are so many questions. How did this come from Constantinople to Belgrade, and then to here? Where is his jaw? Should he be sent back? Should we give him a decent burial? Is this really him? Oh—you cause us so much trouble," she added, patting the top of the glass case.

"I like to think it is him. But you never know. I think back then we Viennese were happy to have any symbol, anything, that showed us having beaten back the Turks. This, I suppose, could be any skull. But I hope not. I haven't seen him for a long while—and I must say I'm glad to see he's all right."

We gazed at the relic for a while. Outside the rain had cleared, and shafts of sunlight illuminated the vitrine and its macabre inhabitant.

"Shall we?" ventured Dr. Mattl, gesturing toward the door. And so, with the guard helping, we gingerly lifted Kara Mustafa back into his cardboard box and stuffed back the wrapping paper and sealed him up with fresh tape, then set him down on the floor by the exit. And then the door was locked, and we walked out into the sunshine. Dr. Mattl thanked us for coming. "And for letting me see the old man. It is many years since I had the opportunity. He's rather like an old friend."

Sometime later I uncovered the existence of a small academic industry devoted to the life and times and controversies surrounding Kara Mustafa Pasha. His headless body still exists, buried in northern Turkey. As I was about to leave Vienna I heard that preparations being made for an international symposium to be staged close to his shrine. Most of those due to present papers were, as might be expected, from Austria.

There has long been friendly disagreement over exactly what Prince Metternich had said—that the East begins at the Ringstrasse, or the Landstrasse, or that Asia begins at one or the other—but it matters not. The point is that the Viennese have long regarded themselves as living at the outer reaches of Europe, the *ultima Thule* of properly European civilization.* Beyond and to the east lie the Slavs, a wild mix of peoples and creeds and customs with whom the Germanic Austrians have had the most complicated of relationships—a series of political marriages (and all too often, actual ones) that reached a Hapsburg imperial apogee that James Joyce once described as comprising "a hundred races and a thousand languages."

We might have tried heading east or northeast, along the Landstrasse or the Oststrasse, ending up at Bratislava, Prague, or Budapest. Or we might have struck out southwest along the Triestenstrasse, and found ourselves at the now-Italian port city of Trieste, a fine medieval-hearted city that had changed hands all too often, but which had reached its own zenith when it had been the Hapsburgs' principal outlet (and connected to Vienna by a direct railway line) to the sea.

But no. I wanted to be in the Balkan heartland as directly as possible; and so we headed instead to a railway station, the Südbahnhof, from which one could dive—more precipitously than via any other route—into the whirling center of the great storm that we could hear and read about all over. I consulted my *Cook's Continental* and, at a small travel agency around the corner from the Staatsoper, bought two first-class tickets on that late-afternoon's train No. 159, *The Croatia*.

We were about an hour out from the city, and sitting in the lace-trimmed dining car, when something about the wine bottle caught my eye. The sun was already beginning to slant down

---

*Once, for a not wholly frivolous journalistic reason, I was driving a Rolls-Royce across Russia and needed someone to tinker with engine's carburator before I took it to places where the gasoline had the look and feel of peanut butter. When I asked Rolls-Royce where this work might be done, the senior engineers, after consulting maps, gave me the address of the official agent in Vienna. "The last bastion of civilized mechanics," I was told. "After that, who knows?"

into the western sky, and a ray must have briefly glinted on the wine's meniscus, showing it to be sloping quite dramatically. The train, it turned out, was climbing a gradient, an unusually steep slope.

I opened the window and looked outside. The featureless and dreary suburban plains of the Danube were all behind us now, and in their place were sharp peaks and tiny villages, nesting storks, velvet meadows and wildflowers, the sounds of cowbells and flashes of distant snow. The train was snorting heavily through a chain of mountains, pushing through the one physical barrier that kept Austria decently apart from the most troublesome of the hundred races and the thousand languages over which at and the Turks and the ever-shifting friends of both had battled and waged war.

3

To the
"Land of the Osmanlees"

Bosnia and the Sava River valley

I T CAN TAKE a dreamy railway journey through a range of majestic Middle European mountains to put the Balkans into their true and proper perspective. For if there can be said to be any ultimate villain behind all the centuries of Balkan misery, it has to do with mountains, and it is this: the fact that between fifty-eight and twenty-four million years ago the northern part of what is now the continent of Africa moved northward and started to collide with the southern part of what is now the continent of Europe.

This episode, which is very broadly known as the Alpine Cenozoic Orogeny, was, and still is (for it continues to this day) one of the most important tectonic events in the making of the planet—something that will bring scant comfort to the wretches who went on to inhabit the regions it created. An uncountable series of geological events took place during the early millions of years of the collision. Some of them—the forcing together and thrusting upward of crustal plates to create the great southern European mountain chains, like the Alps (part of which our train was heaving itself up and over) and the Pyrenees—were by common agreement major. Others—the forming of Italian volcanoes like Mount Etna and volcanic islands like Lipari and Vulcano, the creation of world's best sources of pumice stones, or the making of rock veins from which Roman centurions might win obsidian and so carve razor blades and invade their neighboring countries clean shaven—were perhaps less so.

The collisions between the two great tectonic plates took a very long time. During their later phases scores upon scores of smaller tectonic plates, which had broken off from the vanguards of the principal ones, jostled and collided with one another, rolled over and beneath one another and the wreckage of already collided ones—leaving behind a ghastly mosaic of geology that is more complicated than almost anywhere else in the world.

Two major events tended to dominate the picture, however. The first of these was the relatively simple making of the main southern European Alpine chain. The other, more tricky to imagine, was the steady northward movement of the Arabian Peninsula along the huge fault line of what are now the Dead Sea and the river Jordan. This caused a cascade of what would finally be Balkan-related geology to happen. The Arabian Peninsula moved north and caused the creation of the Zagros Mountains of Iran, whose snow-capped higher peaks can be glimpsed south of the holy city of Isfahan. The piling up of these south Persian hills caused the entire Anatolian Plateau of eastern Turkey to be pushed steadily westward, which in turn caused enormous pressure both on the rising peninsula of Greece and, to its immediate north and most important of all, on the eastward extension of the very Alpine range that our train was currently crossing.

And it was this last that left the Balkans the geologically and topographically wild place they are today—the crushing of one newly formed mountain chain (the Balkan Mountains, largely in Bulgaria), heading westward into another (the Dinaric Alps) that was curving south and eastward. The two chains smashed into another to create a geological fracture zone that became a template for the fractured behavior of those who would later live on it. Like the complicated patterns that are made by intersecting ripples from a number of stones thrown into a pool, with sizes and shapes that can only be confirmed by the deepest calculus, so these two, or three, or four colliding ranges of hills formed yet newer ranges of hills and valleys that then trended in directions that were the varied sums of the trending directions of all their parent ranges, and were extraordinarily complex as a result.

The ranges of hills had unexpectedly steep faces and deep

and curiously isolated valleys, rivers that twisted and turned in corkscrew patterns, defiles that became dangerous culs-de-sac, hidden and unexpected plains, eternally defensible hilltops and impossibly deep canyons, eccentricities of microclimates, and on the coastline (which was of amazing length, and adorned with bizarrely shaped islands, skerries, and reefs) deep fjordlike harbors and wriggling estuaries that proved terrifyingly nightmarish to innocent navigators.

Add to all this the fact that the rock out of which the Balkans are made was not something grand and imperturbable, like granite, dolerite, or marble, but rather the soft young limestone, made in Permian times in the warm Tethyan Sea, that dissolves so readily in the mild hydrochloric acid that is rainwater that even in areas of classic and stable geology like North Yorkshire, it forms areas of fantastic topography—these are the so-called karsts, with their deep caves and gorges and vanishing rivers. A fantastically troubled underneath and a waywardly malleable and porous upper surface: How much weirder a landscape is it possible to imagine?

And that is even before the human population had been grafted onto it all.

One might say that anyone who inhabited such a place for a long period would probably eventually evolve into something that varied substantially, for good or for ill, from whatever is the human norm. I imagine it can be argued that geologically and tectonically stable (and so generally rather tediously flat) regions—like Holland, Kansas, North China, the Australian Outback—tend to be inhabited by the less fractious of the world's peoples—peoples who depart from the norm in being perhaps less aggressive, less bellicose, perhaps less curious, less imaginative. Places that have a more crazed geology, on the other hand, quite possibly tend to attract, or maybe even to produce, peoples who are of a (let us say) more robust character.

Given that the Slavs who moved into the Balkans two thousand years ago were already of fairly robust stock—they were probably Iranian-led and came from the shores of the Black Sea, the wilds of the Caucasus and northern Persia's Elburz Mountains—it is scarcely surprising to find that, once they had vanished into their isolated Balkan valleys and hidden harbors and climatically unrelated culs-de-sac, they became—one from another and all from those outside—a very different people indeed.

Such were my musings on the train. I almost missed the border inspections, of which there were quite a number. We were stamped out of Austria by an efficient and smiling pair of guards, and then into Slovenia, at a place called Maribor, by a posse of gray-suited and rather miserable Slovenes.

These, then, were the first true Slavs we had encountered and if one wanted a reminder that the word *Slav* is a portmanteau term that encompasses as multiethnic and polyglot a group as it is possible to imagine, then this forlorn group of Slovenian frontier guards more than amply fitted the bill. One of them, the passport stamper, was very round and fat, with a shaved head, and he looked like an only very slightly animated potato. One had such sharp features that he reminded me of a weasel. Another was short, dark, and sallow. A fourth was burly and had a beard. The sole woman among them had flaming red hair. There was no apparent ethnic unity to them at all—and all that distinguished them from the people from among whom we had come is that while those behind us had been all Germanic and did all have the same very general kind of appearance, these here in the Maribor railway station were in no way Germanic and all looked quite different. Two of them, though, had crucifixes around their necks, and not one them wrote in (nor were their passport stamps written in) Cyrillic script.

So they may have been Slavs; they may have been, until 1991, part of the Federation of South Slavs that was called Yugoslavia, but they were not, in any sense, Serbs. The Serbs were Eastern

Orthodox by belief, and such were their fraternal links with the
Slavs of Russia they used Saint Cyril's script as their own. In all
other ways—except for their given names, which reflected their
alternative pantheon of saints—the Slavs who were Serbs were the
same people as the Slavs who were Slovenes, as here, or the Slavs
who were Croatians, and whom we would encounter when we
crossed their frontier in few hours' time.

And this was one of the abiding complex absurdities of the
Balkans: that almost all the people who have been so horribly at
odds with one another are all, in essential ethnic terms, the self-
same people. This does not include the Albanians, as we shall
see; but elsewhere, the Bosnian Muslims and the Croatian and
Slovenian Catholics are of essentially the very same ethnic and
genetic makeup as the Orthodox Christian Serbs—a people of
whom, until lately, they were true and literal Yugoslav—south
Slav—compatriots.

These Maribor Slovenes were more properly linked with their
coreligionists far away than with their ethnic kin here at home.
These people, to judge by their crucifixes, worshiped, if they did
so at all, at the same churches as did their brother and sister Slavs
in dominantly Catholic Slavic countries like Poland, the Czech
Republic, Slovakia, and neighboring Croatia, as well as some of
their number in Ukraine and Belarus. They worshipped in the
same churches as their Germanic cousins did in Vienna, too, or in
south Germany. But they did not worship in the same churches as
their compatriots and brother and sister Slavs in Serbia—and
there, sad to say, is the rub.

I would like to say it was the great Gothic Cathedral of the
Assumption of the Blessed Virgin Mary that dominated my view
of the Croatian capital when we finally stepped down from the
train at Zagreb station later that night. It was not. Its two towers,
illuminated by golden floodlight, pierced the night sky from the
top of the low hill on which they and the old Archbishop's

Palace stood. But it was the ordered magnificence of the structures in the square outside the station that first caught my eye. This was Vienna, I thought, all over again. Some of the buildings were faux-Renaissance, some art nouveau, still others born of that Viennese radical architectural school that grew out of—and was, in part, a reaction to—nouveau and was called the Sezession. This may have been a Slav city, but the stylistic influence on its center was pure Hapsburg, from the station itself to the boxy and colonnaded Esplanade Hotel, which loomed fortresslike and severe, to the left of the imposing square. It had been commissioned by the Wagons-Lits company, someone said, for passengers coming in from Paris on the Orient Express (it was always assumed that anyone of any class who arrived in Zagreb would be bound to do so by rail).

The hotel and the cathedral, both of which are relatively modern structures (the first cathedral was knocked down by a furious earthquake in 1880), have something in common—a feature that offered us the first terrible glimpse (and so soon beyond the comforts of Vienna!) of the true horrors of the Balkans.

The imposing, green-washed Esplanade Hotel, as darkly imposing and majestic inside as its outside suggested it should be, turned out, according to the staff, to have been the headquarters during World War II of the Gestapo. And the cathedral, half a mile away, was in some sense a spiritual refuge for those Croats who were committing dreadful crimes either at the behest of the Gestapo or on their own frighteningly warped initiative.

Croatia in the days following the German and Italian invasions was run as a supposedly self-declared and notionally independent fascist state; and though the Wehrmacht and soldiers from the Italian army were everywhere to lend support, it was run principally and with blood-chilling ruthlessness by Zagreb's dreaded home-grown terror organization, the so-called Insurrectionists, the Ustashi.

The men who peopled this appalling organization of unutter-

ably violent Croat separatists, a body that had existed since the
thirties, first came to worldwide attention when, in 1934 in Marseilles, they asssassinated the Serbian king, Alexander I (Alek-
sandr Karadjordjevic).* The uncanny connection between cathedral and hotel is that for an indecently long while, beginning in
April 1941, the Ustashi were receiving their orders from the
Gestapo officers at the Esplanade while at the same time, and
even more chillingly, they were said to be receiving their moral
imprimatur and, for a while, their blessing, from the archbishop
up in the Zagreb cathedral. Sezession mansion and Gothic church
were thus united, at least for a while, in the underwriting of one of
the great bestialities of modern times.

From the evidence collected in the years since the war, it
seems that almost every dire act the Croat madmen perpetrated
against the Serbs—the butchery, killings with knives and mallets
and hacksaws, the throat slittings, the ax murderings either
because the Serbs were members of what many Croatian Catholics
considered the apostasy of the Orthodox Church, or because
they were reckoned to be Communists—was said to be done
under the invigilation and approval of one of the more allegedly
diabolical figures that the modern Roman Catholic Church has
produced.

He was called Alojzije Cardinal Stepinac, and his consecrated
remains, lately blessed by the pope, lie in the cathedral today, in
an elegant tomb not far from a celebrated Dürer bas-relief, and
under the gold stars and azure sky of the cathedral ceiling. His
memory is revered by thousands of Croats still—I watched a line
of several dozen young women with their children waiting to
kneel before his tomb, to kiss his image and mutter incantations
over their rosaries. Yet seen by today's standards, Stepinac seems
hardly worthy of such unswerving Christian devotion. He was by

---

*Along with his host, French Foreign Minister Louis Barthou.

too many accounts to disbelieve a cruel, dogmatic man, a puritan zealot and a bigot, and a figure who was cynically used by the Ustashi to give moral authority to the terrible things they were doing to the Serbs who lived among them.

One side of his zealotry was harmless enough—he was a stickler for the unvarying protocols of church ritual, he took a Franciscan oath of poverty, he believed that Masons were everywhere plotting, and he railed against the immorality—as he saw it—of such innocent pursuits as sunbathing and mixed swimming. But he also made sermon after impassioned sermon condemning those who wanted—as many intellectuals did in those days—an end to the schism between the Eastern and Roman churches. The archbishop's firmly held belief, at least as a young man (and he was first inducted into the Zagreb cathedral chancery when he was only thirty-two) was that the Orthodox Church represented a perversion of holy truth, and all who held to the Byzantine beliefs should be shunned, converted, or worse. His belief mirrored precisely the stated policy of the Ustashi regime, which famously and chillingly said of the Serbs that the only way to deal with them was to ensure that one-third were exiled, one-third were converted, and one-third were killed.

The most egregious example of Stepinac's alleged tyrannies had to do with both conversion and killing. He is said to have directed, and on occasion presided over, the forced conversion to Catholicism of tens of thousands of Orthodox Serbs at the infamous Jasenovac concentration camp, seventy miles away from Zagreb. The conversions were given, or forced, just moments before the camp's Ustashi thugs set about the men with hammers and axes, killing them in such numbers and with such viciousness that even the Nazi Germans—who had taken industralized killing to high art—were hard put to outdo. They were made Catholics, the Croatian church leadership later explained, to ensure that after their deaths they could go to heaven.

By chance a trial concerning the horrors of half a century

ago at Jasenovac was going on in the Zagreb county court on
the day we arrived. A former camp commander named Sakic
was being prosecuted for mass murder and war crimes—an
effort by the eight-year-old Croatian state to make some amends
for, and come to terms with, events that had taken place in the
name of its people. On the days that we spent in the city, a Jew-
ish former inmate named Josip Erlih had been brought in from
Belgrade to testify: He told gruesome stories of men being
machine-gunned to death because they were Jews, or of Serbian
farmers being beaten to death with mallets, axes, and picks, or
of the hanging of large groups of Chetniks, the most prominent
and active of the Serb partisan fighters.

Some 350,000 prisoners had been killed at one camp, he
said—40,000 of them alone Gypsies. Anyone who departed
from the Croatian Catholic norm—Serbs, Jews, Gypsies, gay
men—was regarded as beneath contempt. "There was so much
killing. The Ustashi tried to burn the bodies in the incinerator
but gave it up because of the terrible stench. They tried to make
soap from the prisoners' corpses, but gave up that effort, too,
because the bodies were so frail and there was not enough fat in
them for that."

Mr. Erlih's testimony, given in a quiet courtroom on this ordinary warm spring day in a town that, beyond the courtroom, was
bustling merrily with all the pleasantries of European café society,
was heartbreaking. "Abuse and beatings took place on a daily
basis," this neatly dressed, dignified old Belgrade Jew told the
court, "because every Ustashi officer had unlimited power, and
the possibility to kill without being punished. Day after day I saw
the women and children of Jasenovac going off to be killed. They
knew where they were going, but they did not cry. They were
singing."

And they were singing, too, in the cathedral, on the day we visited.
A small chorus of nuns from a distant nunnery were rehearsing

old compline psalms. There was still a line of housewives in front of the cardinal's tomb, many of them carrying bags of fresh farm produce from the nearby Dolac vegetable market (to which Mrs. Thatcher had once been taken, as stall holders liked to tell me). Had these women any idea, I wondered but was unable to ask, what this man was really supposed to have done? Or had they thought the stories about him to be mere propaganda, dismissing any errors as those of a naive man with poor judgment? After all, there are some who believe that late in the war, when the scale of atrocities grew truly vast, Stepinac declared himself publicly against the Ustashis' murderous campaigns. One biographer says that he harbored Jews in the cathedral grounds, another who interviewed him in the 1950s said that the old archbishop felt himself to be a victim, a cleric placed in an impossible position and forced "to suffer for his church."

Certainly the Vatican has been grateful for his stand against Communism; certainly the Holy See has sympathized with his stated aim of preserving Croatia as a civilized and Western-looking Catholic state, not allowing it to fall prey to either the hated Eastern ways of the Orthodox Church or to the even further Eastern ways of the Muslims. Pope Pius XII made him a cardinal in 1952, and if the Vatican then ever investigated his infuriatingly vague wartime record, which came complete with a diary with a large number of puzzlingly missing pages, it never said what it found.

And then in 1998 Pope John Paul II came to Croatia and announced the formal beatification of the cardinal, and the possibility remains that he may yet be declared a saint. His standing now is very different from what it was when he died in 1962: He had been under house arrest then, accused of having collaborating with the fascists. But then again, in 1962 his country was Communist, and dominated by Serbs. Today it is Catholic, and dominated by his own. The legacy of Alojzije Stepinac is a clouded and confused affair, suffused with dreadful stories, and mired in the classic Balkan hatreds, ancient and modern.

The criminality, or culpability, of the cardinal's wartime role has yet be proved, and may never be; the terror inflicted by the Ustashi, by contrast, is admitted, and recorded, just as the Nazi crimes were, in stupefying detail. The historian Milovan Djilas painted an all-too-vivid series of descriptions of events he saw as a partisan fighter. He wrote, for example, of an incident in 1941 when a gang of Ustashi, together with some Muslim toughs who were along for the ride, rounded up all the Serbs in a village called Miljevina and slit their throats while hanging them over the edge of the community wine vat, so that their gushing blood would take the place of grape pulp. There are stories, too, of Ustashi thugs capturing Serb partisans and tying them down and cutting their heads off with *saws*—sawing their necks, *back and forth*, with deliberate and agonizing slowness.

The common feature in all of these accounts, of course, is that the victims were Serbs. Which might beg the all-too-obvious question that had puzzled me long before I first came to the Balkans: What, if this was Croatia, were the seemingly very large numbers of Serbs doing there in the first place?

The answer goes back to the Ottomans and the Hapsburgs, as so many of the trials of the region seem to do. I had my first proper explanation of it when we picked up a hitchhiker on the main road from Zagreb to a once-important little town called Karlovac, thirty miles to the southwest. She was a young student named Maria Oreskovic; she was twenty-three, a Croat, a Catholic, was studying economics, and when we picked her up, she was on her way home. I told her I knew that Karlovac had played some important role in Balkan history but confessed that I wasn't sure quite what. Maria was only too happy to help. "I give directions," she said. "I show you why my hometown matters."

An hour later the three of us were standing in the courtyard of a curiously tall wood-and-stone structure that stood on a low and windy hill a mile or so out of town. The main tower was square, four storied, about sixty feet tall, and with what seemed to be an open viewing platform under the eaves. Thick brick walls surrounded the small court, and rising from two of its three corners were smaller towers, with galleries connecting them. The building was known generally as Dubovac Old Town, and it was where the Austrian border guards had kept watch over the vanguard sentries of the Ottomans—it marked the very edge of the Hapsburg Empire, and, just a few miles away, the beginning of what Alexander William Kinglake, in that most classic of travel books, *Eothen* (1844), called the "land of the Osmanlees."

The building, five hundred years old or more, is now run as a country inn. It was deserted, thanks to the war that was being fought just a few dozen miles away, and the manager was happy to give us coffee and then, after we expressed a keen interest in looking over the building, lunch as well. I climbed up through the galleries to the very top, and hoisted myself into what was indeed an old reconnaissance platform. It was from here, for three centuries or more, that the *Grenzer*, the frontier garrison chiefs of the Hapsburg armies, stood sentry duty to protect the outer reaches of their immense empire.

Whatever Clemens von Metternich might have said about the Orient having its beginning at the Rennweg or the Ringstrasse or the Oststrasse, the undeniable truth was that the one empire ended here, and the other began here. The Old Town of Dubovac was military headquarters for that vexed artifice known as the Krajina, whose existence is the main reason that there are now, or have until recently been, so many Serbs inside the territory of Croatia.

If the underlying crust of the earth in the Balkans is cracked and shifting along great tectonic fault lines, so the people on the Balkan surface are affected by the faulty lines made by man—and in this region, there is no more important fault line than the Krajina. The word is Serbo-Croatian, and it means "edge," "boundary," "border," "frontier." Officially the region was known as the Vojna Krajina, the Military Frontier District, and it was basically one huge exclusion zone. Outside, to the west and north, were the Hapsburg-held provinces of Croatia and Slovenia; inside, east and south, the Turkish-held statelets of Bosnia, Herzegovina, and Serbia.

The Krajina was probably not hugely different in its concept or nature from exclusion zones created by more recent Communists and Western governments, as barrier regions, or as buffer zones on one side or both of their more sensitive national borders. There used to be an infamous such zone in southern Bulgaria, for example, twelve miles wide: There could be no villages there, no people at all, in the last twelve miles before Bulgaria became Turkey. It was designed so that no Bulgar ever saw a Turk, nor was any Bulgar ever tempted to drop everything and make a dash for it. (The Turks, one suspects, would never want to anyway.)

The Austrians created their Krajina in the last years of the seventeenth century as a direct response to the failed siege, since the throne had an understandable case of the jitters in case another Kara Mustafa might one day make another lunge for its city. In their making of the frontier, however, the Austrians incorporated one signal difference, one which has since made the word *Krajina*, in general Balkan terms, synonymous with the very worst kinds of violence, mayhem, and ethnic purging.

What the Hofburg bureaucrats decided was that, rather than leave the border regions unpopulated, they would allow, and would indeed encourage, the settlement there of Slavs who were fleeing from the strictures of Ottoman rule. And not just Slavs: Serbs. Scores upon scores of thousands of Serbs.

It was the Serbs in Serbia and Bosnia, after all, who were feeling the crushing weight of the Ottoman yoke. It was Serbs who were most violently opposed to anything and everything that the Turks might do. Who better, then—who more highly motivated?—than the Serbs, to ward the Turks away from Austrian territory. And so the Austrians were generous to a fault with the new settlers (especially since the land they were settling the Serbs on was not actually Austrian territory, but Croatian.)

So when in the late seventeenth century the Orthodox patriarch of the Kosovan cathedral town of Pec led thirty thousand of his faithful to escape the wrath of the Turks, and brought them to sanctuary in the Hapsburg borderland, the Austrians gladly acquiesced. They gave the refugees territory, religious freedom, hope. They apportioned them land, they helped them build farms, they allowed them to reconstruct their Orthodox churches and schools and to write their language, they gave them a degree of autonomy the Croats and the Slovenes did not enjoy—and they permitted them, most significantly of all, to arm themselves, to become a territorial defense force.*

By doing so, the Viennese thought, they would spare the haughty and dignified Austrian *Grenzer* the grubby business of ever battling with the Muslims. The closest they might wish to get to the sharp end of the situation was the fortress on top of the hill by Karlovac. "Let the Serbs do our fighting for us," said the smooth and powdered officials at the Hofburg. "They have suffered already, they know what it is like, and they have their dander up."

So, without the very Germanic and thus very foreign Austrians ever quite realizing what they had done, without ever quite foreseeing the implications of their strategy, they succeeded with one stroke of a courtier's pen in sowing the seeds for centuries of ethnic division.

_____

*Soon after the Austrians allowed in the migrants from Kosovo, the Ottoman administrators closed down the Pec patriarchy, fully aware of its importance as the Serbs' spiritual home. Once the news filtered up to the Krajina the Serbs there decided to make their own settlement its spiritual replacement— which is one reason that the Krajina Serbs were so militantly determined to try to keep the land for themselves, and so violently opposed to those Croats who thought otherwise.

For from the early seventeenth century onward, and fermenting quietly on the margins of what would one day become the overwhelmingly Catholic Republic of Croatia, the Austrians created a land of prosperous farmers and merchants who, rather than looking westward across the Adriatic to Venice and Rome, and rather than owing political loyalty to the House of Hapsburg and any intellectual connection to the West, were a people facing resolutely East. The people of the Krajina owed their loyalties instead to Byzantium and Athens and, indeed, to Moscow, and (to underline this point) they wrote and read in Cyrillic script, and would, in this century, become natural ultimate vehicles for the expansion of Marxism. And then again today, when Croatia wanted its independence from Yugoslavia, these, the people of the Krajina, were the people whose loyalty was not to Croatia at all but to Serbia and Belgrade—which loyalty held them back, made them rebel, made them suspect, made them fight.

For each and all of these reasons the hundreds of thousands of independent-minded, well-armed, and very different people who inhabited the long and scythe-shaped Krajina, which stretched from the Serbian border along north Bosnia and down the Dinaric Alps to where Dubrovnik stands today, were to become victims of the Croat slaughter, and, in due course, were to retaliate in kind. On what was considered sacred Croatian soil, a million miseries—and all because of what the Austrians so airily created and ran from their fortress high on a windy hill.*

Maria still had a little while before she was due to go home to baby-sit her younger sister. "Why not come into the Krajina?" she smiled. "To see what it means." And so we drove down from

---

*The fortress near Karlovac was the Austrians' administrative center for only the western Krajina. The eastern half of the frontier zone, in what is now Slavonia, was run from a similar fortress built at the town of Varazdin.

the hillside, and into lush springtime countryside with fields and fat cows and tall grass, and which could for all the world have been Oxfordshire or Connecticut. The flyblown suburbs of Karlovac soon faded in the mirror. Ahead were some low hills, and beyond them, the frontier proper and Bosnia. In between, according to the map, were a couple of slow rivers and a number of villages. Indeed, there was a scattering of houses in a fold in the hills ahead—but houses that, when we first came close enough to see, were all ruined, all smashed, all burned and roofless and wrecked. It was my first sight of the wreckage of this war, and I stared, open-mouthed, at what I could barely believe.

"You get used to it," said Maria, still smiling. "Part of the landscape here. I guess you can say it's part of our history now."

This must once have been a Croat village, on the outer edge of the Krajina itself. There was a small Catholic church, ruined too. The damage must have been done, and probably back in the early nineties, by Serbs who made forays out of their own villages close to the border, just to bloody the Croats' noses, to show them who was master. On some of the walls inside the more spectacularly wrecked Catholic houses I could see the most potent of Serb symbols, a cross with four Cyrillic *C*s (signifying *S*), the two on the left facing backwards, giving the device perfect bilateral symmetry. The letters stand for *Samo Sloga Srbina Spasava*, or "Only Unity Can Save the Serb."

In other circumstances it might have been a rather pleasing, rather elegant device—but before long, and after seeing it a thousand times on wrecked houses and torched cars and on mutilated victims, painted or carved or burned onto their stomachs or faces, it came only to represent hatred and horror, like a swastika. *Ovo je Srbija* was scrawled on many houses here too, lest anyone forget: "This is Serbia."

But of course it wasn't then, and it isn't now. We were still very much in Croatia, and the ruins past which we were driving were simply the scars of a recent war. The Serbs had lost this piece of territory, had been beaten back, had been forced back into Bosnia across the frontier, or far away into Serbia itself, or into Kosovo or Montenegro. At least that's what I thought.

And then we turned left off the main road, and up a winding country lane, under a bower of apple blossoms, where a beautiful young girl stood holding a brown cow by a string through its nose. We drove into the grassy courtyard of a small farm. Two men sat at a rough oak table, smoking and talking quietly in the early spring sunshine. I stopped the engine, and one of the men got up and walked over to us, smiling and extending a welcoming hand. I introduced myself, Maria doing the translating.

We were in a hamlet called Cerovac, this farmer was called Duro Relja, and he was forty-seven. He had lived on this farm all his life. The girl with the cow was his only daughter, a Maria too. There was his wife—he pointed at a darkened doorway, where a shy middle-aged woman in black stood, playing idly with a large pig. His friend here was Milosan Obradovic—"come on over, Milo! Don't be so lazy. How often do you get to meet a man from England!"—and he had come up that day before from Montenegro, an eight-hour drive. Would I care for a glass of *rakija*, plum brandy? His wife bustled over with a bottle. "Homemade," she said in English. "I hope you like."

We raised our glasses—*Zivjeli!* I was taught to say—and talked long into the warm afternoon, while the cow noisily cropped the long damp grass, the lambs bleated on the hillsides across the valley, and the blackbirds sang. His was a hard life, he said: He had a couple of dairy cows, maybe thirty sheep, he sold apples from his orchard, he had a field set to potatoes. He made only a modest living. And then—and at this point Duro Relja rose, and beckoned for me to follow him around the back of his house, the side that faced the valley—there was this.

The back of his farmhouse was wrecked, the walls smashed by a direct hit from a shell, the room inside, the bed still lying there in pieces, blackened and scarred by shrapnel. It had been in 1995, when the Croat forces had occupied the Krajina, and most of the Serbs had been forced out. He pointed to where he thought the gun emplacement had been. He thought he knew the man who had fired the shot. "Some Ustashi bastard," he said.

Wait a minute. Come again?, I thought. A Croat gunner firing at a Croat? What was going on? "But you're a Croat, right? A Catholic, right?" Dura Relja and his friend and Maria laughed. "No, no!" he said. "You never asked us. We are not Croats at all. We are Serbs. We are Serbs who stayed here. They tried to get us out—but here on this side of the valley, everyone likes us. Yes, there was some bastard of an artilleryman who wanted to force us out. And he was only following orders from some politician in Zagreb. I think I know who the gunner was. I know him. I'd see him at the market. I think I could meet him again. But anyway, the neighbors here,"—and he pointed to another farm, which looked relatively unscarred, set on a hillside nearby— "they told us to stay on, if we could bear to. They helped us repair the house a little. They were Croats, and yet they didn't see us as the enemy.

"And of course, we're not. We're all Slavs here. You must have been told that. We're the same people. And there are some places, like this village, thank God, where people think like that still.

"But my God, it was so much easier when it was all Yugoslavia. So much easier. But anyway,"—and his wife filled the glasses again, and emptied the bottle of the colorless, fiery liquid—"let's drink to better times. *Zivjeli!*"

We got up to go. Overhead there was a low rumbling, and I looked up into the violet evening sky. There were four, five, six vapor trails, the thin gossamer traces of a squadron of high-flying jet planes. They were close together, heading east.

"Bombers," said Duro Relja, tensely. "Off to attack Belgrade. The Americans. You English too. Off to kill some Serbs." He pounded his fist on the old oak table, angry now. "It is such a pity. Why can't everywhere be peaceful, like this village here? In Cerovac it all seems so simple. But why is the world going so mad?"

We took Maria home, to a neat house back in the Karlovac suburbs. Her father was mowing the lawn, taking care not to disturb a plastic gnome who fished patiently in a small artificial pool. We turned the car around by a wrecked bridge, one almost destroyed, said Maria, in the 1991 fighting, and which, like Mr. Relja's wrecked farm, no one had found the money to repair.

Almost outside her house we picked up three more hitch-hikers, a trio of teenage girls who were going dancing. They sat crammed in the back of the car and sang the one song they knew in English. It was by Patsy Cline: "Crazy." And they sang it very well.

All that remained now was to make it through the Krajina and venture into the "land of the Osmanlees." I wondered if ours might be like Alexander Kinglake's crossing a century and a half before. He had been ferried over the very same river that we would have to cross, the Sava. And for him it was at a perilous time, too—for while beyond the Sava these days there is violence and revenge, beyond the river in 1844 the problem was the plague:

> When all was in order for our departure, we walked down to the precincts of the quarantine establishment, and there awaited the "compromised" officer of the Austrian government, whose duty it is to superintend the passage of the frontier, and who for that purpose lives in a state of perpetual excommunication. The boats with their "compromised" rowers were also in readiness.
>
> After coming into contact with any creature or thing belonging to the Ottoman empire, it would be impossible for us to return to the Austrian territory without undergoing an imprisonment of fourteen days in the Lazaretto. We felt, there-

fore, that before we committed ourselves, it was important to take care that none of the arrangements necessary for the journey had been forgotten; and in our anxiety to avoid such a misfortune we managed the work of departure from Semlin with nearly as much solemnity as if we had been departing this life. Some obliging persons from whom we had received civilities during our short stay in the place, came down to say their farewells at the river's side; and now, as we stood with them at the distance of three or four yards from the "compromised" officer, they asked if we were perfectly certain that we had wound up all our affairs in Christendom, and whether we had no parting requests to make. We repeated the caution to our servants, and took anxious thought lest by any possibility we might be cut off from some cherished object of affection:— were they quite sure than nothing had been forgotten—that there was no fragrant dressing-case with its gold-compelling letters of credit from which we might be parting for ever? No— every one of our treasures lay safely stowed in the boat, and we—we were ready to follow. Now there we shook hands with our Semlin friends, and they immediately retreated for three or four paces, so as to leave us in the centre of a space between them and the "compromised" officer; the latter then advanced, and asking once more if we had done with the civilized world, held forth his hand—I met it with mine, and there was an end to Christendom for many a day to come.

I was not entirely certain just where to cross the Sava; when I took advice it was from the strangest source. It turned out that a former Australian prime minister, Malcolm Fraser, was staying in the room next to mine at the Esplanade. He told me, when we had a drink that evening, that he was trying (in vain as it turned out) to secure the release of a pair of Australian aid workers who had been arrested in Serbia and charged with spying. His mission not unnaturally fascinated Australia, and there were four journalists from Sydney and Melbourne in the hotel, covering the story.

One of them turned out to be a man with whom I had shared a house in Washington a quarter of a century before, and whom I had not seen since. We spent our last evening in Christendom with him, and he assured us that the most prudent place to cross the Sava was via a half-ruined bridge a hundred miles east of Zagreb, at a place called Gradiska.

And so the next morning we drove there, and under a blazing sun crossed the iron Bailey bridge, our progress monitored by the crew of Hungarian army sappers who had helped to build it. It took half an hour of paperwork and fee paying and delay, but by lunch we were properly stamped—in Cyrillic, naturally—into what was notionally the Republic of Bosnia and Herzegovina, BiH for short, or the Federation.

Except not quite. We had in fact come across the border, across the Sava River, not directly into the Federation, but into that part of Bosnia that is almost wholly occupied by Serbs, rather than by the Croats or Bosnian Muslims—Slavs all, it has to be remembered—for whom the Federation is their supposed home. We were driving, and would be driving for a couple of hours more, through that half-legal entity that was won out of the cliff-hanging negotiations at Wright-Patterson Air Force Base in Dayton, Ohio, and is known as the Republika Srpska—a place where no one, quite frankly, is very welcome. Certainly not two foreigners driving a Fiat that sported license plates showing it was registered in Croatia. It was perhaps not wholly surprising, then, that like Alexander Kinglake all those years before, we passed under the barrels of the sentries' guns with just a *frisson* of apprehension.

4

Looking for a Sarajevo Rose

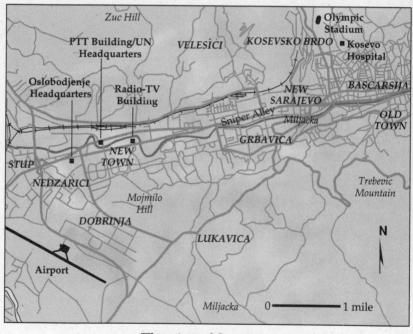

The city of Sarajevo

I WAS TOLD THAT I should see a Sarajevo rose. I had heard a lot about them—not exactly what they were, mind you, but that they were well worth seeing. I asked the Rose with whom I was traveling: She had heard of them, too, but wasn't quite sure either.

Rose knew a good deal about Sarajevo, and like so many who had lived in Europe during its years of siege and near destruction, had followed the downward spiral of the city's fortunes with a grim fascination. In the United States there wasn't the same degree of interest, and I was less prepared than was Rose for what lay ahead. I had heard several people say that after its five years of ruination and despair the city was now in an optimistic mood, and that it thought of itself as the fastest-changing place on earth. On the other hand, some Cassandras I had spoken to back in Vienna and Zagreb said this was fanciful nonsense, and that the city would eventually turn out to be much the same as it always was—a cauldron of all Balkan races and religions but one perpetually on the verge of boiling over. Just see a Sarajevo rose, one of them said, and then you'll have a better idea of whether or not things will ever really change.

In ordinary circumstances it should be about a three-hour drive to the Bosnian capital from the Sava River. But neither Sarajevo nor the Bosnian Republic have known ordinary circumstances for a long time now, and I supposed it would take rather longer to get there. Especially in a car registered in Croatia. (Though one of the Serb border guards who was in a friendly mood said that, since my car was registered in the Istrian seaport of Rijeka, and there was little historic animosity between the average Serb and the average Istrian, I would quite probably "get away with it.")

The first few miles proved amiable enough. For maybe two or three miles, close to the frontier, there were some ruined houses, relics of the shelling from the Croatian guns. But when we turned into the Taxi-Bar café that the frontier sentries had recommended, it had been newly rebuilt and was filled with free-spending patrons, and no one, not even a group of four enormous and bare-chested Serbian men who sat at the next table, appeared unduly interested in my foreign car. I ordered beer and *cevapcici*, a dish of lamb and beef rolls, with freshly chopped chives and red-hot peppers, and which owes much to Bosnia's Turkish culinary influence.

We ordered coffee. "Bosnian?" asked the waitress, matter-of-factly, and when we agreed brought us what back home we always called Turkish coffee, two tiny cups on a brass stand, and poured the thick brown liquid from a *dzezva*, a Turkish brass coffee jug. As we paid the bill—in German marks, the most widely accepted currency in the Balkans—one of the men from the next table came across and promptly turned the coffee cup over, dumping out the remaining coffee, claiming loudly to be able to read our futures from the grounds left behind.

"I see, I forecast, you will have good time here," he said, in fractured English. His companions, contentedly drunk, giggled and gave the two-finger-and-thumb Serb salute—a gesture I was to see in much more threatening circumstances some weeks ahead.

We sped as fast as was legal through the ugly crossroads town of Banja Luka, forty miles from the frontier. There had once been more than a dozen mosques in the town, but so militant were the Serbs who flocked here during the war—as refugees from the Krajina in Croatia, and from those parts of Bosnia that were awarded to the Federation—that every one of them had been knocked down, including the famous Ferhadija Mosque, which was built in the sixteenth century with the ransom money paid to recover a kidnapped Austrian count. These days the town is the epicenter of nationalist Serbdom for what is called the RS—the Republika Srpska—and for those who care to demonize the Serbs, not a place in which to linger. But I got lost, and everyone I stopped to ask—each of whom glanced automatically at my license plates to guess at my persuasions—was helpful, and displayed not a trace of hostility. That was to come a good while later.

To get to Sarajevo there was a choice: either the main road due south, or a smaller country road that wound up and over a range of hills. I had an army map that is customarily given to drivers of SFOR, the thirty-thousand-strong NATO Stabilization Force that tries to keep the Bosnian peace: It marked the country lane in red, as what armies call a Theater-Controlled Route, and even gave it a code-name, albeit an unlovely one: CLOG.* And sure enough, below the main sign that said SARAJEVO was a small yellow tac-sign (a tactical sign) with CLOG in a military stencil. We swung left onto the convoy route and climbed up into the high country.

Here at last was the geology of the Balkans writ large. The hills reared and plunged like the backs of a million mustangs. Villages were tucked away in the deep and forested folds of the ranges. There were waterfalls and tiny lakes, meadows and cliffs and precipitous ridges. There were dozens of churches too, each with the cross of the Eastern Orthodox faith, the tilted crosspiece at the base reminding worshipers that one of the men crucified beside Christ was destined for heaven, the other

---

*The Turks were nominally in control of this sector of Bosnia, and their route names were not especially pretty. A few miles west, in a British-patrolled sector, the recommended routes had names like PELICAN, CUCKOO, DIAMOND, and TRIANGLE. The Americans, over on the east, clearly felt homesick: Their tanks and armored cars drove roads named ALABAMA, GEORGIA, and NEW JERSEY.

not. No Catholic spires here, or minarets. We were deep inside the Serbian Republic, in a landscape that, however cruelly, had been cleansed of all alien callings, and that, like it or not, basked in the temporary peace of its newfound purity.

And then we heard a faraway deep-throated rumble, and high above us were the contrails again: a big bomber this time, an American B-52 dispatched from its forward base in East Anglia, with four fighters from a U.S. base in Italy escorting it, on the way to drop hot iron onto Serbia.

As we came ever closer to what the SFOR map defined with a thick black line and a set of warning symbols as the "inter-entity boundary," there was ruin again—mile after mile of shattered houses, the burned-out shells of what had been homes and farms and barns. The daubings once more—"Cetniki brigade"— showed who was responsible. These had been the houses of Muslims, burned out and cleared by Serbs to make this region pure. By now I was becoming inured to it, but Rose fell silent, stunned.

Whole village house rows were empty—lines upon lines of houses destroyed, not randomly but with concentrated deliberation. I think that is what dismayed us most. This was not a countryside devastated by conventional fighting, in which an army had smashed its way across an urban landscape and laid waste anything in its path. This was selective, spiteful fighting, in which soldiers and civilians with pure hatred in their hearts set about the destruction of personal enemies, the settling of old scores. This was evidence of an abscesslike welling up of years of poison, and its sudden release, with dreadful, impassioned result.

The only houses that were untouched were those once owned by Serb farmers, back in those times when villagers ignored their differences—such as they were: Everyone here was a Slav, it needs to be said again and again—and just got on with the harvesting or the sowing or the raising of barns. But even these intact houses were empty, their owners quite understandably opting not to live on in a village of ghosts. That was one difference about the desertion: The Serbian houses had their windows boarded up; the Muslim houses had no windows.

A Bailey bridge—built by Royal Engineers a couple of years before—took us across a rushing gray river that formed the entity frontier itself, the ruins of the old bridge standing like broken teeth beside it. And then a few more miles of wreckage, before we rounded a bend, passed a Turkish army jeep and a white Land Rover, both with SFOR stenciled on their sides, and found ourselves in a settlement of modern houses, all intact. There was a café, and we bought two beers. The owner was a Muslim. There was a wall calendar in Arabic. "Yes, Muslim but Bosniak," he grinned. "I drink beer. Is okay."

Suddenly there came a furious barking from below the lip of a hill beside the bar, and four breathless men in army fatigues clambered up beside us. They each had a huge dog, restrained by heavy chain leashes, and each had a hunting rifle slung over his shoulder. "Pigs!" one shouted, "Wild pigs!" pointing down to the bottom of the valley. "And we have a wolf. Caught him yesterday."

Rose and I slithered down the grassy bank to a hastily built barbed-wire cage. Inside, and chained by a back foot, was a gray wolf with yellow eyes and teeth an inch long. It jumped up wildly when it spied us, and began a deep growling, like far-off thunder. But when we knelt down next to its cage it fell mute, and sat gazing up at me with what seemed an expression of terrible misery, caught and pinioned like this away from its forest lair. The men who had caught it waved their guns and cheered. "Serbian wolf!" one shouted. And they laughed drunkenly, kicked their dogs up into a cage behind the car, and, waving their guns out of the windows, skidded off down the mountainside.

There was an increasing number of minarets now, as we passed town after bustling Federation town. We stopped for a while in Travnik, a town with a classical Balkan look—squeezed and squashed by geology and topography into an inconveniently narrow valley, hemmed in by steep hills and connected to the outside only by winding switchback roads. My principal Balkan hero, the Nobel Prize–winner Ivo Andric had been born here: He wrote the novel that I have long thought of as the most important Balkan book, *The Bridge on the Drina*; a book that, though it appears to offer high regard for the Serb, was written by what Ivo Andric was invariably forgotten to be, a Croat.* There was a museum to his memory, but as so often happens it was locked, and a bored attendant who might well have been schooled in China offered only the memorably Oriental excuse, heard without cease in the People's Republic: "The man with the key is not here."

The imam of the local mosque was more welcoming, and though almost totally deaf spoke enough German to express his relief that his and six other mosques had all escaped the wartime shelling. He let me wander around inside where it was cool, and I padded across the soft, thick Turkish carpets and counted two dozen sets of prayer beads and as many copies of the Koran, open at different pages. When I emerged into the light the mullah was surrounded by elderly women in head-scarves, and was eating happily from a bag of fries and ketchup that one of the ladies had brought him.

Dusk was gathering when, finally, we came to the junction beside the infamous airport and the even more infamous Mount Igman and, after turning left, saw the twinkling lights and familiar ruins of the city of Sarajevo itself. Soon there were trolley tracks and then, on our right, suddenly rearing out of the earth like some devastated nuclear sarcophagus, the twisted girders and shattered curved gray cement walls and floors of what had once been the towers of the newspaper

---

*I have always thought it a shame that President Clinton never read it or, if he did, that he famously derived his political views on Bosnia and later on Kosovo from another, *Balkan Ghosts*, written by an American journalist, Robert Kaplan.

office, *Oslobodenje*, which more than almost any other ruin seemed to symbolize the awfulness of what had happened to this town.

That is not to say it is the most infamous ruin. The terrible damage done to the graceful and domed old Hapsburg National Library, which used to be the town hall, stands as memorial to a particularly dire moment—the summer evening when, six months after the siege began in early 1992, a torrent of shells poured down on the building and set fire to it, and the ashes of a million burning books rained down on those who tried in vain to save it. The barbarity of that event remains indelibly etched in the minds of all who stayed during the war or who have since returned—along, to a greater or less degree, with the countless other moments of terror and misery that left 10,615 people dead, of whom 1,601 were children. The siege of Sarajevo went on for 1,395 days—longer than the siege of Stalingrad; longer, it is said, than any siege in modern history. And its evidence, physical, psychological, spiritual, is inescapable. It confronts you, assaults you, in every view, with every conversation. It hangs in the air, a deathly mustiness, sour and rotten.

We stayed at the Holiday Inn, which had been built for the 1984 Olympics and which famously stayed open throughout the siege, and in which—since it overlooked a snipers' alley, with the ruins of the assembly building between it and the Miljacka River and the Serb front line—the costliest rooms were those that did *not* have a view. The city outside was busy: Shoppers passed back and forth, the trolleys rattled past every few moments, cars went by at normal speed. No one ran, no one scuttled. There was a small café close by where people sat out in the sunshine, without an apparent care in the world. But when, as often happened, there was a sudden sound—a screech of tires, a car backfire, a shout—everyone looked up; there was a collective wince of memory, a skittishness born of five years of hard experience.

Outwardly there were many reassuring signs that matters

might be returning to normal. But then again, perhaps not. There were four houses of worship within a few hundred yards of the hotel, which before the war had bustled with congregations and showed just how well the fourth faiths, Eastern Orthodox, Roman Catholic, Muslim, and Jew, had managed to coexist. But now the Orthodox church seemed closed, and there appeared to be little business in the synagogue. Only the Catholic Croats and the Muslims, for whom the Bosnian Federation had been established, seemed active.

Much else was moribund as well. On my first morning I went to the railway station. There had been a time when Sarajevo was a lively railway town, the station itself the pride of the Balkans. Ten years ago you could go by rail from Sarajevo down to Ploce on the Adriatic coast, or all the way up to Zagreb, or across to Belgrade, or Budapest or Athens. The latest *Cook's Continental* suggested there might still be some services, a fifty-minute shuttle to Visoko and Zenica—but it warned otherwise that "many long-distance services have been suspended," and even such details as were published were "from unofficial sources and therefore subject to confirmation."

And the station was, of course, a total wreck. The facade was normal enough, except for some old shell damage. Inside a few stores were working, and there was a desultory crowd waiting, as if in a Samuel Beckett play, for something—a train, a bus, a long-lost friend—that never seemed to turn up. Once under the tracks and up the stairs to the platforms, however, the sadder reality of Sarajevo station became readily apparent.

There were six tracks, and grass grew up from all of them. The station clock stood still, unwound, unpowered: It was stuck at some minutes after five, the time one of the shells struck home in 1992, just when the siege began. A few carriages stood idly, their paint peeling, their windows shattered, as if they were waiting for restoration in a rail museum. In one corner a large diesel truck had been coupled with rusty steel cables to a carriage, and someone said that it might leave later that afternoon, its tires straddling the railway tracks, and make a journey to one of the city suburbs, half an hour away.

At first I thought there was no one there, that the station was quite dead. But behind a coal heap I found four miserable-looking men, all from Sri Lanka, who said they had been living on the platforms for the past six months. They spoke English, and explained that a middleman in Colombo, to whom they had each paid six thousand American dollars, had promised them he would smuggle them into Germany and find them work.

They had been brought west by cargo ship and by freight train to Turkey and then—of all places—to Banja Luka, which is where the middleman himself had wanted to go. They had eventually wound up here in Sarajevo, where the agent had left, had given them the slip. They had been on the platform ever since, with no money, no prospects, no work, no passports, no friends. Except they knew a man named Bobby, one said—he was a Nigerian, a student at Sarajevo University, and he came down from time to time and brought them cigarettes. They begged for food in the station square.

I felt desperately sorry for them—though heaven knows, I suppose I should have felt sorrier for the Sarajevans themselves. I let one of them use my cell phone to call his mother in Colombo, and when the number rang and a familiar voice replied in Sinhalese, his friends crowded around him, smiling, laughing, trying to pass on messages to friends and relatives, reassuring everyone back home that all was well even though it manifestly wasn't, and that all would be well even though it clearly wouldn't be. I couldn't see that they had much reason for optimism, though they seemed to cling to the memory of the promises made by the man who had brought them here, There was no work to be had in Bosnia, there was no money. Nor was there much by way of law or due process or some structure by which they could get redress and hammer their lives back into order.

I gave them a little money, and when I walked back down the steps toward the tunnel I saw that one of them, the boy who had called his mother, was weeping. "I am so homesick," was all he said, and waved and turned away.

Sarajevo is a town given over almost entirely now to "the internationals"—the aid workers and the foreign financiers and the staff of the man who essentially runs the town and who is called, with true Gilbertian flummery, the high representative. I would receive letters for some while after I left Sarajevo from functionaries who worked at the Office of the High Representative, and I imagined them to be courtiers to a man who wore spurs and a cuirasse and a plumed hat, and ran all Bosnia as his personal fief. In fact he was a rather modest Spaniard named Carlos Westendorp, and those who worked for him were similarly unassuming. They worked to rebuild the wrecked country and its capital in the businesslike way of true Eurocrats, wearing suits as they did so, keeping rigidly to an eight-hour day, being chauffered around town in long white four-wheel-drive cars, living in apartments that were no more or no less modest than those they had left behind in Brussels, London, or Rome, and taking leave at frequent intervals and traveling to do so always in business class. There were said to be thirty thousand such "internationals" in Sarajevo—seven hundred alone in Mr. Westendorp's office. The Bosniaks who did not work for them, who remained outside the charmed circle, seemed to hate them, or at least envy them; and those who had managed to find work with the international community—as translators, drivers, functionaries—found their working habits strange, their approach irritatingly demanding.

Rose had a friend in town, a young woman named Anja, who had fled during the worst of the war and had gone to live in Paris. Now she was back, with two languages, working as an interpreter for the high representative. She was paid a handsome salary in

convertible marks to translate technical documents into and out
of Bosnian, and out of and into English and French. But she
didn't like her job, and nor, she said, did many of her Bosnian
friends. It was simply too hard.

"I think we are a pretty lazy people," Anja told me one day, as
we drank coffee in one of the tiny and impossibly crowded bars
that have recently sprung up like weeds out of the ruin. "It is
part of our Ottoman heritage, I guess. All I do is drink coffee,
get my hair done, talk. We Balkans like to talk. We've never had
a tradition of working like this. And so you see what happens
here now. There's no energy to do anything real. There are just
a lot of get-rich-quick schemes. Lots of sponging off the internationals. Black markets. And drugs—lots of drug smuggling. And
girl smuggling. And people—workers to Germany, that sort of
thing."

I told her about the four men I had found at the railway
station. "Typical," she replied. "Everything in transit, nothing permanent, anything that'll make quick money. That middleman—
bound to have been a Bosniak. I probably know the guy. Cute, if
you like that sort of thing. We may see him tonight in Jez [a café,
named for a local type of hedgehog, and much favored by the current Bosnian mafia]. You know, Sarajevo's not a good place. It
ruins itself with fighting, and then it gets ruined again by all these
foreigners. They mean well, but they don't understand. Maybe the
foreign soldiers do. Maybe people with guns understand this
place. But not many others. It doesn't work by normal rules.
There's a sort of anarchy here. And then there's all the anger, one
people against another, and those against a third.

"You have it in Ireland, yes? It goes back years, yes? But in
your case it only concerns two sets of people. Here it concerns
three, at least. And the foreigners too. And all the groups you'll
have forgotten about long ago."

She went on to tell me about an old boyfriend, a young jew-
eler who had come from that strange area of Bosnia known as

the Sanjak of Novi Pazar, a fingerlike extension of longtime Turkish rule sandwiched between Kosovo and Bosnia. It was still largely Muslim—not because its inhabitants were Albanian (as they were in Kosovo itself), but because its people had become Islamicized after so very many years of living under Ottoman occupation. These people had a long history of being ostracized too, she said, had been caught up in the fighting because they were "different," because they were Muslim, because they were sharp traders who made money and, in her words, "behaved like Jews or Chinese."

Her own boyfriend, wearying of threats by the Bosnian Serbs and the jealousy even of the home-grown Bosnian Muslims and Croats around him, had emigrated to Istanbul. There, she said, he felt safe—others from the Sanjak had been going to Turkey for years, and there was now a more sizable Balkan community in the city than one might imagine. She urged me to go and see him; I promised that I would.

I felt at first that I didn't much care for the Sarajevo internationals. They all looked so smug and well-dressed, I thought; they took all the tables at the city's few good restaurants; their numbers drove up the prices of the best flats; and their shiny white Range Rovers and Land Cruisers rode just that little bit taller than all the other cars in town, lending them a hauteur which I thought they didn't much deserve. Parasites, I thought unkindly, not helpers in the real sense. These weren't the people who dirtied their hands bringing help to a benighted place, like the doctors of Médecins sans Frontières, or the vanguard teams from the UN Refugee Commission. These were the assistance commissars, and I resented them. But then again I knew only too well that I was an international too, and I lived far better than most of the inhabitants, and that I was hardly dirtying my hands with the reality of this town or any other. So how could I talk?

The Independent Media Commission, which was set up to try to give some direction to the stripling country's fractured and fractious press and broadcasting industries,* struck me as probably offering an example of the internationals' *schtick.* It had been set up in 1998, the language of its establishment hinting at the bureaucracy involved, since it had been done ". . . under the Authority of Annexe 10 of the General Framework Agreement for peace, and Article V of the Conclusions of the Bonn Peace Implementation Conference 1997. . . ."

The thinking behind the commission was simple enough: The output of the various radio and television stations in what in 1998 was a three-year-old country is, not surprisingly, deeply and intensely partisan, to the point of becoming dangerously inflammatory—so let a body of neutral observers, the commission, monitor the stations' output, try to curb the excesses of the wilder members of the fraternity, and use persuasion, sanctions, and perhaps even force to oblige them all to behave. A perfectly laudable aim: The idea that a new country should have a robust but responsible press can be nothing less than the universally acceptable wish of reasonable men.

The offices are on the third floor of a half-wrecked building close to the front line, beside a threadbare riverside park. A dozen white cars were parked outside, and a chauffeur was polishing the windows of the largest of them. Inside all was tidy, quietly busy. The air-conditioning hummed; secretaries, dressed as they might be in Brussels or London, stepped in and out of offices, looking serious. I was eventually shown into the office of a former sergeant in the British army parachute regiment, who laughed and shook his head when I asked if knew anything about the press or broadcasting, but whose desk was now covered with memorandums, in a Babel of tongues, giving those

---

*In 1999 Bosnia had 280 radio and TV stations, and seven hundred transmitters—one for every five thousand people, thus making its population the most broadcasted-to in the world.

few back up in Brussels or Geneva or New York who might be interested news of the latest skirmishes in what he called "Bosnia's war for truth." He appeared outwardly calm but said that he was in fact perplexed, overwhelmed. He had his work cut out for him.

"Sometimes it is hard to take these broadcasts seriously," he said, waving a sheet of paper at me. "Look at this—it's a transcript of a station in the Serb Republic—TV St. George, run by Radovan Karadzic's daughter, as it happens—which claimed the other night that, listen to this, Mujaheddin fighters on the Muslim side are kidnapping Serbian children, and feeding them to the lions in the Sarajevo zoo! I ask you! This is the kind of thing we deal with all the time.

"We've got Croatian TV, with huge transmitters down in Herzegovina, just up in the hills beyond Dubrovnik—great waterskiing, by the way!—uttering all kinds of bilge, which the Serbs get terribly worked up about. There is RTV-BiH, which is hopelessly Muslim-biased. The Serbs don't like that either. Canal S is very pro-Serb, and so is STV, which we want to shut down because it broadcasts endless stuff directly from inside Serbia about how wonderful Milosevic is and how cowardly NATO is.

"Some of it we permit, because we're all for free speech. But some of it becomes too irresponsible—just rabble-rousing. That we try to take a hard line about—but we have to follow procedures, of course, and it all takes time. It takes eight, nine steps, so far as I know.

"First we ask those stations that break our code—and it's mainly TV stations; the people here are fanatic TV addicts—we ask them to say they're sorry. Then we issue a warning. Then we make an order against them. We can fine them. We can suspend their broadcasting license. We can go into their building, seize their equipment, close them down, take their license away forever. It is all very formal—but we do have the power."

But I put it to the former soldier that all of this wasn't going to do much good if, moments after a broadcast like the one he told me about, a gang of Serbs came down to the Sarajevo zoo bent on killing young Muslims who might look as though they had thrown Serbian children to the lions. He shook his head wearily. "That's what I mean. We behave like reasonable people here. Not everyone else does."

Later in the day I drove a couple of miles west out of town to the sprawling and scrupulously well-guarded headquarters of SFOR, the huge multinational armed force that is charged with trying to keep the peace inside Bosnia. After an hour spent acquiring permission—during which I had to stand directly in front of a Turkish armored car that trained its 50 mm cannon directly onto my windshield—I found myself in the Ops Room, with a dapper Argentinian brigadier who clicked his heels and said how sorry he was about the Falklands War, and with his colleague, a young British colonel who was also an Irish hereditary earl—and who might have stepped straight out of an Evelyn Waugh novel.

We sat in the sun and drank tea—no beer before seven, SFOR rules—and I told him about the troubles that the IMC had enforcing anything. "It falls to us, then," said His Noble Lordship. "Very simple, really. If push comes to shove we don't bother to go through the whole rigmarole of warning them and asking them to stop. We don't go to their offices—no point, really, if you want to act decisively. We just go up to the hill where they have the transmitter—there's usually no one there, or perhaps just a *chokidar* and we find the switch, and flick it up. Bingo! Turns everything off. And then we put a couple of sentries there so they can't go back and turn it on, and if they do, we blow it up. Quite simple, really. Miserable for the sentries in winter, of course. But it's the only kind of thing some of these chaps understand. A bit of decisiveness."

So, were the internationals a good thing, on the whole? "They mean well. That chap Westendorp—good fellow, reasonable man. But he's dealing with terribly unreasonable people. I think they sometimes forget that. That's where we come in. We keep the three sides apart. And we make sure that everyone behaves. Who's the bigger dictator—the high representative, or the general, the SFOR commander?" he asked rhetorically.

"I guess they're both pretty much dictatorial in their powers. The civilians are the benign ones, I guess. They don't have the muscle to be malign. We do. It's not very easy to argue with us. Have you seen some of our tanks? And we can whistle up planes in two shakes of a lamb's tail.

"No—a strong hand is needed to run a place like this. To keep the lid on the pressure cooker. And for now we're the strong hand. Us in Bosnia. Our chums down in Kosovo before long, I guess. You seen any news today?"

In a bar later that evening I met two policemen, dressed in navy blue uniforms and with an impressive array of badges, flashes, and medals. They were Americans, one from Kansas City, the other from Wichita Falls, Texas. They had been seconded to the UN and had spent the past twelve months in Bosnia, trying—"yes, trying"—to train young Bosniak policemen. The biggest problems had to do with drug smuggling and passport scams. The pair thought that Sarajevo was probably now one of the largest drug-smuggling centers in the world. The raw material came on what they called "the Mujaheddin highway" from Afghanistan or the Burmese Golden Triangle, and it was refined and distributed from warehouses among the ruins of central Bosnia. "Everyone's in on it," drawled the Texan in a tone of languid desperation. "It's not just a Muslim thing, you know."

But anyway, he continued, it wasn't his problem anymore. He was leaving Bosnia the very next morning and going home to Texas. He had just had his final plate of kebabs, the *raznjazici*, and now he was going down to the Turkish bazaar by the old library, to buy one of those "darned cute carved shell cases." A small cottage industry had developed at the east end of town, and merchants peddled the intricately worked cylinders of brass, 155 mm being the largest and most expensive. He thought he might take two. One for each side of the fireplace in the den. "Then I can tell the story. Don't get much better than that in Wichita Falls, I can tell you."

Near to the restaurant was what used to be known as Princip's Corner. Rose and I had argued heatedly that morning as whether the more important event in Sarajevo's history was the five-year siege of the 1990s or whether it was what happened eighty years before, on June 28, 1914, at this corner, at the end of the street to the north of second bridge across the Miljacka River. (I was for the earlier event, which, after all, I pointed out, involved the whole world. To the siege, most of the world turned its back.)

The heir to the Austro-Hungarian throne, the Archduke Franz Ferdinand, and his morganatic* wife, Sophie Chotek, had just been driven there after a meeting at the town hall, now the ruined National Library. A man named Gavrilo Princip fired at the couple with a small pistol, killing them both. A black tablet was later erected at the spot, noting that "Here, in this historical place, Gavrilo Princip was the initiator of liberty, on the day of St. Vitus, the 28th of June, 1914."

What the tablet omitted to say, of course, was that the two victims who fell here in 1914 became the eight million that fell all across Europe in the Great War triggered by their assassination. And what it also chose not to say was that Princip was a Serb, and

---

*Though an explanation has little place in the the Balkan story, the word *morganatic* does have a compelling origin. It refers to a marriage in which the only benefit is the "morning [*Morgen*] gift" of the spouse, the token reward offered for consummation. Nothing else—such as a title or a fortune—is to be given or inherited. In Germany morganatic marriages were sometimes known as "left-handed" marriages, since it was the custom for the groom to offer his left hand during the ceremony, instead of his right.

the most extreme of nationalists. The date he chose was itself pregnant with significance: June 28 is not merely Saint Vitus's Day—it is the anniversary of the Battle of Kosovo Polje, when all Serbs celebrate their battle with (and defeat at the hands of) the Ottoman Turks—the date also chosen by Slobodan Milosevic, seventy-five years later, to begin his own Serb campaign, which culminated in so much contemporary bloodletting.

But all this, for the tourist, was now moot. Those who once came to read the tablet and to ponder the notion that Princip had somehow initiated "liberty"—that he had somehow performed some noble deed—no longer have no opportunity to do so. The tablet is gone, torn down by the Bosnian government in 1996 simply because Princip was a Serb nationalist, no different in his way from the artillerymen and the snipers who, in the name of Greater Serbia, made life for Sarajevo's Bosnians so wretched and so dire.

The town government had long ago torn up the paving stones bearing Princip's supposed footprints. So anyone who visits today will find nothing to see at the corner that bears his name. Perhaps Sarajevo has come to believe that its siege was the more important event in its history, and that what happened here on that Saint Vitus's Day, though it may have had effects that rumbled across the rest of the world, had but little impact on this ancient Balkan town. I asked Anja what she thought: She was very much a child of her times, and said that in her opinion whatever Gavrilo Princip had done was far too long ago to be of any importance.

People are still working among the ruins of the *Oslobodanje*. A long while ago the besieging Serbs had it in mind to use the building—grand and up-to-date as once it was—as their head-quarters. But after their gunners failed to dislodge the workers from it, they simply shelled it into what they thought was oblivion. The crumbling sarcophagus of the main tower is still terribly dangerous, with slabs of broken cement swinging from rusty girders, and glass falling in torrents whenever there is a high wind. But the office building beside it, like the printing plant below, is still more or less intact; and if you pass through the back doors and in front of an elevator that is still peppered with bullet holes, there is a half-intact glass door and, beyond it, a scattering of desks, computers, and workbenches—a newspaper office, as messy and smoke-filled as any anywhere. It was from here throughout the war, as it still is from here today, that the bulk of Sarajevo's more independent-minded newspapers and magazines were being edited, published, and printed.

Zlatko Dizdarevic was the paper's publisher when the war began, and his columns, published each week, were gathered together as one of the most moving testaments to the conflict. "This is not a war," he wrote famously at the start of one column. "This is a horror that has no name. It is a black hole in the spectrum of all reasoned thought."

Dizdarevic is a Muslim, born in Belgrade, and he is married to a Serb. He looks older than his fifty years, very much a European, sitting behind his desk in tweeds and a sport shirt. He knows that the spotlight has shifted away from Sarajevo, and he understands that the world has other wars, other concerns.

His own concern that day had nothing directly to do with Bosnia either: He was wondering whether it was right for the NATO bombers to have attacked the Belgrade television station, as had just been reported on the wire service. He wasn't sure what view to take in his next column.

"It is all to do with principles and realities, you know. Of course I am not in favor of anything that harms free speech, that amounts to censorship—as this bombing was meant to do. It was meant to silence the station, of course. But the reality of the situation is so different—that station was pumping out so many lies, it had to be silenced. But then again—we say they were lies. But were they? How do I know that what that nice Mr.

Shea* in Brussels was saying was true? They were only bombing Belgrade to halt the spread of what they consider a perversion of the truth. So even the reality gets a little clouded at times. Often, in these parts, actually."

I asked him how things were in Sarajevo today. He looked downcast. He, too, had heard the Serbian broadcast about captured Serbian children being fed to the lions in the local zoo, and it made him wonder if matters were ever really going to get better.

"At times I feel really nostalgic for the Tito era. Maybe we were less free. But Tito kept the lid on all this crazy nationalism. As a newspaperman I hate the censorship, the very idea of a government-controlled press. But so much about Tito's time was good, compared to this. Better even than now, while we have SFOR to protect us, and that nice, well-meaning Mr. Westendorp to help us rebuild.

"In theory I feel now that the Balkans need not be the black hole of Europe—I feel that a real mixing of the cultures here could be a good thing. They've mixed them pretty well in America, in London. Why not here? I keep asking myself. I am just not convinced that we here are pathologically unstable, that we need a heavy hand from outside to keep us in check. I feel that all this trouble is due simply to criminal manipulation—a few really, really bad people have made a business of stirring things up. They are profiting, and we are all losing."

But did he see any hope? "Not until we have something like the denazification programs they had in Germany after the war— because we do have real Nazis here, you know. Real fascists. Terrible people. They need to be found and rooted out. The politicians they control have views that are rooted in the nineteenth century. They need to be elected out of office. We need

---

*"Jamie" Shea, the formidably professional voice of NATO, and spokesman for its policies, during most of the bombing campaign.

new people, a new generation. And economic recovery. Then the Balkans might have some hope. But not the heavy hand of outsiders—not for long.

"Even I have some nostalgia for the war, you know. A terrible thing to say. But in those days there was some semblance of fatalism, all being in this together. Now we are divided again—feeding children to the lions, for heaven's sake!—and we pretend that things are going to get better. I don't think they are; I am afraid I truly don't. Three years ago, when I was writing those columns, I was optimistic, and I knew that I would get my children, whom I had sent away for the siege, to come back and help rebuild.

"But now I won't ask them back. One of them is in Kansas City. One is in Italy. I don't want them to come back here to live. Bosnia is not a good place, not for one with hopes and dreams. Everyone who is young and full of hope wants to leave. There is a sickness about this place. This is a place for old people now. For memories, and most of them bad memories."

That night was the last we spent in Sarajevo, and we took Anja out to dinner and then to a smoky bar that was filled with men she knew, all drug dealers or arms dealers, or men who could sell you an Australian passport and smuggle you across the frontiers and get you out and away. And we were going back to the hotel when I remembered that I hadn't seen a Sarajevo rose, and I asked her what it was.

She laughed, looked down at the roadway, and pointed at a spot a few yards away under a street lamp. "There!" she said. "Take a look."

A Sarajevo rose is the scar of a shell burst, a deep central core surrounded by a ring of smaller depressions made by the exploding shrapnel. Some wit had had the idea, a year or two before, to fill up all the remaining scars with pink molten plastic. There are now hundreds of them, pink road sculptures commemorating each cannonade of shellfire, pretty in their own macabre way.

I told the young woman that I had been told to look at a Sarajevo rose and ask what it foretold about the future for Bosnia. What did she imagine?

"A lot more like this, before too long," she said. "This is not the end—it is just a stay. I just hope it is a very long one. But I am not so sure."

And she scuffed the pink plastic with her shoe, got back into her shiny white car, and sped off into the Sarajevo night.

We sped off too, down what during the siege had been the ragged and dangerous western escape route toward the sea— and along which the internationals now left for weekends of waterskiing at Split. There were high mountains along the way, covered with snow that was melting into the road tunnels and making the road treacherous. It took two difficult hours to reach, just before the Croatian frontier, the ruined old Herze-govinan town of Mostar, where I knew we would see one of the saddest sights of all, one of the low points in this world of misery and ruin.

5

The Fortress by the Sea

Herzegovina and southern Croatia

E VERYWHERE IN THE WORLD the Muslims ever went, they left as a legacy something, most often a piece of architecture, that was and still remains entirely beautiful. The great palace of the Alhambra in Granada. The domes of Cordoba and the caravanserais of Iran. The *hammam* of Kiraly in Budapest. Timur's mausoleum in Samarkand, or that of the Samanids in Bukhara. The shrine to the Imam Reza in Tabriz. And the countless mosques and minarets just about everywhere.

Even the simpler, humbler structures in the small, unnoticed towns have an astonishing beauty, an integrity, an assuredness of style and grace. The day, some weeks before, when we had driven south after being among the north Bosnian Serbs, and as we finally came to Travnik nestled in the hills, I remember remarking to Rose on the simple loveliness of all the minarets, rising as they did with such precision and economy from the more ordinary buildings of the town.

No more graceful, precise, and economical structure could there ever have been, I used to think, than the bridge across the Neretva River, in the Herzegovinan capital of Mostar. It had given the town its name: Stari Most, the Old Bridge. It was quite a modest structure, crossing the deep and swirling green river with just a single graceful arch, no more than fifty yards across. It rose from two large buttresses that seemed to have been annealed into the very limestone river cliffs. Its underside was a perfect upward swoop of carefully chamfered and fitted blocks, its upper parapet a low-pitched roof, its walkway shining with the passage of a million slippered feet.

From a distance it looked like a simple arabesque decorating the river valley. Up close it was a busy, teeming place, with cafés on each side, and bazaar shops selling beaten copper and brass, and in the old days stern Turkish policemen wearing the fez, and Serbian janissaries in their baggy trousers and brocaded waistcoats. It was more than four hundred years old when the latest round of Balkan wars began, and it did not survive them.

We saw it begin to crumble, piece by hallowed piece, in the summer of 1992. The fighting here, once properly established, was between Croats and Muslims—groups that, for a short while, had actually dreamed up the imaginative idea that they might form an alliance against the Serbs. The Balkans, however, are a place where the only alliances tend to be those with parties from the outside: Within the region everyone seems bent on eventually fighting everybody else, and almost all alliances turn out to be deeply cynical, very, very brief, or, like this one, complete fictions. (The Serbs themselves had once very much wanted the city of Mostar, and indeed had envisioned all the land of Herzegovina and south Dalmatia as far as the ancient port city of Dubrovnik itself as belonging, in their wilder dreams, to some utopian vision of Greater Serbia. But in the early summer of 1992 the Croats beat them in battle here and drove them away from the bank of the Neretva for all time. The stage was then set for a war for control across the river, between the Muslims on the western side and the Croats on the east.)

The bridge was built well, and for a while it stood up to the barrage of shellfire from the Croats on the hills above town. The Muslims, with a mixture of pride, affection, and simple economic need, tried their best to protect the old structure with automobile tires, hung over the edge as fenders, to minimize damage from shrapnel. But they were no match for the sustained and willful cannonade. One day late that autumn, and with an exhausted and exasperated roar that could be heard above the gunfire, the old bridge collapsed, its last stones—which had been painstakingly carved by Turkish masons in 1566—crashing into the river canyon and being swept downstream with the current. One should not mourn lost architecture so much as lost people, I suppose: But this was one of the loveliest bridges in the world, and it seems peculiarly terrible that it was in our enlightened times that we decided to demolish it, and to ruin a work that had survived so long.

Rose and I stopped for lunch on our first day in Mostar at a café on the west side. The road beside us led up to where the bridge had been, and some obliging urban planner had stretched chicken wire across the entrance to stop people plunging into the waters below. The gentle curve of the mantel rose up from the stream and hung there in midair, like a broken tooth—as did its brother mantel on the far side. An old lady waved at me from the buttress on her side of the river, inviting me to her caftan shop, indicating that I might double back upstream and use the new replacement bridge—"Built by 36 Regiment, Royal Artillery, in 1994, a Gift of the British People to all the People of Mostar." I pointed to my watch, and to the *sirnica*, the cheese pie that the waitress had just brought, and indicated that I would think about it.

I saw her later, and when I chided her for greeting me in German, and said that I was in fact English, she launched into what sounded like a timetable recitative: "Ostend—Dover—Ashford—Westminster—Greenwich—Norfolk—Harwich!" She had been to England once, and had traveled by train. She thanked me for the bridge, as though I had built it personally. She explained that she had very much hoped I wasn't German, as it was Germany that had first given formal recognition to Croatia and Slovenia, and she, as a good Muslim, could not abide the Croats. "Besides, see what they did to our bridge!"

And to the rest of the town besides. The front line, still visible a hundred yards or so west of the Neretva, is as frightful a zone of destruction as I was to see anywhere in this war. It stretches along a wide street called the Boulevard Hvratski Branitelija, where the Croats had sited their artillery in the great buildings on its western side, and the Muslims had been holed up on the east. The scale of destruction makes it look like Dresden, or the London docks after a night of incendiaries, in World War II. Such walls as still stood were pockmarked with a million shell bursts; great jagged gaps show where building burned and crashed; there were weeds, pools of stagnant water, flies, and forgotten relics from those who lived and worked here—a sofa, a pair of spectacles, a baby's pram, trousers.

And in the open spaces behind there were graves, too, with hastily carved markers—Haris, Ivan, Milhija, Jovan—leaning drunkenly at all angles. This must have been a hellish place. But now the fig trees were in bloom, and blossoms drifted down from a plum tree, and in the scrubby banks leading down to a rushing rivulet there were purple larkspur and buttercups. The Balkan landscape, usually so unforgiving and harsh, can display moments of tenderness, too, and when it chooses to, nature can always reclaim the worst of human excess.

But between Mostar and the coast the landscape is as classically unforgiving as any rain-shadow country can be—it is harsh and dry, with scrubby stands of forest and low and barren hills, and there are said to be innumerable snakes. Rocks, snakes, and guns, the locals say, are what the householders of Herzegovina know best. There was only a cursory frontier check at the town of Gabela, where we passed back into Croatia, before the car heaved up one final range of hills and then we saw, with breathtaking clarity, the coastline and the Adriatic.

Here at last was the coast road from Split to Dubrovnik, along which I had driven on my way to India in 1977. Here at last I thought, was civilization once again. Here was normal life, and an extraordinarily beautiful one at that.

The road onto which I was now turning left, to head down to Dubrovnik—is in truth one of the loveliest in all the world—it makes California's justly celebrated Route 1 seem banal by comparison, because in the Pacific you are beside the ocean alone, whereas here you look down on *islands*. Not long ago this

very coastal highway was a proud symbol of well-tempered normality. Until 1991 you could drive for four hundred miles, from
Trieste to the Albanian frontier, without so much as a customs
post or a police check, and certainly no need to show a passport. And yet you did all this across lands that until recently
had been a muddled mosaic of once-competing suzerainties:
You drove through large territories that had been variously
Austrian, Italian, Roman, Venetian, Serbian, Ottoman, Slovenian, Croatian—and microscopically independent, too, as once
Dubrovnik had been (when it was called Ragusa), and as poor
Montenegro had been, when it had its own king.

The creation of Yugoslavia ended all this colorful inconvenience, at least for a while. Under the astute presidency of Marshal Tito, and for eleven more years after his death in 1980, this
was a single country, and once you had left the Italian town of
Trieste and had passed through the relatively mild strictures of
Tito's Iron Curtain, you were on a coast road that told of his
skillful eradication, or so it seemed at the time, of all the con-
trary statelets of the years before. Their relics were there—the
churches, the mosques, the Venetian crests—but their attitudes
and hatreds were not. This was a road for all the southern Slavs,
and for those who cared to come visit.

But then came 1991, and the borders went up and the fighting
began. Today between Trieste and the Albanian frontier, you are
compelled to pass first in and out of Slovenia, then in and out of
Croatia, then in and out again of a tiny strip of Bosnia near a quay-
less and so quite useless port called Neum,* then once more in
and out of Croatia, then in and—if the Albanians are feeling

---

*The Bosnians, having no other outlet to the Adriatic, negotiated an
arrangement with the Croatians allowing them to use the port of
Ploce, where the Neretva flows into the sea. There is a railway terminus at Ploce, and notionally at least Sarajevo's ruined station can be
reached in six hours, with a change at the frontier.

cooperative—out of Montenegro. Five frontiers, ten passport stamps if the guards are in a liverish mood, ten openings and closings of the car if the customs men are similarly inclined. An amusing inconvenience to foreigners, at worst. Another aspect of the dystopian nightmare of the Balkans, to those who live there.

On this day, though, we had only to endure the single inspection coming in from Bosnia to Croatia—from BiH, as the Bosniaks know Bosna i Hercegovina, to Hrvatska, as the Croatians officially call their country. From the junction it was an hour to the outskirts of Dubrovnik, and to the jewel-city of the Adriatic that has been practically emptied by the war that has been raging at its doorstep all these years.

We assumed we would stay at the Excelsior or the Argentina, both of which stand a little south of and a little above the city walls. The view from either was magnificent, magical. The entire city-state could be seen, glowing by night (when we arrived) like a golden star at sea, or by day hemmed in by blue water and with its huge walls and towers rising from the waves, majestic, timeless, and imperturbable. Of all the city-states of the Mediterranean—like Venice, Amalfi, Pisa, Genoa—and of others beyond, like Bremen—Dubrovnik still has the look and feel of being all of a piece, so compact, so contented and confident of its standing. It was subjugated by Napoleon in 1808 and turned over to Hapsburg control in 1815—but for more than a thousand years before that, this exquisite walled city, doing business either under its own name, which means "city of a grove of trees," or until 1918 under the Italian name of Ragusa, was powerful, rich, and free to all asylum seekers (including Richard the Lionheart, who arrived after a shipwreck), a place of nobility, beauty, and style.

It was when we were looking for a hotel, strolling along the streets above the harbor and planning to ask for rooms at a place called the Villa Dubrovnik (which turned out to be closed and barred, a victim of the war like so much else around here), that we came across an ancient and, from her dress and appearance, evidently Croatian woman who was giving an evening hose-down to her equally ancient and rather decrepit dog. She spoke English with a notably cut-glass accent and demanded in an imperious manner that we clamber up the stairs to meet her and Wookie, as the beast was called. When we got there she extended a frail and blue-veined hand.

"A very good afternoon," she said, and then began a staccato, nonstop *curriculum vitae*. "I heard you speaking English. I get to see very few people these days. I like to speak to people. But there are none here now, because of this blessed business. I lived in Chelsea, do you know, for thirty years. I would shop at Gorringe's all the time—you know Gorringe's, don't you? Now I eat *Dinkel* all the time—I would be dead by now if I hadn't discovered it. It comes from Germany—I have heaps of it, literally heaps.

"Would you answer that telephone?—I am getting dirty calls from a man who breathes down the line. It is rather disagreeable. I'm ninety and then some. He must think otherwise, though goodness knows why. And I'm descended from a Serb who fought at the Battle of Kosovo. All these things may be of interest to you. So will you stay awhile? And might I interest you in some *Dinkel*, and perhaps a cup of tea?"

She was called Jelka Lowne, and she was well known at this end of Dubrovnik. "The mad Englishwoman," they called her, though she was neither very mad nor at all English. Her husband, an engineer with the British Post Office, had come from Kent. She had lived in England from 1935 until he died in 1963—they had a apartment opposite the Chelsea Town Hall, which is when she shopped at the now long-defunct (but among the well-heeled London elderly, still much missed) department store. They had then moved up to Coventry, which she gamely said was "a very decent sort of town."

She lived in some congenial squalor, with books and newspapers all over an unmade bed, congealed gruel in the bottom of a saucepan, dishes piled up in the sink, unopened letters from a branch of Barclay's Bank in stacks everywhere. "Some difficulty with a trust fund," she said—"perhaps you'll be able to help sort this out?" Wookie, a large and ever-bounding black dog who had the most unattractive mange and seemed to be at constant war with his coat, guarded his mistress with unfailing zeal, and whenever she rose to do anything—to open a letter, to make a cup of tea for us—came rushing to her side, panting, eyes gleaming, back leg scratching furiously. "My only friend," she explained. "No one comes to Dubrovnik anymore. This frightful nonsense is driving them all away. I had some friends from Sussex who used to come, and they would bring me tea and Marmite. But they write to say it is too dangerous. I say fiddlesticks—is that the word? I have been away so long!— but they don't come anyway."

She told us of her famous ancestor, a General Hrebeljanovic, who had fought at Kosovo alongside the legendary Serb leader Prince Lazar. On seeing my interest, she went to a locked drawer, extracted a manila folder and pulled out a sheaf of papers that she said would prove her ancestry. I was amazed and delighted.

Hrebeljanovic, from all accounts, was Prince Lazar's family name, and so there was every likelihood that this lady—and her papers had the *look* of authenticity about them, though I had only a cursory look—was related not merely to a general at the Battle of Kosovo, but to the great Czar Lazar himself. At least this is what I wanted to believe, for here I was, taking tea with her: It struck me as splendidly incongruous and almost impossibly serendipitous. Lazar, after all, was the one true hero of Serbian history, the man who in 1389 had his head cut off by the Turks in Kosovo after choosing to die rather than surrender, a man whose death all Serbs have since been avenging, and whose memory all Serbs have since been honoring. And here, sitting in a tiny overheated room on the Adriatic coast with her boisterous dog Wookie and nibbling at puffed *Dinkel*—here was a

woman who claimed to be his supposed direct descendant! It
seemed, of course, too good to be true.

But then so much else did too. Almost everything about Lazar
himself is clouded and enfolded by myth and legend, as is usually
the way with heroes who become the subject of songs and epic
poems. The Serbian tradition of the blind Gypsy, traveling from
Balkan town to Balkan town, playing the one-stringed instrument
the Slavs call the *gusla*, and reciting the long series of poems
known as the Kosovo Cycle, endures to this day.

> *Lazar, glorious emperor,*
> *Which is the empire of your choice?*
> *Is it the empire of heaven?*
> *Is it the empire of earth?*
> . . . .
> *"Kind God, now, what shall I do, how shall I do it?*
> *What is the empire of my choice?*
> *Is it the empire of heaven?*
> *Is it the empire of the earth?*
> *And if I shall choose the empire of the earth,*
> *The empire of the earth is brief,*
> *Heaven is everlasting."*
> *And the emperor chose the empire of heaven*
> *Above the empire of the earth.*

His choice made—so the myth has it—he was promptly exe-
cuted and his head cut off by the Turks who would then go on to
defeat his Serbian army. His body was dried, he was dressed in the
cloak with lions rampant which he was said to have worn on the
battlefield, and a red-and-gold cloth was placed over him. His
remains were placed in an open coffin in a monastery nearby. The
monastery, at a place nearby called Ravanica, became for three
centuries the center for a cult following that attracted hundreds of
thousands of Serb pilgrims from all over the Orthodox dominions.

Three hundred years later Czar Lazar's withered and headless body and his red-and-gold-shrouded bones left Kosovo for the relative safety of the north. They were taken there by the Orthodox patriarch of the Pec monastery, the holy man who was leading a column of thirty thousand Serbian faithful to a safe haven in the Slavonian and Croatian, the frontier land that had been gifted by the Austrians and that would in time become the Krajina. And then they went to off another church near Budapest, and in 1697 to yet another at a place called Srem. Finally, in 1942, after the Croatian Ustashi fascists stole some of Lazar's rings, the Germans—who had no love for Orthodox Serbs but did have some respect for tradition and holiness—helped take the relics to relative safety in Belgrade.

And there they stayed until 1987, when, at the urgings of Slobodan Milosevic, their priestly guardians allowed them to begin a rabble-rousing progress around all of Yugoslavia. The remains of Czar Lazar Hrebeljanovic—his coffin lid of transparent plastic, his thin brown hands, withered and frail, visible, sticking out from under their covering—were one of the early devices used to whip up the froth of nationalistic fervor that would keep Milosevic in power, and all Yugoslavia in turmoil. The czar's bones were central to the glorious mythic memory that Milosevic was to cite in his infamous speech on Saint Vitus's Day 1989, at the old battlefield near Kosovo Polje, the Field of the Blackbird. "Six centuries later again we are in battles and quarrels. . . ."

"But the odd thing," whispered the ancient and now tiring Mrs. Lowne, "is that I am hardly a Serb at all. I am a Croat, really—I am Catholic, for a start—and I am part Hungarian. Yes, I have Serb blood—who doesn't, in these parts? But it is droll, don't you think, that a living descendant of the greatest of all remembered Serbs is a Croat-Hungarian, living beside the sea in old Ragusa. I suppose that shows what six centuries of interbreeding can do.

"And that's what makes this nonsense"—and she spread her arms wide, gesturing toward the distant war—"all seem so utterly crazy. We are all Slavs, for heaven's sake. We are all the same people. Why do we fight so much among ourselves? I have seen so much in ninety years. And it is ending no better than when I was a child. That is so sad. So sad."

We stood up to leave. Her dog had caught the melancholy mood, I thought, but he jumped up and began racing furiously around the moment that we made a step for the door. Wookie's sudden excitement snapped her from her glum mood, and she became animated, too. "Will you stay? Will you stay?" she asked. She found and pushed into our hands a large bag of puffed *Dinkel*—which turned out to be the German version of the grain known elsewhere as spelt—and then asked forlornly if whether, instead of staying at a hotel, we might consider staying with her, in a shack at the end of the garden. We went up and looked at it, but it was like a potting shed, full of broken implements and yellowed copies of ancient English newspapers, and it smelled of mold and Wookie's leavings, so we thanked her and politely said perhaps another time. I needed telephones, I said, and a good long bath—particularly a bath, after all the exigencies of Sarajevo and Mostar. Mrs. Lowne sighed, and then drew herself up, recovered, and became her old imperious self again. "Then stay at the Excelsior, do," she said. "I know both of the managers. The man at the Excelsior is a cultured man. The fellow at the Argentina is perfectly nice but quite frankly, *a bit of a peasant.*"

Wookie stood stock-still beside Mrs. Lowne as we made our way down her garden stairs and off to the hotel. "Think *Dinkel,*" was the last thing she said. "I think I would have died a hundred times over if I hadn't eaten it for so long." We had an enormous bag of it, her parting gift, and it lasted us for a week.

There is a large map screwed to Dubrovnik's old city wall, just inside the Ploce gate. It records, with black diamonds and red stars, where every artillery shell and mortar bomb and incendiary device fell on the Old Town, during the eight months of the siege that began in 1991. The map is covered with symbols, like insects on flypaper; and it is a testament to the pride with which Dubrovnik itself and Croatia beyond regard this incomparably beautiful place that so much is now repaired. The city burghers once apologized that they had had some difficulty matching the exact color of the ancient clay roof tiles that had been destroyed, and indeed, from the distance of our window at the Excelsior, the roofs within the walls did have a mottled, mosaic appearance. But I thought it rather added to the magnificence of the place, the mite of imperfection underlining the otherwise impeccable.

The siege of Dubrovnik still seems to me to have been a pointless act of savagery. Just as with the Croats' wrecking of the lovely Turkish bridge at Mostar, and just like the systematic wrecking of Muslim houses in the villages in Bosnia, it seemed yet another indication of the brutish, unnecessary spitefulness of this wretched war. What military need had there ever been, "for heaven's sake," as Mrs. Lowne would have put it, for the Yugoslav army to fire artillery rounds from within the safety of the Montenegrin mountains, directly into the center of one of the world's most revered architectural sites? It was a monstrous crime, as unthinkable before it happened as would be the bombing of Oxford or Kyoto. But the Serbs in their army seemingly felt no attachment to a town that was 90 percent Croat anyway, and in a country that had declared its independence: And so in the middle of October 1991 they unleashed their guns, and the battering of the almost undefended former city-state began in fearful earnest.

The dramatic geography of this southern portion of the Dalmatian coast turned out to be both the deadliest curse for the fate of the town and yet, in the end, a blessing, too.

The Dinaric Alps here are almost at the waterline, and plunge precipitously down into the sea within a mile or less of horizontal distance—they are, in other words, almost cliffs, and very high

cliffs at that, almost sheer. The borders with Bosnia and Montenegro—not that there *were* true borders back in 1991, when the siege
began, but only the unformed lines of future states—wind among
and in some cases along the top of those cliffs—meaning that
artillery pieces could be placed high on the mountains overlooking the Old Town, and from safety positions in front of the soon-
to-be-declared Croatian frontiers, fire a barrage of shells down
into the city with unceasing impunity.

A Yugoslav army bombardier would watch with glee as he
conducted his sport—firing shells into the parking lots below,
for example, and gawking as the ensuing fire leaped from car to
car to car, as the successive fuel tanks exploded like firecrackers
on a string. The artilleryman could be confident that there was
virtually no chance of retaliation: From down below his firing
positions would be no more than a couple of dots on a horizon
that loomed neck-breakingly high over the town. But the Serbian firing master had merely to peer over the cliff-edge and
select which building—which Catholic church, which shop,
which apartment house, which segment of the thousand-year-
old wall—to destroy, then load, aim, and fire! As with some diabolical arcade game he then had only to peek over the cliff
once more to watch his whistling outbound shell land, and perform its gruesome task.

But the steepness of the Dinaric hills had for the attackers a dis-
advantage too. Soldiers could not clamber down the slopes rapidly
enough ever to invade the city below—the descent would be too
dangerous in and of itself, and besides, the men would be picked
off one by one by snipers firing from below. The ground was open:
Only a few cypress tress afforded any protection, and cypresses,
though now abundant on the hillsides, grew here as solitary spec-
imens, not in forests that might give an invading army cover.

So no land invasion of Dubrovnik ever took place—only the
merciless nightly shelling. On one spectacularly horrible day in
November 1991 the besieging army, using wire-guided missiles,

destroyed and sank, with deliberation, every single boat that was moored between the moles of the old Dubrovnik harbor: The television pictures of this most wanton act, the blowing up of sailing yachts in one of the best-loved sailors' harbors in the world, did much to nudge Western opinion, at least for a while. *Why are they doing this?* wailed half the world. *What danger could a small schooner or a sloop from Marseilles ever pose to the Yugoslav army? What harm have these old walls ever done to the memory of the heroic fighters of Kosovo? What, for God's sake, is the blessed point?*

And in the end the Serbs gave up and went away. They never breached the walls, never sent men down on ropes or in parachutes to invade and occupy the old city, never extended their influence beyond the boundaries of their own areas in Bosnia. Croatia won its independence; the shelling was stopped for good. Dubrovnik was safe, at least for a while—safe, and able both to rebuild itself physically and to rebuild its reputation as a place of tranquillity and serene loveliness. It has been, by all accounts, difficult beyond words.

We had dinner, several times running, in one of a number of cafés that line Ulica Prijeko, a narrow street parallel to the Placa, the magnificently wide, shining marble pedestrian street that runs between the cathedral and the monastery that, respectively, mark each end of town. The food was perfect*—lobsters and crayfish and fresh garden salads and pancakes, and a red Croatian wine called Dingac. But there were no other customers, except for a group of internationals down from Sarajevo for the weekend, and a group of archaeologists, investigating Roman sites on an island nearby. A genial but out-of-work jazz musician named Ben, who normally played saxophone in a group called

---

*More so than the menu, which offered, among other delights, Cackerels, Bogues, and Pilehards. The last I recognized as pilchards, the oily Mediterranean fish; the others I never dared to order.

the Dubrovnik Troubadours, was sitting nearby: Not for another year or so, he said, would the town revive.

"People are frightened—and who can blame them? I lie in bed at night, when the sea is quiet, and I can hear the NATO bombs dropping on Montenegro. We always have the fear that there will be fighting in Montenegro once again, and that the remainder of the Yugoslav army will be back in the mountains again, making trouble for us. It is not so good."

But he perked up when I told him I lived in New York. He was due to come to play in Weehawken, New Jersey, in a few weeks' time: The Croatian-American Fraternity Union paid the fares and then was sending his band on to Pittsburgh, where a quarter of a million Croats live. He slapped us both on the back, and folded us in his arms, and led us off to his tiny bar beside the Church of St. Blaise. We sat there drinking slivovitz (plum brandy) until two in the morning, when his exceptionally disagreeable and very ugly dog bit Rose in the ankle, and we decided to limp back to the Excelsior.

A few days later I met a man who looked, with his wild gray hair and straggly beard, and sounded, with his strange theories and propositions, charmingly but disconcertingly mad.

He approached me almost out of the blue and proceeded to tell me a story that for a long time afterward made me wonder whether he was certifiably insane, and whether or not to write about him. I asked others, too, and indeed, on the very eve of planning the writing of what follows, I received an E-mail from a professor at Yale University who urged me in no uncertain terms to ignore all that the man said, and to give him no credence whatsoever.

But one aspect of the man's story, even to the skeptics who insisted that I not give him a second thought, did ring uncannily true—a truth that bothered me, made me wonder. And so in the end I decided to ignore the Yale professor's caution and tell what happened when I met a Swedish mathematician named Jan Suurkula. We met by chance at an airport, and although he knew nothing about me or why I was in Dubrovnik in the first place, he proceeded to tell me in some detail his particular interest in (*a*) unified field theory, and (*b*) its connections, if properly harnessed, with the lessening of human chaos. Since there was a very great deal of chaos in the area just now, he said, I would surely be interested in anything that might lessen it?

His basic thesis, though hardly simple, was easily stated. Proving the unified field theory, the notion that all the main forces of physics—electromagnetism, time, space, and gravity—are somehow linked together in a kind of all-encompassing multidimensional geometry, has been the Holy Grail of great scientific thinkers for most of this century. That human beings might somehow contribute to, or somehow affect, the frail gossamer threads that link all these physical elements together is what mathematicians like Dr. Suurkula have come to believe.

He and his similarly minded colleagues, of whom he said there were many thousands in almost every country in the world, were now working to make sure that human interaction with these forces was channeled for the good of all humanity—and quite specifically, so that humans could control their own destiny by harnessing forces within themselves to mitigate the chaos-tending forces of physics: that some humans, in other words, had the power to reduce chaos. "And to stop war," he said brightly.

"You are, of course, here for the congress?"

I said that I hadn't the faintest idea what he was talking about.

"The Croatian peace conference. Perhaps the most important conference going on in the world today. You are not attending?" he said, incredulous.

"We are on the brink—the very brink, you know—of bringing about peace in the Balkans. There are two hundred of us here just now. We only need a few more people. This why I am coming down from Sweden. People are coming in from all over. America.

Italy. England. South Africa. We need just a total of, let me see"—
he took out a chewed pen and scribbled a quick calculation on the
palm of his hand—"two hundred and fifty-four people. Once we
have them, all assembled in one room, then peace will happen. I
assure you. It always works."

I must have looked more than a little mystified, for he sat down
beside me and with an accomplished bedside manner, began to
explain. These, it is important to say, are Dr. Suurkula's words, not
mine. No product endorsement here. Just mystification and,
because of one singular fact that was to emerge later on, a degree
of impressed acceptance.

People, Dr. Suurkula said, can learn the secret of channeling
their internal energies in a way that will communicate vibrations
that will, or may, intersect with all the invisible webs that link the
various fields of unified physical geometry. The secret to making
that intersection useful, allowing people to make, by their mental
powers alone, a measurable electronic effect on the way the physical world works, is to gather together a certain critical number of
people so that, just like the critical mass in an atomic pile (or
bomb), their presence and common effort creates a kind of mentally powered fission.

I blinked in disbelief, but the strangely beguiling Dr. Suurkula
went on. I asked a question: How many people might be needed
to make up this so-called critical mass. He was, it turned out, just
coming to that.

The number of people required to have a measurable effect on
a population varies directly with the size of the population that
needs to be affected. Measurements made over the last thirty
years, in a variety of towns and cities and countries around the
world, had shown incontrovertibly that, by chance—or in fact
probably not by chance—a perfect mathematical device invariably
comes into play. For the critical mass seems always to be reached
when the number of people assembled in one place, all of them
manifesting the same vibrations at the same time, is equal to the

square root of 1 percent of the population that is to be affected.

This curiously satisfying mathematical coincidence was noticed first of all in the mid-seventies, in Providence, Rhode Island. The town used to be a wayward place, the car-theft capital of the United States, a place of murder and burglary and enough crime to make the local police chief throw up his hands in despair. But then Dr. Suurkula's friends—people whose names are familiar in this world: John Hagelin, Matti Pitkanen, Neil Phillips, Paolo Menoni—decided to become involved, trying to see if they could direct the powers they believed they had, in a way that they thought might help. They assembled enough of their like-minded colleagues to reach the number that equaled the square root of 1 percent of the Providence population—which, since it stood at 160,000, was the neat and precise number 40—and put them in a local hotel room and then— well, that, Dr. Suurkula said, was the part that a rationalist, as he assumed me to be, might well choose not to believe.

Too true, I retorted. I had not believed overmuch of what I had heard so far. Fair enough, he replied, and continued anyway. What these forty people in Providence then did, he said, was to indulge in several powerful minutes of *simultaneous yogic flying*.

Of course, I said to myself: Transcendental meditation. I might have known. My cynicism went into immediate overdrive. These people, I said to myself, were completely nuts. These here were part of a pathetic troupe of disciples of the now fabulously rich and probably totally cynical confidence trickster (as I saw him and his like) known as the Maharishi Mahesh Yogi, who had been the spiritual adviser to some of the Beatles and now lived as a wealthy recluse somewhere near Amsterdam.

Like so many others I had come across elsewhere over the years, and like the disciples of the Baghwan Rajneesh and Sai Baba and a woman called Maya whom half of social Hong Kong seemed to be following, they had been gulled into handing over huge sums of their own savings to be taught the nonsense that

mental-energies-can-be-harnessed-and-made-to-bring-about-uni-
versal-peace, and were now performing in the Balkans, of all
places, the same stupefying rituals—which culminated in something so perfectly silly, not to say unattractive, as managing to
lift (for several continuous seconds) their backsides off cush-
ions while sitting in the lotus position—that had made them a
global laughing-stock. And now they were here trying to per-
suade innocents like me that by such madness lay the road to
peace, that I might perhaps join them, or give them money, or
write laudable things about them and so help them to win ever
more credibility. The exploiting of a such a tragedy as this—it
was all too shabby, too cynical, too tasteless.

Dr. Suurkula clearly saw the anticipated doubt on my face
and tried to dispel it with a barrage of statistics. The forty people who performed simultaneous yogic flying in Providence, he
said, had achieved great success. The number of car thefts and
robberies in the city had dropped by 42 percent over the next
week, he said, and has remained lower ever since. Had I heard
any further discussion of Providence being the car-stealing capital of the United States? No, I said, I had not. "Well, that was all
to do with us!" smiled the man, and launched into a barrage of
facts and figures.

"Look at what we did in Jerusalem in 1979," he said: 230 people—the Israeli population is 5.3 million—performed yogic flying on the eve of the Camp David talks, and a peace agreement
was signed. Then again, and most ambitiously, seven thousand
people met and performed the rituals in a gymnasium outside
Washington, D.C., and, their power being harnessed to improve
the lot of the then 4.9 million people of the planet, the Cold
War ended, the Berlin Wall fell, and the atomic stalemate, which
had dogged the global population for half a century, was ended.

His conversation then veered into areas I could not possible
understand—the nature of the five sub-atomic particles, the
coincidence of the five levels of Vedic-inspired consciousness,

the overlapping circles of energy, the works of Niels Bohr and Erwin Schrödinger and Albert Einstein, the role of the mantra in stimulating internal vibration. And then, on the verge of losing me, he wondered whether I might not come down to the congress and see the preparations under way to bring peace to the Balkans.

The Dubrovnik Peace Project was being held in an airy resort hotel, the Mincenta, at the north end of town. There were no tourists in sight, just scores of the earnest-looking and friendly people—Germans, Israelis, Britons, Italians, Americans—who were delegates to the conference and who seemed to spend much of their time languidly strolling from workshop to workshop, or intently reading the messages (for cheap flights home, for organic food shops in town, for phone cards) posted on a bulletin board outside the conference office. It might have been a low-key trade show, or a book festival, and the delegates all sales representatives for health-food manufacturers, or sandals, or Peruvian sweaters. There seemed to be no leaders, as such—just instructors and lecturers, and once in a while, men who were so well-known in the field that the crowds parted before them, and there was a quiet collective gasp of awe.

Dr. Paolo Menoni, whose pair of impeccably made business cards pronounced him to be *Avvocato* and *Insegnante di Meditazione Trascendentale*, was one such, and he broke off what he was doing—which seemed principally to be talking to a group of excited middle-aged ladies—and sat down to talk of the urgency of the mission, the crisis it had now reached, the need for everyone to come and assemble so that peace might be brought into being.

"You may be skeptical," he said, "and I would understand that. But you should know there are now no fewer than fifty-seven proven cases in which what we do—meditating, yogic hopping, skywalking, yogic flying—has truly brought about peace. Read the paper in the *Journal of Conflict Resolution*, back in 1988: It showed without a doubt how this really works.

"Your William Hague, leader of Mrs. Thatcher's Conservatives, he believes in meditation, in the benefits of what we do. So does the president of Mozambique, Dr. Chissano. Believe me, this is catching on."

And Dr. Menoni took me through the back of the hotel to what had once evidently been the large socialist-style dining hall where happy Slavic vacationers took their gruel and goulash. In it were hundreds of mattresses, readied for the evening flying session. There was a chart on one wall, showing the numbers taking part each day. Two weeks before the numbers had been low, 75, 90, 56. Then, after an appeal went out on the Internet, and concerned would-be fliers heard about the critical need to reach the super-radiance number, people started drifting in, and the figures crept up: 130, 178, 203, 217. Now, according to Dr. Menoni, two figures were vitally necessary: 254, which was to stop the war in Croatia and Bosnia, and 345, which was to bring peace to Yugoslavia.

I pointed out that there was actually no war going on in either Croatia and Bosnia, which perplexed him a little. But the figure of 345—that was indeed the square root of 11.9 million, which was more or less the population of Yugoslavia (more or less: The official figure appears to be 10.59 million). If perhaps the pleas and telephone calls and telexes that were then being sent out from the Mincenta did lure the faithful in sufficient numbers, then perhaps—*just* perhaps—peace might break out.

I left them just as they were beginning a session. Scores of earnest-looking and very friendly middle-aged men and women—there seemed rather few youngsters in the group— were taking off their shoes, signing up for the coming attempt, and taking up positions on their various mattresses. An instructor mounted the podium, muttered a few words of Sanskrit by way of universal greeting, and told everyone to begin mouthing their mantras. And then another pair of instructors looked at me, to suggest that I might leave, and drew shut the curtains. As I walked away a low, rhythmic chanting was beginning, a humming and a thumping and the sound of a growing ecstasy. And then I turned the corner, and there was the Adriatic, and in place of human ecstasy, the sound of waves crashing on the shore two hundred feet below.

Later, when I returned to the United States, I asked the editor of the *Journal of Conflict Resolution*, Bruce Russett, if he thought there was any merit in the ideas of transcendental meditation, and of the Dubrovnik Peace Project—whether there was any sense behind the notion of harmonic vibrations and superradiance numbers and the power to influence unified fields and to bring about peace by means of human electronics. Yale University's Dean Acheson Professor of Political Science, for such was his other title, was acerbic in his reply, which came in the form of a long E-mail:

> My considered opinion is that what the TM folks are peddling is snake oil. The premise that TM can help its practitioners reduce their own conflicts is reasonable; the premise that it can reduce conflict among nearby nonpractitioners is absurd.
>
> It is true that *JCR*, which I edit, did long ago publish an article by the TM folks purporting to show big effects in the Jerusalem area. Even then I regarded the premise as absurd, but after a lot of internal debate decided that the empirical work should be judged on its own merits, separately from the plausibility of its chief assumption, and let it see daylight. That was in the December 1988 issue. A critic took a stab at demolishing their statistical analysis in the December 1990 issue, but in my judgment just missed driving his stake through the heart. Nonetheless, I have seen nothing since that persuades me that they have any general capability to do what they say; to the degree their Jerusalem experience does fit it is almost certainly a lucky coincidence, and they don't tell us about all the tries elsewhere that didn't work. I much regret

having gone out on a limb for this, and would advise extreme caution to anyone else.

And yet. It so happens that the week during which Dr. Menoni was calling for new volunteers—the week when Dr. Suurkula arrived at the Mincenta Hotel, the week during which the numbers of those performing their various yogic feats was climbing up into the one hundreds and two hundreds—during that very week, the first week of June, there were significant moves toward peace being made in Belgrade, Moscow, London, Brussels, New York, and Washington, D.C.

And on the very day that the group did manage to assemble 345 yogic fliers, Slobodan Milosevic did accept the peace proposals from NATO. Peace of a sort was beginning to break out in the Balkans at precisely the moment that the Dubrovnik Peace Project was doing its hardest and most sustained work—when, as its leaders would claim, the vibrational forces were working at their maximum.

Maybe it is all absurd. Maybe what happened in the Balkans, like whatever happened in Jerusalem, can be dismissed as a lucky coincidence. Maybe there are those in the various great churches around the world who believe that their particular prayers or other spiritual intercessions did what was necessary. The possibility that human beings, harnessing some kind of invisible and indefinable energy, can on occasion influence external affairs with which they have no physical connection—the idea intrigues, and remains intriguing, long after the absurdity of the performance has vanished into memory. There is just a faint and lingering thought from Dubrovnik that says, all too quietly—Well, why not?

The frontier with Montenegro is half an hour's drive from the outskirts of Dubrovnik. From the main road it is possible to see—impossible to avoid, in fact—the zigzag track that was cut up the Dinaric hillside to where the American secretary of commerce, Ron Brown, was killed in a plane crash in the spring of 1996. He had been in a U.S. Air Force Hercules, and according to reports at the time, had flown into the most terrible sudden storm and the pilot, not having the benefit of any navigation aids at the primitive Dubrovnik airfield, had flown his aircraft straight into the mountainside. Brown, along with thirty-four other members of an American trade mission, was killed.

The incident has been mired in argument ever since. Ron Brown was a black man, the highest-ranking of his race in the Clinton administration. He had been under investigation for supposed financial irregularities. And ever since his death there have been suggestions, or claims, that he might have been murdered. (Acting on a report from an air force pathologist that a wound at the top of Brown's head could have been caused by a gunshot, the NAACP launched an investigation into the circumstances of his death.) A rash of theories, suggesting various kinds of conspiracy, flared up about a year after his death, coincident with the more florid suggestions about President Clinton and his various political problems. But, as with the White House scandals, the suggestions about improprieties surrounding Brown's sad death quickly faded away. No one talks about the event much anymore, except in Croatia, where they have put up a memorial, and the shepherd who found the wreckage occasionally talks about the crash, and surprises listeners by saying that no, there was no storm, terrible or otherwise, on the March afternoon in question.

The most visible consequence of the tragedy, so far as Croatia itself was concerned, can be seen in the makeup of the fleet of the nation's small airline. Mr. Brown had hoped that the directors of Croatia Airlines would order Boeing aircraft, and the dispatch of his trade mission was in part to help them make up their minds to do so. But after the accident the line decided not to buy American at all, and if you fly these days from Dubrovnik to Zagreb, or to Rome, you will do so now in a smart

new A–340 Airbus, built by a consortium of European manufacturers, in France.

The flag with the red-and-white checkered shield of Croatia, the
once-notorious *sahovnica* that was also the wartime symbol of
the Ustashi, fluttered over the little shack that housed the border control point south of Dubrovnik. There was no southbound traffic on the road at all—a road that still bore the scars
of the fighting of the early nineties—and the skeleton staff at
the checkpoint were surprised to see anyone venturing into
Montenegro. The senior immigration officer was a woman, and
she grinned uneasily.

"Are you sure you are wanting to go on?" she asked, with gen-
uine concern. "Dangerous people ahead."

But we said yes, she hastily stamped our passports, and ordered
her assistant to raise the barrier. We edged ahead into the no-
man's land and rounded a corner beyond which stood a cluster of
temporary shacks with the red-white-and-blue flag of the Federal
Republic of Yugoslavia snapping in the breeze above them. There
was a thick steel pole across the road here, too, and behind it a
group of heavily armed and camouflaged policemen and a big
artillery piece that was pointed not toward us and any possible
enemies back in Croatia—but back down the hill into Montenegro. For if these men perceived any threat at this frontier, was
likely to come not from outside the country, but from within.

6

Western Approaches

The Republic of Montenegro

A BLACK MERCEDES was waiting on the Montenegrin side of frontier, with two tough young Yugoslav women inside. They were called Dali and Vesna, they were university students from Belgrade, and they were known in the trade as fixers—members of an elite corps of unsung heroes who operate in all distant wars, the local helpmeets without whom almost no foreign correspondent could ever ply the craft.

I was delighted to see them. A friend at the BBC had organized their arrival, since it was said that they knew the least troublesome way to travel into the interior. It was for this kind of local knowledge that the fixers prove so invaluable—the best of them being legendarily undaunted by the most arcane of requests, and by the risks that are frequently involved.

An editor in London or New York might send an urgent message to his correspondent on the ground: Find me a young and attractive Albanian refugee who speaks serviceable English, who is pregnant after being raped by a Serb paramilitary, and find her in the next hour. The correspondent without a fixer would have little idea which way to turn. The correspondent with one, on the other hand, would turn immediately to the fixer to arrange everything, and in all probability it could and would be done.

The fortunate journalist would then make the broadcast or write the article, and in due course get all the glory, receive the "herograms." But the fixer would receive none of this—no recognition for him or her other than the daily fee that had been agreed beforehand. The going rate in the Balkans, at least from the British and American networks and newspapers, was two hundred German marks a day.

Economic distress is most often the reason that fixers take the work. The kind of circumstances where fixers are needed—such as here, the outbreak of a complicated war in a difficult and unfamiliar part of the world—rarely embrace periods of economic contentment and social harmony. And such circumstances thus have a way of driving into the fixer corps numbers of extremely well-educated and overqualified young men and women who, because of the situation that the reporters have come to cover, are temporarily down on their luck. There was a twenty-five-year-old doctor working in the Balkans as a cameraman's assistant; and Dali and Vesna here in Montenegro were both highly intelligent women, one taking a graduate degree in political science, the other studying to be a pharmacist. They didn't much like the drudge work—but they needed the money. The four hundred marks that Vesna received for two days' acting as gofer for a visiting correspondent was more than her father earned in a month.

Besides doing work they didn't much like, and for reasons they didn't care to reveal, and rarely winning credit for the tasks they performed, the fixers not infrequently got into trouble. While we were in the region a Kosovo Albanian fixer working for a British journalist was killed by a NATO bomb fragment, and a Macedonian fixer was murdered by Serb soldiers, along with the two German reporters who had hired him. There were long news reports noting the deaths or injuries to the correspondents, but no initial mention of the locally hired helpmeets. Their fate was reported only much later, in the laconic list of the unfortunate also-rans.

Dali and Vesna needed to have a particular skill on the day we met—and it was for this specific reason that they had been asked to meet us. They were get us into the Montenegrin capital past the very hostile and rather dangerous Yugoslav army checkpoints. They had devised a simple and probably foolproof scheme for doing so.

The fact that such a problem existed at all says much about the curiously ambiguous situation of the mountainous, geologically chaotic and astonishingly beautiful state of Montenegro—home, it is said, to the tallest people in Europe, and probably also to the toughest. Officially it is a part of Yugoslavia, one of the country's two constituent republics, Serbia being the other.* There is a constitutionally guaranteed equivalence: both Serbia and Montenegro send twenty deputies to the federal upper house of the parliament, both Serbia and Montenegro have their own governments and their own presidents, and both maintain armed police forces. But there the similarity ends. Whereas in Serbia the interests of the dominantly Serbian federal administration can be said to coincide almost perfectly with those of the local people, almost the very opposite holds true in Montenegro.

The Montenegrins in the main may be Orthodox Christians, like most of the Serbs; but they are fiercely independent, they have a fiery reputation, and they are a people of the sea and the mountains and not the rivers and the plains. They would never, they insist today as they always have, accept subjugation by anyone. They got rid of the Turks—just the only Balkan people ever to do so. They had employed the simplest but most effective of guerrilla methods for doing so—methods that would be duplicated hundreds of years later, half a world away, by such strategists as Ho Chi Minh in Vietnam, and Mao Zedong in China.

The men—vastly tall, utterly impressive—were extraordinary snipers, and they used guns ten feet long against the invaders. When the Turks first invaded the capital of Cetinje, as they did

---

*Kosovo, on the other hand, like the relatively unknown northern territory of Vojvodina, is regarded as a formerly autonomous province within the Republic of Serbia. It is thus administratively junior to Montenegro, which, if one accepts the validity of Yugoslavia's 1990 constitution, is a coequal member of the Federal Republic, along with Serbia.

three times, the defenders of the local monastery touched off their powder magazine, destroying the place, killing themselves—but driving all the terrified Turks away. On other occasions the Montenegrin women would trigger landslides, and avalanches in winter, and create all kinds of havoc among the Turks' supply lines. The children were involved in the fighting too—setting fires, firing catapults, ferrying ammunition and water to the men in the firing lines. The entire country, knitted together by family, by blood, and by loyalty to the very idea of Montenegro, became fully involved if anyone ever dared set foot inside their hallowed territory. The people knew little other than God and war, and it was the gravest of insults for one Montenegrin to sneer at another: "I know your people—all your ancestors died in their beds."

They had gotten rid of the Turks; and, I was to be told almost every day that I was inside this happy little former kingdom, that if they had to get rid of the Serbs as well, then they would do so without any hesitation at all. A man walking beneath the cathedral walls in Kotor was the first to say about Belgrade's Mr. Milosevic, "Let him try it—just let him try it. He'll have the bloodiest fight he's ever known."

All across Montenegro there seemed a sudden eruption of anger toward the Serbs. "Every evil in the Balkans has come from them," a café owner was quoted as saying. "They are scum," said a painter. They had "stolen" the Montenegrin language (which has four more letters in its alphabet than plain Serbian), they were "genocidal cowards," they "lacked a civilization," they were of (the greatest insult of all) "Turkish descent."

Which is why the Montenegrin police force and the Yugoslav army, both of which have constitutional responsibility for the territorial serenity and integrity of the five thousand square miles of Montenegrin territory, are at perpetual and often dangerous odds with each other. The Montenegrin police are, first, loyal to their president, a dapper young matinee idol named Milo Djukanovic;

the Yugoslav army is loyal to the federal president, who at the time of writing is Slobodan Milosevic. The two men (despite Milosevic having been the Montenegrin president's political patron) glare at each other with ill-concealed distaste.

Djukanovic eyes Milosevic with suspicion, wary of his long-term intentions, openly challenging him to dare to try to tinker with, or worse still, try to annex, his rumbustious little republic. His ministers talk openly of declaring independence: There is already a Montenegrin airline, there is talk of Montenegrin passports, and a currency tied, like Bosnia's, to the German mark.

Milosevic in turn rails back at Djukanovic, reminding him (with some accuracy) that he and the federal army he commands could crush him and his insignificant nation in a heartbeat, if he chose to. But the Montenegrin president has managed so far to remain sturdily—some would say cheekily—independent of Belgrade: He has astutely given himself two guarantees that this interesting situation may last.

First, the young president has worked hard, via a series of foreign expeditions and state visits and countless ambassadorial soirées, to ensure that he retains the sympathetic interest of as much of the international community as possible. It has been a strategy that has seemed to work—for during the Kosovo war all of those capitals, from Washington to London, from Helsinki to Canberra, which condemned the policies of the Yugoslav government were invariably careful to add "except, of course, for Montenegro." They recognized President Djukanovic as somehow different, not a man to be tarred with the same brush as the leader in Belgrade.

Then again, and in tandem with his courtship of foreign governments, President Djukanovic has spent much time and energy courting the attentions of the foreign press. He has appeared to believe that the generals in faraway Belgrade, however much they might wish to rid themselves of his turbulent presence, would simply never dare to touch him with the whole world looking on. (But of course Milosevic did just that in Kosovo and Bosnia, quite careless of world opinion—meaning that Montenegro's present optimism may turn out to be ill-placed.)

Whatever Djukanovic's chances of ultimate success, whatever his chances of long-term survival, he was certainly extraordinarily popular with the access-demanding foreign press. Even at the height of the war it was perfectly easy for a foreign corespondent to gain entry into what, it has to be remembered, was and at the time of writing still is, an integral part of Yugoslavia. The bureaucrats in Podgorica, the country's dull little modern capital, saw to it that anyone who wished to come in, could—in sharp contrast to the situation in Belgrade, where correspondents were turned away in their droves, and those who were allowed in had to function under the most controlled of conditions.

In Montenegro reporters and photographers were given an essentially free rein, and they received all the care and attention and interested help that a sympathetic government is able to give. This, considering that there was a war going on, was almost a correspondent's heaven. It was most unusual, and all who went to Montenegro during the war reveled in the freedoms—but at the same time wondered just how long they could last.

Those of us who were allowed to come in were handed a prettily-produced booklet about Montenegro, attached to which was an open letter, one of the more remarkable I can remember receiving. It was from the presidential palace, above the signature of the Montenegrin Secretary for Information, and was dated April 24, 1999:

> *Respected Ladies and Gentlemen and Dear Colleagues,*
> *As never before in it's* [sic] *history, Montenegro has become host to many media representatives, reporters, photographers and cameramen from all corners of the world.*

Unfortunately, at this time Montenegro has not attracted you here because of its exquisite beauty, or for you to escape from "the realities of the world." Montenegro itself has become "a center of tensions and crises." That is why all the citizens of Montenegro watch over and guard their peace. This is why we feel free to ask you, as friends of this country and its people, to cooperate with us and help us in the preservation of the stability of the country.

In the performance of your regular, daily, professional duties do not ever forget that peace, liberty and the independence of our country is preserved by the Yugoslav Army and the Ministry of Internal Affairs of the Republic of Montenegro—together. The Yugoslav Army in the performance of its duties as the exclusive Yugoslav Defense Force respects the decision of the federal Government to declare a State of War. In this sense, the Yugoslav Army undertakes all necessary measures that are under its authority.

We sincerely request that you do not do anything that would not follow in accordance with the legal regulations of our country. Bear in mind that photographing or filming of uniformed soldiers, military formations and facilities, as well as trespassing within areas under Military security are forbidden.

Concerning the organization of your daily assignments, you should consult the Republic Secretariat for Information so that we can supply you with the necessary instructions.

You should take special care during your departure from your temporary residence and when working on locations you should consult their security representatives, as to whether or not filming on the site is permissible.

We are certain that by doing so and in working together, we will eliminate all possible future disagreements. This will contribute to your personal safety and also the preservation of peace within the Republic.

Yours sincerely,
BOZIDAR JAREDIC

Montenegro was indeed a nervous country, living on a razor's edge, hoping neither to be seen to be supportive of the Belgrade regime, nor wanting to incur its wrath. The writers and cameramen who had come to Montenegro were skittish and nervous, too—and never more so than when any one of them encountered a patrol or a roadblock of the Yugoslav army.

It was because there was a good chance that on our journey from the Croatian frontier to Podgorica we might well come across the army that we had asked for an escort by this pair of Amazonian fixers.

They could make sure that if were stopped by any soldiers from the VJ—the Vojska Jugoslavije, the force that was the successor of the Yugoslav Federal Army—we would not be arrested, fined, our possessions stolen, our clothes stripped from our back, or ourselves beaten, tortured, or worse. This had already happened to other reporters in Montenegro: We didn't want it happening to us.

As if to underline the schism between the army and police, the plan that Dali and Vesna had hatched required the cooperation of the constabulary itself. They had arranged that a police car would be made available to us in the town of Herceg-Novi, five miles in from the border. A VJ checkpoint was known to be sited on the shore of the Gulf of Kotor, about three miles farther on. The idea was that we would drive in the Mercedes to the police station, we would transfer to the police van and hide under blankets on the floor while the women remained in the car, and then the two vehicles, with an extra police jeep for security "in case things get rough," would drive toward Podgorica. It should be, said Dali, exercising the colloquialisms of her last employer, "a piece of cake."

And indeed it was. We drove through Igalo, past where Marshal Tito once had a lavish villa, and down to the edge of the gulf—surely one of the loveliest inlets of water on any coast anywhere, with the bluest of seas surrounded by meadows draped with forests, and by an infinity of hyacinth-pale mountains and

white cliffs laced with waterfalls. We stopped in a café at Herceg-
Novi, and drank a couple of reinforcing beers. A boy offered
me a piece of candy, which I noticed was called, for no apparent
reason, a Negro.*

Three policemen came up and shook our hands. They spoke
little English, but offered their view that the Serbs were up to no
good. I held my tongue: Some opinions were best kept to one-
self, even at risk of seeming stupid, as all foreigners everywhere
are naturally assumed to be. They motioned to a large white van
and showed us some sacks we could lie beneath. On top they
piled guns, and as we set off I had the stock of a very large
machine gun jammed into my stomach. The women, we
assumed, were behind us, the escort vehicle ahead.

We sped along the road for five minutes or so, and then we
slowed to a crawl. I heard the window open, and one of the
policemen hushed us to make sure we didn't move. I held my
breath. Someone opened the front door, there were some gut-
tural exchanges: *"Dobre din. Zdravo."* Check? *"Niz naiu. Hvala."*
And then the door was slammed.

"Pravo," one of the soldiers said—drive on. We accelerated
again. The car went around a right-hand bend, and then one of
the young policemen whooped with delight. "Is okay now. You
safe." The policeman added that he knew a quick and easy way to
tell a Montenegrin reservist from a regular Yugoslav soldier—the
reservists were able to go home at night and wash, while the regu-
lars could not, and so always smelled. "And those boys on the barricade—they smelled, I can tell you!"

The Montenegrins, according to my now-dog-eared 1918

---

*Only outsiders call the country Montenegro. The official name is
Crna Gora, and by some accounts means the same. (Others say it
refers to a Prince Crna, long dead.) The mountains on the coast, however, are decidedly white.

National Geographic, are "of tall, large and erect figure. Their characteristics are those of liberty-loving mountaineers who have lived apart and distrust strangers. Their women are brave, loyal and as implacable as themselves. The word of a Montenegrin is never broken."*

The first man we met in Montenegro, though he may well never have broken his word, was in all other ways very different from the *Geographic*'s confident description. He was short and stooped, had interestingly protruding eyes, lived in a household swarming with people, adored strangers, and—unlike most Montenegrins, who belong to the Orthodox Church—was a Roman Catholic priest and—*very* unlike most Montenegrins, who are steadfastly loyal to their genes and their hormones— was unashamedly flamboyant. He was called Don Branco Sbutega, and I was given his name in European cities from London to the Golden Horn as one of the most agreeable of people one could ever want to meet. A Pole I knew in Zagreb had insisted that I have tea with Father Sbutega, though cautioned that I would find he was "not a friend of this reality," whatever that was likely to mean.

He lives beside his church in a small waterfront town called Dobrota three miles north of Kotor itself. An aged housekeeper and an immense Airedale terrier named Hook live with him— the latter, he explained, was the son of the resident dog at the Russian embassy in Belgrade. When we called, in midafternoon, his housekeeper insisted he was asleep. But there came a roaring from an upstairs bedroom, a demand to know who we might be, and, on hearing we were British, he came partly dressed to

---

*Gone are the days of such trenchant portrayals. From this same issue we learn that the Lapps "are the roundest-headed people in Europe," but have unfortunate children whose faces are "frequently drawn and ugly, as if with age."

the window and bellowed down: "Come up immediately. I worked for the BBC. I will give you strawberry jelly." We could hear him chortling, "This is too wonderful, too wonderful."

He was extravagantly theatrical, not at all priestly, and once were we assembled in his living room, seemed a little tipsy. He reminded me of Anthony Blanche, or at least the Nickolas Grace version of him, in *Brideshead Revisited*; I thought he might stutter and roll his eyes, and refer to the Serbs as "wuffians" or "hobbledehoys." He certainly called me "dear boy," and praised Rose's beauty endlessly. He was somewhat suspicious of Dali and Vesna, because they were from Belgrade, but warmed to Vesna when she admitted to being Montenegrin. "Then you are most beautiful, too," he said.

His father had been a Croat, and he himself, he said, was descended from the Montenegrin royal family. "So I cannot be anti-Serb really—for it was Serbs who largely peopled this place. But anyone who might be an ally of that madman in Belgrade—he or she I could not abide."

He clapped his hands for the old black-clad woman who had been his housekeeper for twenty years, and she brought out a dish of dew-fresh strawberries, a bowl of red gelatin dessert, a large number of bottles of beer, and a young man with whom Father Sbutega had been spending the afternoon. He was tall, handsome, dark-haired, and muscular—very much the Montenegrin—and in his late thirties. The two spent much of their time with us continuing an earlier conversation in Montenegrin about various foods and the degree to which Turkey had influenced their making. It was possible, both agreed, to buy good halvah and baklava in Montenegro, as well as a divine *cevapcici*—the perfect blend of East and West, North and South, and all in a place that had never been subjugated by any outsider.

His interests in the current war, he said, were only humanitarian—and indeed, some days before when I had tried to telephone him, he had been off helping French aid workers take a convoy of food to the refugee camps that had been opened just over the Albanian border. "But they are inside Montenegro," he said. "Isn't that too strange? People are coming in as refugees from Kosovo to Montenegro—in the same country. We're a part of Yugoslavia, for heaven's sake!—and yet other Yugoslavs are asking us to take them in and look after them. But there are VJ units everywhere here, and lots of the people here are Serbs. How can they feel safe?" He harrumphed with disbelief.

"I guess they know we're Montenegrins first, and we won't put up with any nonsense. But it makes this war seem even crazier than it is."

He positively *loathed* the war, he said. He would rather talk instead of civilized things. Like London, for example. How was his old friend Cardinal Hume? (Not good, I had to tell him—and three weeks after I left Basil Hume died, which left Don Branco "devastated," as he put it.) He had come to know him when he filled in at a small church in Brixton, at a time when he was doubling working for the BBC Russian Service at Bush House in London. "Tell my friends there. They will remember me." He still listened to the BBC faithfully, every day. Except that he was very busy. "I have eighty parishioners," he said. "Very demanding people. I have far too much to do." And he waved his hand wildly and put on a panic-stricken expression.

Then he brightened. Would we care to come and look at his chapel, to see the work he had done? And so, joined by Hook, who bounded along merrily ahead of us, we trooped through a low door into an immense Aladdin's cave of wild mosaics and gold trim and rich red carpeting: the new Chapel of Dobrota, Don Branco Sbutega's legacy for the Catholic people of the Montenegrin coast. It was an extraordinary place, bizarre, vulgar in the extreme, a fantasy chapel that might have been in Las Vegas, or at Portmeirion, or on the set of a Hammer film. Don Branco sat and happily played the organ—"The Wedding

March," "Silent Night"—while we stood, awestruck, looking up at ornate single eye under the apex of the dome, which gazed down coldly at the congregation below.

Outside, on a bus shelter, was the Serbian cross, and a vulgarism denouncing the Catholic Church. Beside it was a swath of graffiti, the reminder that this territory, like Kosovo, was "Serbia forever."

"That's what they think," growled Don Branco Sbutega. "But let them ever dare to try and take on the Montenegrins. They have good reason to be scared. Not of people like me of course—I'd just run away. But the people up in the hills. All they know up there is guns and fighting. They've been doing it for hundreds of years. And they always win."

Before climbing up the hills to the desolate karst plateau, I had a small mission to undertake down on the Adriatic coast, at a seaside town called Petrovac. I had heard something of the place—a tidy little resort, though not quite so fashionable as the near-islet of Sveti Stefan, where film stars used to pay thousands of dollars a night to be housed in perfect Adriatic peace, in a jumble of houses and cypress trees on the sea five miles away. Petrovac was much less assuming than that, a pleasing seaside mix of the acceptably new and the delightfully ancient. A friend in London, a well-known magazine editor, was married to an architectural writer who had come from Petrovac, and both he and his brother, now a lawyer in Scotland, wanted to know how their old family house was getting along, and how their neighbors were, from whom they hadn't heard all through the war, and about whom they now were a little worried.

Everyone in the dusty outskirts of Petrovac knew the family—"The boys did very well, went to England, you know," said one old man I met in the street, who was leading a donkey on a string. He gave directions, and we found the house, part of it now turned into a butcher shop, part a warehouse. It was built of limestone, weathered, substantial, and still in good shape. The neighbors lived behind it, and were sitting in a courtyard drinking Turkish coffee. They sat us down immediately, assured us they were fine— but that the telephones, run as they were by an administration in Belgrade, were not working too well. So I called Scotland on my cell phone, and within minutes there was a babel of Montenegrin passing across the ether, and to celebrate the moment someone broke out a box of *lokum*, the gummy and flower-fragrant sweet-meat that elsewhere is known as Turkish delight.

The neighbors, grateful for the contact with the outside, then seemed to feel it their duty to tell us stories—did we know, for example, that there were families of black people living farther down the coast at Ulcinj? The coast had fallen to the Turks for a while, and back in the sixteenth century the bey of Algiers brought African slaves to the walled port city they built at Ulcinj and made them work with the corsairs, who, with the official blessing of Topkapi, were then trying to wreak havoc among the trading ships of imperial Venice. The slaves had in time inter-mingled with the local Montenegrins. Part of Ulcinj town, they said, remained noticeably African in appearance, "rather like the *souk* in Djibouti."

We whiled away the warm afternoon in the sunshine, listen-ing to the stories, hearing waves crashing on the pebble beach, idly watching the fishermen stocking their lobster pots or sort-ing through their hauls of oysters, and gazing up at the moun-tains we would soon have to climb. Both of the capitals of Mon-tenegro were somewhere up there, in the sea of rocks of the karst lands.

One was the present capital, the unlovely socialist-realist city of Podgorica that had until the late eighties been known by its tem-porary honorific of Titograd, and that spread out into a wide river valley at the southern edge of the mountains. The other, the old capital, was high in the mountains, remote and unreachable, and said by all to be one of the most curious capital cities in all the world.

It was called Cetinje, and it had been founded in the fifteenth century around a huge and isolated monastery. For nearly five centuries it was the seat of power of a series of regal (but popularly elected) Orthodox bishops—all of them, after 1697, coming from the same family, nephew-bishop succeeding nephew-bishop. In 1910 the then ruling bishop, Nicola Petrovic, declared himself King Nicholas, and reigned for eight years before the Austrians deposed and deported him. The capital itself, confused by war and turmoil, lived on as the administrative center of the tiny country—by then absorbed ignominiously into Serbia—until 1948, when the heads of state and government moved across to the duller and less romantic commercial center at Podgorica.

Cetinje stands in curious and glorious isolation in a basin of rocks just below the holy Black Mountain, Mount Levcen, where there is a mausoleum to one of the more revered of the bishop-princes, but which it is now impossible to visit because the Yugoslav army has a radio and radar station on its summit. But getting to the capital itself was interesting enough: You may go by road from Podgorica itself, or still by the old way, from behind the city walls of Kotor and up the cliff face via a dizzying switchback of a track, called the Ladder of Cattaro, that is more suited to mules than for the kind of passengers—diplomats, bureaucrats, and the like—that a capital city ordinarily attracts. The track, though it has been widened and metaled in recent times, still has the capacity to scare.

I must make sure I went to Cetinje, Father Sbutega had said, for more than mere historical amusement. While there I might find the answer to a matter that had recently been intriguing him—but a matter in which he, as a Catholic, had no direct and vested interest. If, he said, the Montenegrin people were over-whelmingly of the Orthodox faith, then at which Orthodox church were they supposed to worship? Because as he had heard on the ecumenical grapevine, there were now *two* Eastern churches in Montenegro, both competing for saints and competing for sinners. And as he had heard tell, battle royal was currently breaking out between them.

The mountains around the old capital are bone dry, the limestone too porous to hold water after rain. The fields are tiny, crops do not thrive, the trees are stunted—there is a lunar bleakness to the place that makes one wonder why anyone lives there. In every fold of rock, they say, there are six kinds of snakes—the poisonous *sharka* is the worst, but the *boskok*, which according to improbable local lore leaps from trees and strangles passersby, is also less than endearing. But nevertheless, and however harsh the landscape, there are small stone houses, patches of scrub, a wizened lemon tree, a donkey or two: Somehow people manage to eke out a living.

And in the midst of it all, sheltered in a crater in this Montenegrin sea of tranquillity and slumbering in the eternal sunshine, is the tiny old city, a place of miniature palaces and churches and pavilions, with small squares and rows of little blue-and-white houses. It is like the capital of Toytown: You half expect the figures—a mayor, a fireman, a constable, a fishmonger, a baker, his excellency the ambassador—to be made of plastic, and move from place to place only when the gigantic stubby fingers of a child reach down from the skies.

The charming absurdity of the place is hardly mitigated by learning that one of the principal episcopal palaces is known simple as Biljarda—Billiards. One of the heroic clergymen who ran the country, the Prince-Bishop Peter II,* had a billiard table

---

*The cleric was a keen military man as well, in common with most Montenegrins, and liked to show his skills by having an attendant toss into the air a lemon, which he would speedily shoot and destroy. "A singular accomplishment for a Bishop," wrote a British diplomat who met him.

hauled up the Ladder of Cattaro in the 1830s, presented it to his people as a great wonder of modern life, and named his palace after the game. In the same building there is a three-dimensional map of the entire kingdom, made a century ago by the Austrian generals for whom the chaotic mountainscapes meant utter bewilderment, and a two-dimensional map was not good enough. There is an opera house nearby, and the feat of building it up in this remote notch in the Dinaric Alps must have rivaled that of the German rubber baron who carried his own, ready-made, into the jungles of Brazil.*

The old royal palace is now a museum, from where His Royal Montenegrin Highness King Nicholas presided benignly over his people for sixty-eight years, fought five wars on their behalf, and turned Cetinje into a diplomatic clearinghouse for the Balkans and the glittering social center of the southern European world. The palace is a dollhouse version of what a fanciful monarchy should be like: There are flattering portraits and chased-silver guns, vast fireplaces, and a library of specially made and presented books,† polar bear rugs and chairs with the monogrammed letter *N*, immense silver tureens given by brother emperors, a dinner service from Napoleon III, pictures of visitors who would go on to head the royal houses of Europe from Norway to Sicily, and endless arrays of medals, orders, ribbons, scrolls, and honors in glass cases everywhere.

And there are marriage certificates, too, and faded daguerreotypes from the more primitive lands into which his fecund majesty

---

*About which Werner Herzog made a film, *Fitzcarraldo*, some years ago.

†Including Cyrillic volumes printed by a press set up in Cetinje in 1493, just twenty years after Caxton invented the idea of movable type. But as befits the weird mix of scholarship and war characterizing the Montenegrin, the lead type had to be melted down soon after and made into bullets instead.

had dispatched the best of his three sons and nine daughters to be married and help create new dynasties of their own. Not for nothing was King Nicholas known as "Europe's father-in-law": one of his daughters married the king of Italy, another the king of Serbia, a third was the mother of the future king Alexander of Yugoslavia, and a fourth became a German princess.

Most notable of all was the cascade of events that followed the marriage of the his daughter Militsa to the Russian Grand Duke Peter. It was Militsa who, in common with many in the fevered court at St. Petersburg, became obsessively intrigued by the outer reaches of religion, by mysticism and the occult. And it was Militsa, this young Montenegrin woman, who in 1908 conspired with her sister-in-law Anastasia to introduce to the Russian czarina a vibrantly eccentric monk named Grigory Yefimovich Novykh, a wandering Siberian peasant who was generally known by a nickname meaning "the debauched one": Rasputin. The devastating influence that Rasputin was to have for the next eight years on the Russian imperial throne is only too well known—that the modest little royal palace of Montenegro played an unsung but profound role in the ruin of Russia is droll indeed.

Everyone, the Russians included, had embassies here, and most of the buildings remain. They are suitably small structures, but they all display an elegance and dignity appropriate for housing the representatives to a full-fledged if somewhat Ruritanian kingdom. Most are like small country mansions in the old Caribbean or Scotland, made of gray or red-and-white stone and with roofs of flattened tin. The British mission remains, with a brass plaque on the gate, and is now a music school. The French embassy is the grandest, not least because it was a building supposedly destined for the governor of Algiers, but got swapped, thanks to the efforts of a cunning Montenegrin in Paris: The office in North Africa is still said to be one of the dullest in French diplomatic hands. Court intrigue and amusement was rife in the landlocked declivity of Cetinje; the embassies vied with one another to give the best garden parties, to import the choicest wines, to have as guests the prettiest girls. Life there was said by diplomats to be comfortably pointless but enormous fun.*

The huge Orthodox monastery of Cetinje is next door to the royal palace, and I was just stepping across to it when I asked our guide if it was indeed true that there wcrc now two rival Orthodox churches in Montenegro. He nodded and then looked rather sheepish, as if the rivalry were too unseemly to discuss. There was, he said, a new Montenegrin Orthodox Church; the old one, the Serbian Orthodox Church, had its headquarters in the monastery next door. It might be better, the guide warned, if I went to see the new one first—simply because if I admitted to seeing the established church first, then the patriarch of the new church, a touchy man, might well refuse to receive me. It sounded like William Boot's visits to the rival Ishmaelian embassies in Evelyn Waugh's *Scoop*: I was intrigued, and so took directions to the house of His Beatitude the Metropolitan of the Montenegrin Orthodox Church.

It turned out to be a small suburban house a mile from town, with net curtains and a lawn sprinkler. His Beatitude was asleep, but a delicate and fussy little acolyte in a black surplice welcomed us in, offered us Turkish coffee, and gave us magazines to read, and suggested we might wait for a little while.

A brief minute later, with a flourish, the young man threw open a door and in walked a magnificent figure, who bowed and handed over a scarlet visiting card. In English on one side, Cyrillic Serbo-Croat on the other, was written the name and title: HIS BEATITUDE THE MONTENEGRIN METROPOLITAN, THE REVEREND MIHAILO.

---

*The diplomats who were posted to Cetinje worked rather little—one result being that it was not until 1995 that someone noticed that a formal state of war still existed between Montenegro and Japan. It had been declared in 1905, and no one had bothered to lift it. It has been now.

He was very tall, dressed in a long omophorion of black silk with a burgundy lining, with a delicate black velvet chasuble on top and a large metal and enamel cross on his chest. He had pure white hair and a long, well-trimmed beard, though a dusting of dandruff had formed below it on the black velvet. He wore a dauntingly imperious expression, and I could well believe he was touchy on occasion. But on this one he was polite and welcoming: He dismissed the boy-priest and his coffee, curtly demanding slivovitz instead. He bowed to us and raised his glass. He seemed very much the showman.

He talked expansively, in broken English and good Italian, about the needs and aspirations of the Montenegrin people to have their own church, to break free of the tiresome domination of the Serbs, to resume the church's once autocephalous state, with its own Montenegrin leadership, as they had enjoyed until their king was deposed at the end of the Great War. There were fully 667 Montenegrin churches back in the old days.

"But now we are small, our congregations are tiny. Officially we have no churches, because the Serbs have gone to court to forbid us from establishing ourselves. But as pride in our country grows again, so pride in our religion does too. I am filled with optimism. Look at the two-headed eagles in our coats of arms—see how the Serbian eagle has folded wings, while our eagle has its wings spread, ready to fly? Well, that is how we are—ready to fly."

But there were problems, he said. The right of a new Orthodox church to exist was determined by the supervising body of the Orthodox communion, an office in Istanbul—which Mihailo kept referring to, confusingly, as Czarigrad, the capital of the czars— and so far they had refused.

And he took us downstairs to the tiny chapel he had set up on the ground floor—half a room, really, with a linoleum floor and a few icons stuck on the wall. He held services there once a week, and perhaps forty people came. "But at Easter we had fifteen thousand at an open-air service—the Serbians only had five thousand, and most of them they brought in by bus from Herzegovina." He became visibly agitated as he said this. He denounced the Serbian church leadership as "rude" and "psychologically disturbed," he accused them of trying to engineer his downfall, of bringing pressure to bear on the authorities in Istanbul, trying to deny his attempt at independence. "They are behaving like barbarians—the Barbarians of the Balkans. They must realize that tolerance is the spirit of the age."

But in truth Bishop Mihailo's mission seemed more compounded of rhetoric than revival; the power of his Serb opposition seemed overwhelming, and there was little by way of ecclesiastical business going on in his small suburban house—the telephone never rang, the fax machine on his desk remained silent all the time we were there. Perhaps his claims of a large Easter turnout were true; perhaps the Serbian religious leadership was employing unfair tactics. But Mihailo was losing ground, by all accounts. I could well imagine that after we left, His Beatitude—especially after his fortifying afternoon plum brandy—went upstairs again and crept back into bed.

At the Cetinje Monastery, by contrast, there was bustle and business, and it took some minutes before the abbot, the young and straggle-bearded Father Luke, came out into the courtyard. I was about to ask him the status of Mihailo when he suddenly said: "Wait—you are English. You know something of Saint Kieran of Clonmacnois? You can tell me something I do not know about the Venerable Bede? You know that today is the feast-day of Saint Augustine of Canterbury? Wait, wait here!"—and he bustled off into the gloom of the monastery and emerged a minute later with a postcard, an image of Saint Augustine published in Woking, in Surrey. "There! I have a collection. You may have it."

Father Luke of Cetinje proved to be a walking encyclopedia of the Eastern Orthodox Church, and a man as keenly confident of his own Serbian religious rights as Mihailo seemed to be of his Montenegrin claims. "The difference is—we have history on our side. We are the oldest Serbian church—we are older than the church at Pec, which you will know as the holiest of all places in Kosovo.

"The first saint, the founder of the Serbian church, was Saint Sava—and he was born in Montenegro, though he died in Bulgaria and people think of him as perhaps Bulgarian. But he was not: He was one of us. It is through connections like this that we know we are the rightful religious establishment here, and for an old fool like Mihailo to try and claim to be a founder of a new Montenegrin movement is just silly. Just politics. Besides," he said darkly, "look at Mihailo's record. He was in Rome, you know, head of the Greek Orthodox movement there—and he was defrocked."

I asked him what he meant, and he grinned and whispered something about unpriestly behavior. His remark, certainly rude, underlined what Father Sbutega had suggested: that battle royal was raging among the Eastern churches in Montenegro, providing an ecclesiastical parallel to what was still going on, raging like distant thunder, in the surrounding skies.

The thunder was growing louder now, the war was gathering pace. In Podgorica the journalists were getting excited, the fixers being asked to make ever-more-daring excursions as the demands of the editors outside became ever more extreme. *Get over the border deep into Kosovo. Find the Kosovo Liberation Army headquarters. Interview disaffected Serb soldiers on the frontier.* Only one radio reporter seemed bored by the whole affair, a middle-aged man who declared that he had had enough of fighting and proposed to sit out this particular war. He stayed in the hotel bar all day and sent his team of fixers off to ferret out any developments: Not surprisingly they found very little, for everything that was happening—and that meant a great deal—was doing so in Albania, in Macedonia, or in Kosovo itself.

Montenegro itself may well be poised for its own grisly little war: That much was abundantly clear, so deep and growing is the loathing now between the Montenegrins and the Serb forces among them. As I was preparing to leave there was talk about how Serbia might try to take control of the little repub- lic's frontiers, something the Montenegrins would not tolerate and against which they would undoubtedly fight; and I had met heavily armed young men back in Cetinje who were training, preparing to do real battle with the ten thousand Serb soldiers who were in their midst. A mood of fatalism and fear was all of a sudden gripping this exquisite little corner of the world: All, I felt, would soon end in tears.

Yet however worrying in the long term, the short-term fate of Montenegro seemed in early June to be but a sideshow to the main event—Podgorica suddenly seemed like a backwater, and I was running out of time. So Rose and I found a car, asked Dali and Vesna for the best tactics for avoiding the Yugoslav army checkpoints on the way out, and headed promptly south for Lake Scutari, and the one non-Slavic country of this corner of the Balkans, the Republika e Shqiperise: Albania.

7

The Lifting of the Gate

Albania and her neighbors

W HY SHOULD WE turn our country into an inn," Enver Hoxha once asked, "with her doors flung open to pigs and sows, to people with pants on or no pants at all, and to the hirsuit [*sic*], longhaired hippies who would come here to supplant with their wild orgies the graceful dances of our people?"

That was in 1970, when Albania was an impoverished and lonely workers' paradise, when the ghost of Joseph Stalin was the only foreign hero the nation was allowed, and when Enver Hoxha, whose madness had created all this misery, was still fifteen years away from the grave. But eventually he did die, Albania did find another and more tolerant government, and the country did begin reach out for the world from which it had been so self-estranged for so long. And though Albania is still an anarchic and fractious place today, many matters—a sense of freedom and a refurbished economy in particular—are slowly improving. The legacy of Hoxha's four decades of unmitigated harshness, however, and his frowardly and unyielding hatred for all things foreign, clings like summer mildew.

True, no frontier barber with a blunt and bloodied razor stands ready, as once he did, to hack off any unauthorized ponytail or goatee. No "compromised" border guard is there, freed briefly from his labor camp, to pore through your every book and private letter, searching for the vaguest hint of written disrespect to Comrades Stalin or Hoxha, or to any others whom Albania chose to regard as like only unto God.

One can get into Albania with perfect ease these days, on payment at the frontier of what some officials insist is fifty-seven dollars in cash for a one-time visa (but only fifteen dollars if you are Irish). It doesn't seem to matter these days whether you are pig or sow, long-bearded or hairless, whether you wear pants or miniskirts or even neither, or even if you are habitually inclined to the practice of indolence and the consumption of dope. But though things have improved since the times of Hoxha, there can be no feelings of relief at the Albanian frontiers of today either—none of relief, and certainly none of joy.

A flimsy and half-broken plywood pole with blue and gray markings, a pool of muddy water that was alleged once to have been disinfectant, a shredded blood-red flag with Skanderbeg's black double-headed eagle, and a warped and flaking sign saying, barely legibly, *Miresevni ne Shqiperi*—"Welcome to the Land of the Eagle": With such devices and delights alone does the Republic of Albania greet today's visitors who enter the country by road, and as we did, from the north.

As the two unshaven policemen thumbed clumsily through our passports, in a room that stank of urine, its only furniture a ripped sofa whose innards were teeming with blowflies, I gazed back north, almost with yearning, to the far frontier. It looked so *civilized*, just a few hundred yards away. There was the red-and-white steel pole that had been lifted for us; there, nearly out of sight on the far side of the little stream, was the newly built steel-and-concrete shed for customs examinations; and there above was the red-white-and-blue flag of Yugoslavia, fluttering next to the Montenegrin two-headed eagle, in white. The car that had brought us south, a brand-new air-conditioned Toyota, had turned around, was leaving, the driver going back to Podgorica. Two Montenegrin border policemen were cheerfully showing off to him the salmon they had caught in Lake Scutari—with only two or three travelers crossing this frontier each day, life for the guards was pretty easy.

Someone else, I could see, was using a cell phone. A tall Montenegrin policewoman was tapping her feet to the rhythms—barely audible from here—that sounded from a radio she had placed on a chair. In spite of the strange, nervous situation that had been triggered by the war, Montenegro looked from this modest distance like a bastion of European normality: What lay ahead of us by contrast seemed stranger, more foreign, and poorer, than any place I had been for a long while.

I suddenly felt a delicate, feathery touch on my arm, and started. It was a nut-brown Gypsy boy, dressed in a wildly bright cowboy shirt, begging for spare change. He had broken away from a group of the urchins just beside the frontier line: They were hoping for foot passengers, like us, who had to leave our Montenegrin car behind and walk across no-man's land to the waiting Albanian taxi. A tiny girl rushed up and planted a dry kiss on my arm and smiled up at me beseechingly: I gave her and her impish friends all the remaining dinars I had, and a few American quarters, and they scuttled away in a flash of color, giggling.

I liked Gypsies, and had ever since my childhood days when my father would me take fishing in Norfolk, along with a policeman friend of his who had been a bit of a *didicoi* himself. I liked the Gypsies' magnificent insolence, their devil-may-care look at a life that, considering that they lacked everything the rest of us had—like a state, a permanent home, a capital, a single language, heroes, myths—must have been fairly bitter, but from which they always seemed to come up grubby-faced but grinning. They were persecuted everywhere: In Albania in the days of Hoxha's bizarre Stalinist regime they had been herded en masse into unlovely apartment houses, which was better at least than what had happened to them in Nazi Germany, or in Poland or Bulgaria, where they were gassed or just ignored and made to change their names.

Names were important in Hoxha's Albania. Whether you were a Gypsy or not, you could call your child only by a name selected from an officially approved list, and the list changed each year. The names were often Illyrian, or pagan, and sometimes just made up: Many Albanian adults these days bear the first name *Marenglen*, which comes from the first letters of Marx, Engels, and Lenin.

Such madness was only the more trivial side of a tyranny that has left ineradicable scars on almost all of Albania's three and a half million people, who remain as a result one of the most backward and ruined peoples of Europe. The Sigurimi, the dreaded security police, had a network of no fewer than forty-eight prison camps inside the republic—and this a country hardly bigger than Vermont, about the same size as Kuwait or Djibouti, and which had as many people as Chicago.

Hundreds of thousands of people, turned in by huge numbers of informers and spies, vanished into the camps and were either murdered or worked to death. Whole families were punished for the "crimes" of one—if a young man dared listen to a foreign broadcast, or tell a faintly amusing but disrespectful story about Enver Hoxha, his entire family, parents and grandparents included, would be sent to a Sigurimi camp, either to be brutally tortured or allowed to starve. Children were taught to spy on parents: The entire country was caught up in a web of mutual distrust, the only constant being the genially cruel presence of Friend Enver, Comrade Enver, the man whose statue was on every street corner, for whom almost every street was named, and the man who made magic, could make flowers blossom in his footsteps or the rains come at a single word.

No one was allowed to own a car: A visitor to Tirana in 1971 noted the presence in Skanderbeg Square of just one sleepy traffic policeman who jumped up at the appearance of anything with an engine, and if he saw the same car twice in one day greeted it like a long-lost friend. Most of the people traveled in ancient buses, on trains that belched smoke and sparks, or by pony or oxcart. The senior bureaucrats had cars, as did those few foreign diplomats unlucky enough to be posted to the grim fastness of a Tirana they could barely ever leave: Otherwise the city was a capital where 150,000 people lived in squalor and misery, amids a welter of free-ranging livestock and the ever-present spies from the Sigurimi.

There was, officially, no religion—Albania under Hoxha had announced with pride that it was the world's first truly atheist nation. Mosques had been turned into sports halls and swimming pools, and one majestic Catholic structure in Scutari had become a tire warehouse. But in fact, in spite of the strictures and the spies, people did manage to worship, as they seem to in all those countries that try to ban religion: Services were held in private houses, and foreign religious broadcasts, mainly from Italy, were listened to avidly, late at night, and quietly.

Then came December 1990 and the return to Albania of the nation's favorite daughter, Mother Teresa, arguably the world's most famous nun. Her return (she was actually born in Macedonia, though her family was of Albanian stock) triggered an eruption of repressed religious zeal that was as impressive in its scale as in its ecumenical breadth. The result was that today Albania, albeit still poor and corrupt and lawless and sometimes frightening, is at least a country that worships, and its churches and mosques are filled.

It is, moreover, the only European nation that sports a majority of Muslims: Seven out of ten Albanians visit the mosque—the Turks had evidently done their work well, and Hoxha had hardly outdone it during his forty years. Friday prayers held these days at the Mosque of Mahmud Dashi in Tirana's Skanderbeg Square are as impressive for their rituals and the numbers of the faithful as are any services in Lahore, Dacca, Dubai, or Istanbul: This country that was godless in the eighties had become more than amply full of gods at the century's end, with more, in all likelihood, on the way.*

_____

*Since American Christian evangelists have recently made Albania a target for their proselytizing zeal, and young churchmen from Kentucky and Ohio are to be found, with their short-sleeved shirts and ever-ready smiles, standing on street corners everywhere from Scutari to Elbasan.

*   *   *

The driver had been arranged by telephone from Podgorica. He was an elderly man with a lopsided and toothless grin and three days' worth of gray stubble on his chin. He drove a twenty-year-old Mercedes—there are said to be some twenty thousand Mercedes-Benzes in Albania, all stolen in Germany and licensed in such a way as to ensure they can never leave the country again. He attempted to speak to us—but his Albanian was far too strange and difficult, even for Rose, who could normally pick up foreign tongues with unusual dispatch. She spoke excellent Italian and French and was competent in a host of lesser tongues, but Albanian quite foxed her.

She was not alone. Edward Lear, who traveled in Albania in 1848, was infuriated by the one European language he could not fathom: Among the "clatter of strange monosyllables," he wrote, he could discern only strange near-Anglicisms, "dort beer, dort bloo, dort hitch, hitch beer, blue beer, beer chak, dort gatch." Although there are just two properly official languages today—that of the Gheg people in the north,* and that of the Tosk in the south, with the occasional addition of a third known as Arberesh, which is spoken mainly by Albanians now living in Italy—there are also said to be five main alphabets, one of which has more than fifty letters.

The road, once we had left the frontier zone, was a ravaged and torn-up thing, much like a cart track—and the only vehicles we saw during the first few miles, as we bumped along the low plain on the eastern shore of Lake Scutari, were in fact drawn by mules, and were little more than immense haystacks on wheels. The scenery was dull, except for one curious phenomenon that became so commonplace that it almost seemed worthless to remark on it—the presence of hundreds upon thousands of mushroom-shaped pillboxes.

---

*Which, along with Serbo-Croat, is the language spoken by most of the Kosovo Albanians.

Enver Hoxha had ordered them to be built. He panicked one summer day in 1968 when the Soviet tanks invaded Czechoslovakia: He withdrew from the Warsaw Pact in protest, and then suddenly realized that his friendship agreement with faraway China did not make any provision for defense. His country, alone in its Stalinist isolation anyway, was ripe for picking should any neighbor—Greece, most probably, or some vile American agent, or maybe the Russians with whom he had so spectacularly fallen out—choose to invade. And so he built pillboxes—eight hundred thousand of them by most accounts, smooth-topped gray cement mushrooms, with a gun slit at one side and a stairway down the back, and dotted them all across his country, defying anyone who might enter the nation illegally to get more than a few hundred yards before being cut down in a hail of gunfire. Albanians today find them a grotesque embarrassment, and they have no real idea why they were built and who they were to defend Albania against. "Everyone," one man in Tirana was quoted as saying.

Scores of thousands of these igloolike bunkers remain—they line every main road, they cluster at the approaches to all cities, they appear every few yards along the much-used highway between Tirana and the port city of Durres,* where any invasion was thought likely to begin. Their gun slits point in all directions: Rose pointed out many that were built on hillsides but with the slit directed not out from the hill, but uselessly backwards, so that any fire would hit the grassy slope that can't have been more than five feet away.

---

*Durres is the Albanian terminus of the great Roman road to Istanbul known as the Egnatian Way. It was twelve feet wide, raised in the middle to allow rainwater to run off, and it had staging posts every dozen miles so the soldiers could change horses. Little of it remains, though the straight line of the Durres-Tirana road looks very Roman indeed.

Some are large, some miniature; they appear sometimes singly, or in twos and threes, or as forests of two dozen and more. None are used, nor do they ever appear to have been—though one assumes that on occasion they bristled with guns and men waiting silently through bitter nights for some of Hoxha's imagined invaders to land. Nowadays a few of them, made no doubt of substandard cement, have crumbled like sugar in the rain. Others have been dug up from their foundations and lie upside down in the fields like stranded tortoises, monuments all to a terrible and costly folly of a sadly paranoid mind.

The rutted road and the trainless railway beside it hugged the shore of the lake. Far to the west rose the Montenegrin mountains, violet in the late-morning sun. Behind them, I knew, lay the sea, and Ulcinj and its community of Slavic Africans. Once in a while an Italian military vehicle—a jeep, the odd armored car, an ambulance—hurried past, the machine-gunner on top looking nervously around. The troops had the acronym AFOR stenciled on the sides—we had seen SFOR and IFOR in Bosnia, and knew that if soldiers ever did go into Kosovo, a development that was looking likelier by the hour, they would be designated as KFOR.*

These men, mostly newcomers, were under the command of a British general based down at the port of Durres. They, together with Americans and Germans and Spaniards, were posted to Albania both to help keep the country stable, as well as to secure its borders, help organize the refugee of all, to be on hand should the NATO troops be ordered to invade. They had, I thought, the uneasy look of readiness about them, and as we pressed on south their convoys became more numerous, and there were tank trans-

---

*AFOR for Albanian Force, KFOR for Kosovo Force—but in Bosnia, SFOR for Stabilization Force, and IFOR for Implementation Force. This last referred to the soldiery sent to make certain that the provisions of the Dayton agreement on the internal frontiers of Bosnia were fully and properly set in place.

porters and helicopters, too. The balloon, it seemed, might soon be about to go up.

We passed through a dozen dusty, forlorn-looking villages, with names that were every bit as expectedly odd as the Albanian language itself. On the way to what outsiders call Scutari, but which the Shqiperian people call Shkoder, we passed either through or close by Hani i Hoti (where we had crossed the frontier) Goraj-Bidisht, Kopliku i Sipermi, Mec, Drisht, and Renc. The names of the people were odd as well: I had only just learned that one pronounces *Enver Hoxha* to rhyme with *lodger*, when we stopped for lunch and Italian coffee at a town called Grude e Re, and I picked up a local paper only to be confronted with stories of a Communist party leader and former tinsmith who was named Koci Xoxe. The driver, happily, did not wish to make conversation about him—and indeed, he kept his own counsel for most of the journey, until we reached the outskirts of Tirana when he made it unmistakably clear, mainly by signs, that he wanted twice as much money as we had agreed to give him.

Tirana looked like a city of the Wild West on the day the carnival comes to town. We arrived at dusk on a Saturday evening, and tens of thousands of Albanians—perhaps the whole city, it looked so chaotic and busy—were on hand for their evening *passeggiata,* milling around, wandering idly in front of speeding cars, tussling with one another, shouting at children, playing in the fountains, gazing into shop windows. There were impromptu amusement parks, bicycles for rent, street stalls, kebab sellers, open-air hairdressers, peasants hawking fresh fish, cobblers and shoeshine boys, farmers selling hunting birds, mullahs on their way to prayer. I half expected to see fire eaters and tumblers, jesters and harlequins. It was like Rome's beautiful and madcap Piazza Navona on a Saturday night—thronging, exuberant, a scene from a Fellini movie, from a summer night's dream, and if the players were ragged and poor—well, what of it!

The women were vividly dressed, the men by contrast dull and dusty—though it was possible to tell in the crowds the northern Gheg people, who if they wore hats at all wore domed white skull-caps. Their Tosk rivals, on the other hand, wore the fez, also white but with a flattened top. Gypsy children were everywhere, darting in and out of the crowds, pestering the strollers, brushing dust from the car windscreens, begging for change. And money changers were at every street corner, offering huge bundles of leks without a care in the world for the police who, ten years before, would have rounded them up and sent them off for torture and hard labor.

Albania's capital was like a city with the safety cap taken off. It positively bubbled and bustled with the newfound enthusiasms of freedom, more than any of the other great cities—Berlin, Prague, Budapest—that had lately been released from the burdens of Marx. It was chaotic, it was poor, it was grubby. But everyone seemed to be smiling, carefree, optimistic, there was an infectious effervescence about the place, as if everyone knew that a great awakening was under way. I knew that I would like it from the moment that our car lurched into Skanderbeg Square, and there was the hero Skanderbeg himself, iron dark and nobly bearded astride his horse, reminding all Albanians that he, not the appalling Hoxha, was the true national hero.

It was five hundred years ago that he, then plain Gjerg Kastrioti, managed the awesome feat of welding into one all the disparate Illyrian tribes of the day, and fighting for twenty-five years—in vain, as it turned out—against the invading Turks. Like Prince Lazar up in Kosovo, the great Alexander Bey, Skanderbeg, is best remembered as a force for unifying and ennobling his people's cause. That both men lost to the superior numbers and the superior military skills of the Turks has never managed to quench, even five and six centuries later, the popular fondness for them.

Skanderbeg left the double-headed black eagle as his legacy, and both it and his image and his statue, around which scores of small children were playing, serve as reminders of pride in

unity and the glories of an Albania whose identity has never
been crushed by the foreign dominations they have had to bear
all too often. By comparison Enver Hoxha has left no legacy at
all, nothing of which one single Albanian can be proud—certainly not the hundreds of thousands of grim cement igloos,
dotted pathetically across the land.

We stayed at an empty and echoing mausoleum of a hotel,
the Dajti. The rooms were small and dusty; I had read once that
the Albanian fleas were the biggest and fattest in the world, and
so shook the sheets to make sure they were clean. Downstairs a
feisty receptionist got rid of the driver and cut his anticipated
bill in half. "A northerner," she said. "A cheat. Be careful. There
are a lot of cheats here this days."

I thanked the woman, once the driver had scowled his way
back to his car and swerved out of the gates. I told her she was
kind, and by the way, very pretty too. She grinned and blushed—
and suddenly a man standing at the counter who had been chat-
ting with her earlier took a step toward me. I shrank away. The girl
raised her hand, waved off the man.

I had been more foolish than I realized. Later that evening I
was told that the possessive pride of many Albanian men is such
as to keep all foreigners perpetually on guard. Pay no compli-
ments, I was warned. Never flirt. Be sure never to smile too hard
or to wink at anyone. Be scrupulously careful of any too-friendly
remark that might perhaps, if understood, being fatally misin-
terpreted.

The old customs and blood feuds between families remained
a powerful force in Albanian tradition. I was told of a young
man from a southern village, a university-educated, English-
speaking engineer named Tony who worked in a factory in
Tirana, who had met a young woman at a carnival earlier in the
year and had playfully pinched her backside. She had thought
little of the incident, had laughed it off—indeed, had been
rather flattered. But a few days later she made the mistake of

mentioning what had happened, in passing, to her brother. The brother in turn told their father, and then a sudden thundercloud descended.

The family patriarch decided that, in line with the ancient customs of his clan, the girl's honor had been besmirched. Vengeance should now be wrought. An example should now be made.

"And so, despite the protests from the girl," I was told, "her brother and another boy from the family took the bus down from Kukes, where they lived up north, and they went down to the village where the young man lived. They rounded up all the young men in the family—not just the bottom pincher, but all of his brothers and his cousins in his village—and they took knives to them and sliced off their noses. Just cut them off, there and then. No questions, no arguments. They told the men why it had happened, that it had been ordered by the clan leader to make their position known, and that the mutilated fellows should never dare set foot in Kukes again. And they took off and went back home.

"Everyone understood. There was no question of a crime having been committed, except for the bottom pinching that started it all. There was no question of an investigation or of any further punishment. That, so far as everyone was concerned, was an end to the matter."

Except it wasn't quite. The young engineer, who would then come to the Tirana office wearing a small handkerchief taped to his forehead, which hung down and obscured the gaping and cartilaginous hole in his face, saved up money to have plastic surgery in Italy. His employer begged him not to: The sum he had saved, a thousand dollars, may have been difficult to come by, and a third of the Albanian average annual income, but it would not buy a satisfactory replacement. But the boy went anyway, and had something grafted onto his face that looked much like a big toe, only lopsided. He had since gone back to his village, ashamed ever to show himself again, taking comfort only in the knowledge that his brothers and cousins looked at least as ugly as he did.

I was told the story of Tony by the one friend I had in Albania—an Irish-Canadian engineer from Calgary, whom I had encountered many years before on Sakhalin Island, in the Russian Far East. He name was Shaun Going, and he ran a company called DRC, Inc., which specialized in "construction and disaster services." What that meant, basically, was that wherever in the world was in need of urgent repair, for whatever reason—war, earthquake, hurricane—he and his men would swarm in and make good and mend. He had been in Sakhalin trying to put up houses for the oilmen who were beginning work in a place ruined by years of Communist neglect. Now he was here in Tirana, building encampments for the refugees. And he was readying himself for Kosovo because, he knew, "just as soon as the war is over, people will need to have new houses, new offices, new everything. I have the men and the equipment, and I can go in like a small task force. It's exciting stuff!"

Shaun Going was an eternally amusing, energetic man, the kind of perpetually upbeat figure for whom nothing seemed ever to be a problem—though I knew from Sakhalin Island that his business had been run fairly close to the wind, and that he had never amassed the kind of fortune that one suspected could be made out of the world's endless supply of disasters. Here he had a worthwhile contract with NATO, and he had already, "through contacts," acquired a plot of land in Pristina, the capital of Kosovo.

"The moment the soldiers get there," he said excitedly, "they're going to need showers, latrines, offices. I'll send in a team within hours of the invasion. I'll build them all they need in double-quick time. Then I'll hang around, bring in more people—rebuild the housing. I guess it's pretty bad over there, huh?" And he gave me a slew of telephone numbers, and asked me whether, if I managed to get into Kosovo, I might call him with an assessment of the damage that had been done. "I need to know

how much to bring in, in the way of material, men, you know. A
call from you, from someone on the spot, would be very helpful."

Mr. Going was a hustler, all right. But on the other hand he
seemed to be having so much fun doing what he did, he seemed
to take so positive and optimistic an attitude to it and was clearly
so well liked by so many of the Albanians I met—"Mr. Going is the
King of Albania" I was told, unprompted, by a total stranger who
had heard of him—that it would seem churlish to suggest that he
was a man who exploited human misery. And besides, who was I,
or who was any writer who came to these parts to see and write
about wars and disasters, to pass any judgment at all? Wars and disasters throw up all kinds of humanity, and Shaun Going was one
of those you meet on the periphery, not as noble as the fighters
perhaps, but yet with his own kind of nobility, for sure.

He took us to a restaurant called the Black Rooster, which has
a courtyard with a thatched roof that was kept wet and dripped
sheets of water into old stone runnels, and we ate trout from Lake
Ohrid—a fish so rare, and from a lake so clear and deep that
Enver Hoxha banned anyone but himself from fishing it, on
penalty of thirty years' hard labor. The fish was interesting, but
rather more so was the man Shaun brought as his guest—an
American named Greg, who came from North Carolina, said he
was a journalist working for *George* magazine in New York, and by
his own admission paced the streets of Tirana at all hours of the
night gathering, as he put it, "financial intelligence."

I never quite knew what to make of him. He was tall, languid,
educated, he spoke with an elaborately courteous southern
drawl and he dressed impeccably. He had a strange accent, an
odd manner: He kept referring to "the province," which he
claimed to visit regularly, when he was speaking of Kosovo, and
on those few occasions he used the word he called it Koss-*oh*-vo,
with a long second *o*. He referred to his present home as being
in a nation called Alb-*ah*-nia.

He gave the impression, as I am sure he half-intended, that

he was some kind of American spy—which, when I compared him with the handful of real spies I knew, he almost certainly was not—or else was an extremely inept one. His journalistic contacts were far fewer than he suggested at first, and when I pressed him he could cite only having done an occasional piece on local casinos for a Texas-based journal devoted to gambling. I was puzzled by him, and after spending half a day wandering the back streets of the city with him and getting hopelessly lost, I concluded that he was probably one of those Walter Mittyish characters who are often thrown up by the atmospheres of strange cities like Tirana—sad men who attach themselves, limpetlike, to the journalists and other temporary figures who briefly settle during the crisis, who eke out an existence in a more drab and banal way than they pretend, and who then, and before they are discovered, pack up and move on somewhere else. I had seen such people before, in Kabul, in Beirut, in Buenos Aires, and he seemed to fit the *modus operandi*. But then again, maybe Greg was indeed a senior spymaster for the Albanian desk back at the circus, and I had been royally duped.

Tirana was, in any case, infested by a veritable army of "internationals," as they had been snippishly called back in Sarajevo. They gathered each evening beside the caricaturably Hockney-blue pool at the EuropaPark Hotel, which was managed by Viennese and had been created for the sole use, it seemed, of foreigners willing to pay hundreds of dollars a night to stay and help Albania get back on its feet. I had lunch there once: A courtly Italian aid official with highly polished shoes and a suit of the coolest linen spent a good fifteen minutes choosing the perfect Montepulciano to have with his *osso buco*, in the process puzzling the tall Albanian waiter, whose badge suggested that his name was Elvis. What relevance any of this had to do with the poor, corrupt, lunatic nation beyond the clipped privet hedges and the security guards, I do not know: but I was happy to settle the bill and leave, and get into the car bound for the frontier with Macedonia.

Shaun had arranged that a huge Gheg villager named Monday*, once a heavyweight boxing champion, would drive us across to Skopje. Shaun also supplied us with one of his fleet of cars, which unlike most Albanian cars did have the right permission and insurance certificates that were needed to leave the country. And so we headed off out of Tirana, which fell away in no more than five minutes, once we had maneuvered our way around the massive fortifications at the American embassy. This, it seems, is a city without suburbs: Just like Pyongyang, with which it had few other similarities except for the screwball nature of its former regime, you are at one moment in the city—and then you were not. As with North Korea, so here with Albania. A row of mean houses comes to a sudden end—and then the countryside begins. One moment there is noise and confusion and fumes and traffic jams—and the next the sweet smell of new-mown hay, the sound of sheep bells, the patient plod of cowherds, and, in this case of this Albanian journey, the crags of the mountains of Kerrabe, which stand between the capital and the valley of Elbasan.

It was a dangerous, white-knuckle forty miles—for despite this being the Via Egnatia, the most direct Roman-built route between Durres and Byzantium, Monday and the equally huge friend he had brought along for company had no choice but to swing the car through a score of hairpin turns to hoist us over the mountain range. The summit was less than three thousand feet, but the view was stupendous: On the western side of the escarpment we could see all the way across the Durres and Tirana Plain, clear to the Adriatic and the island of Corfu. To the east we were confronted by range upon range of more dis-

---

*His name was Edmund, but since most Albanian names have to end with a vowel, Monday seemed most suitable.

tant blue hills, and just below the immense steel mill that the Chinese had built in more comradely times. It was quiet now, with no billowing clouds from its smokestacks: It rusted quietly in the sun, like Albania a victim of years of ruin and neglect.

Beyond the steel mill the countryside became wilder and ever more remote, and Monday urged us to watch out for bandits, gangs of men with guns who would swarm out of nowhere in an ambush, and take everything in a paroxysm of thievery. I had friends who had made this journey before, one of whom was left beside the road in only his underwear—his car, money, passport, clothes all gone with just a war whoop of delight, all lost in some isolated mountain lair. The region is lawless, dangerous—and I only felt confident that this journey would succeed because of two realities: First, Monday was a very large man indeed, and was known to thousands of Albanian boxing fans and respected by all of them; and second, there was a major war presently in the making, and the road and the fields ahead were swarming with east-bound soldiers and equipment, most of them American.

We came across the first of them while we sped down the valley of the Shkumbinit River, between the towns of Librazhd and Perrenjas: A pair of American Humvees was parked under the trees beside the stream, the soldiers gazing in rapture at a group of young Albanian girls in bathing suits. Then suddenly the air was filled with thunder and a pair of U.S. Army helicopters zoomed low above us, their rotors setting the trees thrashing in their wake. They were bound for the shores of Lake Ohrid, to a rendezvous point for the battle to come.

And then we saw more, many more, as we breasted a rise above the western side of the lake itself. The road forks just beyond Perrenjas, and one can go either to a border crossing south of the lake or another at the northern side. Since we were due to take the road north up to Skopje, this latter northern frontier post seemed the better choice, and so we turned to the left—and climbed up onto a treeless moorland country of tussock grass and stunted bushes that could have been in Scotland, and needed only a sporraned piper to look the part. We rounded a bend—and then saw ahead of a huge concentration of American armed forces, parked in a great circle in a field beside the road.

It was a landing strip and a refueling base for the Macedonia-bound squadron of Apache helicopters. Twenty of the sleek and menacing looking machines, known as AH-64s, and said by the Pentagon to be among the finest tank-killing, infantry-disrupting slow-speed attack aircraft ever designed, had been in Albania for the previous ten weeks. They had proved perfectly useless: One of them had crashed; two men had been killed; the rest of the crews turned out to be poorly trained and quite unsuited for the kind of duties the Joint Chiefs of Staff had assumed they could carry out. So now, as a soft option, they were going to Macedonia, and if not to prosecute a war, then at least to help secure a kind of peace.

And whether they were going proudly or in some kind of disgrace, their simple presence here, the sight of such a muscular part of the American military machine in so backward and bucolic a corner of the world, was hugely impressive. Giant fuel pumps, scores of armored cars, dozens of jeeps and Humvees and radio vans and sentries were posted over ten acres of clifftop. And one by one, the needle-nosed machines thundered in from the west, were refueled with speed and efficiency, and then spiraled up into the sky once more before heading east, across the frontier. We could have watched for hours, and a few Albanian children, held back by the men with guns, were evidently doing so. The sight of so much hardware, the roaring of engines, the smell of jet fuel, the impression of power and money and might—it all had a mesmerizing effect.

But ten minutes later we were at the border, lining up behind a group of armored cars from an engineering support battalion based in faraway Kentucky. The Macedonian frontier guards were making every solder present his passport, stamping each man in as though he were a tourist, making sure the vast green vehicles that roared and spluttered in the heat had all the proper registration and insurance documents. Their commander, a young African American from Texas, scratched his head in disbelief. "I figured we'd cross frontiers like they weren't really there," he said. "What could they do if we just put the hammer down?" He patted the inch-thick steel flank of an armored car. "Do these guys think they could they stop a baby like this?"

But the officer behaved himself and patiently waited until the forms had been filled and the stamps all stamped, and then the convoy roared off into what was once called Thrace—and what until 1992 had itself been a part of Yugoslavia, but that was now called either FYROM, or by everyone but the angry Greeks, Macedonia.

We followed twenty minutes later, only to discover the convoy stranded, perhaps in that notorious commanders' nightmare that comes about when you are, as they say, "lost at the join of four maps." They were turning around in a fog of smoke and dust, heading for an overnight rest camp. We passed them, and the young black officer waved sardonically.

"See you at the front!" he yelled. "If you manage to find it," I shouted back.

By dusk we are in the smart little mountain town of Tetovo, thirty miles shy of the Macedonian capital. I had made a phone call: There were no rooms in Skopje, and so it seemed sensible to spend the night here. We found a motel beside a gas station, with rooms both for us and for Monday and his friend. It was a noisy night. The waitress, a glamorous blond who served us drinks while wearing a dress that might have been sprayed on, whose top half was so sheer as to be almost transparent, made extravagantly noisy love in the room next to ours. And then at four in the morning there came the crashing, screeching, grinding noise of steel tracks on an asphalt road. I looked out of the window: A column, miles long, of German Wehrmacht tanks and armored cars and self-propelled guns was grinding its way northward, just below the window. The great invasion was getting noisily under way.

8

The Sound and the Fury

NATO force movements into Kosovo, July 1999

I T WAS A LITTLE after four o'clock on a cool and starlit Balkan summer morning, the water meadow by the border was quiet and deserted. The main road beside it was quiet, too, but, as our eyes became accustomed to the dark, so we could see that the northbound lane was lined with scores of jeeps and armored cars and, lying on the dew-damp asphalt, hundreds upon hundreds of sleeping soldiers. A scattering of the officers who would command them were in the back of their Land Rovers, hunched over maps lit by pools of red light from night-lamps. Some were smoking. All were fidgeting. Everyone was waiting.

The operation had been code-named Joint Guardian. It involved the rapid establishment of a peacekeeping force in and throughout the cities, villages, plains, and mountain ranges of the Yugoslavian province of Kosovo. The operation was vast in size and scope, and it taken military planners much of the previous six months to work out how best it might be carried out. It involved principally large numbers of heavily armed forces from Britain, the United States, Italy, Germany, Norway, Denmark, and Holland, most of whom were either waiting here or were parked at marshaling sites within a few miles of the frontier zone.

It now required only a decision from NATO headquarters outside Brussels, and the formal issuance of an order by the forces' commanding general on the ground, Sir Michael Jackson, to set the vast machinery of this operation—by far the biggest European military operation since the end of World War II—in motion. That was what everyone—and half the world outside—was waiting for. We stamped our feet to ward off the morning chill: In a head-quarters back at an airbase near Skopje, commanders waited for radio messages, and for the green light, for the signal to go.

Rose and I had arrived from Albania on the evening of Thursday, June 10. The next day, Friday, was when the forces were first scheduled to make their entry, but it turned out instead to be a hectic and surreally confused day, with the Russian government indulging in a subtle and dangerous power play that caused angst and irritation among the Western allies, and ended up causing a twenty-four-hour postponement. But now matters had been at least partially resolved. The Serbian forces that were supposed, under the terms of the previous week's agreement, to be leaving Kosovo, were now in the process of doing so. It was vitally important that there was no vacuum between the departure of one force and the arrival of another. To avoid the possibility of anarchy, or the seizure of the province by any one or more of the guerrillas and paramilitary groups with which the region was blessed, or cursed, depending on your viewpoint, NATO now had to move very fast. So it came as no surprise late on that hectic Friday afternoon when we were told that H hour, the moment when the Allied forces would formally start to roll into Kosovo, was now to be 5:30 in the morning of Saturday, June 12. British forces, it was decided, would be the first to go in. A battalion of Gurkhas* first, then paratroops, and behind them a great deal of very protective heavy armor and a number of extremely large guns.

In anticipation of what we would be likely to see, the two of

---

*Soldiers from Nepal, who were originally recruited by the Crown during the days of British rule in India, and who have since continued to be eager members of the British army, finding themselves on duty in curious places—the Falkland Islands, Cyprus, Hampshire, Kosovo—that must be utterly alien to their own traditions.

us, along with an Australian colleague from a newspaper in Melbourne, managed to reach the Kosovo frontier line shortly after three o'clock. There, beside the Blace water meadow that I was now seeing for the third time, along with a scattering of others who were curious to witness the denouement of this long Balkan crisis, we waited, and waited, in the cool and deceptive peace of this strange Macedonian dawn.

The more obvious preparations had begun to take place just after nightfall. At about 10:00 P.M. a long column of heavy armor began moving along the main bypass to the north of Skopje, past the main hotel where the immense collection of foreign reporters were staying, and past the slums and shanties that, by happy chance, were largely occupied by some of Macedonia's half million Albanians.* The first few vehicles—huge British Challenger tanks manned by engineers, and with earthmoving equipment mounted on the front, as well as Warrior armored cars and self-propelled guns—came and went without the onlookers doing much more than staring, open mouthed in awe. But by midnight, when the column had swollen to an endless roaring river of iron, it seemed as though someone had said to the Albanians it thundered past: *These tanks, these are for you, these are going to help liberate your people.* And once that realization had sunk in, the people on the street began to go wild.

By 1:00 A.M. a huge mass of people, with hundreds of little children all way past their bedtime, stood beside the road cheering madly, waving flags, blaring horns, tossing pieces of ribbon and newspaper confetti at the passing tanks. The crews looked from

---

*The ethnic makeup of Macedonia can hardly be said to augur well for the newborn country's long-term stability: the Macedonians themselves account for about 1.5 million, the Albanians (most of whom live in the west, close to the Albanian frontier) 500,000—and there are significant numbers of Turks, Gypsies, and, most ominously of all, Serbs.

their turrets in happy puzzlement—men from Lancashire and Devon and Belfast and Hawick, witnessing scenes of adulation and hope that had not been seen in Europe since perhaps the liberation of Paris. It was an astonishing, deeply moving sight; and I shall long remember turning away to go back for an hour's sleep, and hearing the strange harmony of the sounds the came from behind me—on one hand the roaring and grinding of the tank columns, and on the other the ecstasy of cheering from those who were watching them, and willing them on, to the frontier.

The eastern sky began to lighten at about half past four, and although the columns of soldiers remained quiet, unmoving, or just begin to stir uneasily, I thought I heard the distant thud of helicopters from behind the eastern hills. Later on it turned out that a small number of aircraft had indeed had set out, an hour or so before the deadline: A single squadron of men from the British Special Air Service and a thirty-strong team of paratroopers known as a Pathfinder Group crossed the border under cover of dark. They stationed themselves on hilltops, building a half dozen or so small observation posts from which they could see and direct the movement of the invasion force to come.

We knew none of this at the time; and in strict legal terms by moving before the designated deadline the NATO side may well have breached the so-called Military Technical Agreement that had been signed three days before, by General Mike Jackson on one side, and the Yugoslav Colonel-General Svetozar Marjanovic on the other. But if this was so there was certainly no one on hand to complain: and none of the Chinook helicopters that took off from the Macedonian airfield at Kumanovo, nor any of the fifty-odd fighters they disgorged, made any contact with an enemy. If there had been Serbian soldiers in this corner of southern Kosovo, they had clearly slipped well away during the night.

By 5:00 it was fully light, and all the soldiers were waking—at the side of most Land Rovers troops had lit small Sterno stoves and were brewing tea. Men were checking their weapons, stowing their sleeping bags into their rucksacks, tuning their radios. There was an air of quiet deliberation about them all; a few made rather feeble attempts at gallows humor; for the rest it was more comfortable to be quiet.

Ahead loomed the chimneys of the old cement factory at the improbably named Serbian community of General Jankovic. Near it, in the middle distance, were some houses—all of them roofless, burned, and empty, all the visible evidence of the local Serbs' apparently systematic emptying twelve weeks before of the Albanian border villages. The water meadow, where I had stopped in 1977 and where, just three months ago, tens of thousands of wretched refugees had tried to camp, was almost pristine now. The mud had gone, and there was thick grass in its place, and except for a few huts put there by the aid agencies, there was little now to show for the brief period when it had enjoyed such notoriety as the squalid first resting place for the people driven from their Kosovo homes.

Then, at 5:05, a sudden burst of activity. A smallish, sprightly British officer, a brigadier named Adrian Freer, detached himself from the throng and marched quickly toward the Macedonian border guards. His own sentries, tough young blades from the Parachute Regiment, made sure that these guards—men who had never behaved well toward the refugees, nor toward the press, and who even now were angrily trying to keep everyone away from the frontier—fell away; within seconds he was at the line itself, demanding through an interpreter to speak to his Yugoslav army opposite number with whom, as he put it, "I believe have an appointment." He was looking for the brigadier commanding the 243rd Mechanized Brigade of the Yugoslav army, the man who had been ordered to tell the incoming Britons where any mine-fields might be, how safe it was to proceed along the road ahead.

But the commander was nowhere to be found. The minutes ticked past. No one came. A few sentries on the far side could be seen talking urgently to one another, and then leaving their post on the double, passing out of sight. On this side the brigadier was joined by a strange-looking officer in a tricorn hat that was covered with what looked like gold-thread curtain tassels. He turned out to be a Dutch brigadier, the holder of some important staff job at NATO, and was known universally as Haen the Hat. But even his arrival did nothing to scare up the Yugoslavs, and at 5:10 a coldly exasperated Adrian Freer shrugged, turned smartly around, and marched back toward us and his men.

He assembled us in a small group, and said quite simply, and with a graceful courtesy perhaps known only in a British-managed invasion: "I have attempted to make contact with my opposite number on the Yugoslav side, but as you can see I have failed to do so.

"My orders are now to clear and secure the Kacanik Defile and to open the Kacanik Corridor. So, gentlemen and ladies—if you would be so kind as to step to one side, I now propose to carry out my orders. Would you kindly let my convoy pass?"

And he gestured with a prearranged signal to Capt. Fraser Rea on the leading Gurkha Land Rover Defender, while at the same time another radioman mouthed a coded one-word order into his microphone.

There was a cry from the column: "Attack! Attack!" and in the one unforgettable moment that followed, two entire brigades of the British army, the Fifth Airborne and the Fourth Armoured, which together make a terrifying monster when roused, got formally and majestically under way. A hundred engines started and began to roar, and from tents and lairs beside the road columns of Gurkhas materialized and began marching swiftly alongside the vehicles that started grinding steadily north.

The Macedonians melted to one side, one of them pausing long enough to raise, rather theatrically, the orange-and-white pole that marked the entrance to no-man's land. And then in the soldiers streamed—mortar carriers and machine-gunners, engineers and bomb-disposal teams, spotters and radiomen, mine clearance specialists and explosives experts, sharpshooters, antitank snipers, military policemen, and hundreds upon hundreds of tough, fit, menacing-looking members of the infantry. Captain Rea had the distinction of being the first to cross the line: The two thousand men of the forward element of Operation Joint Guardian were just moments behind.

As they moved in, so at the same time came what remains in my memory the most dramatic moment of the morning. There was a tremendous roar from behind and then, rising in unison from behind the southern hills, a wave of helicopters that dipped their noses together and, flying fast and true, streamed in toward us at the frontier. The first was an Apache, perhaps one of those we had seen refueling on the Albanian border two days before. As it steadied itself in the crosswinds a hundred yards or so before crossing, it dropped a package that briefly flashed in the sky beneath it, and from which drifted down a myriad fragments of silvery foil—chaff to deceive any radars ahead or perhaps merely to impress the cameras.

Whatever its function, the tiny explosion in the sky was the signal for the other machines to move in—and this they did, fourteen heavy-lift helicopters, eight Chinooks and six Pumas, with six Apaches swooping and curving, riding shotgun alongside them. "I've never seen anything so beautiful," said a paratrooper, marching fast underneath them. "Just so long as they don't shoot at us," said another private, well aware of the Apaches' mixed reputation.

The Chinooks, great double-rotored monsters, were all carrying vehicles slung by wire cables underneath their bellies. There were light tanks, artillery pieces, armored cars, ambulances—and they swung far out into the sky as the machines banked at each curve in the Lepenec River valley. They roared into the distance, settling down their cargoes hurriedly on the far hillsides and by the distant bridges, and then they thundered back for more. Within half an hour more than a thousand troops had been hoisted up into the high ground above the Kacanik Defile, the men joining the observers who had been prepositioned during the night. Now, with machine-gun nests set up and the portable radar stations and antiaircraft installations fully functioning, the oncoming convoy could swish smoothly north and up toward the Kosovan capital of Pristina, fifty miles away. That, we all assumed, was the target for the day: Indeed, when I had had a beer with Mike Jackson the day before, he had said I would be a "sissy" if I didn't meet him in Pristina by sunset on Saturday.

Once the first airborne brigade was safely inside Kosovo, those of us who were being allowed in as civilians—a lot of press, some doctors, a handful of returning refugees working as translators went in next, in a ramshackle convoy of cars and vans.* There was some chaos, as had been predicted, with the press inevitably getting under the feet of the torrent of incoming soldiery. (Sometimes quite literally: A brigadier's armored car, its driver frustrated at not being able to squeeze past an Italian television van blocking the route, suddenly accelerated, tearing off the van's door and very nearly running over the irate producer's feet. But when the armor vanished over the horizon even the producer seemed amused: He'd get the car door repaired on expenses, he said, and the shoes he was wearing weren't exactly his Sunday best.)

There were some delays, as small suspect bombs were detonated, as a party of Yugoslav militia were disarmed and sent packing, as a group of Gurkhas got into a heated argument with some heavily armed members of the Kosovo Liberation Army, who wanted to be photographed linking arms with the small and wiry Nepalese who appeared to have liberated them. Forty members of the MUP, the dark-uniformed Yugoslav special police, were escorted north by another troop of Gurkhas; they

---

*Mine was a tiny Fiat I had rented in Tetovo the day before, the firm asking only that I give them my Hong Kong identity card as guarantee that I would return it. A colleague, based in Moscow, then borrowed it from me, and as is often the way in a war, I am not entirely sure what happened to it. My ID card, however, has since expired.

said they were afraid for their own safety, scared that the Albanians might begin reprisals. One of them we spoke to was sweating profusely under his thick serge uniform. "Perhaps I'll never come back here—I just don't know," he said, before the Gurkhas dropped him off in a safer part of the countryside and told him to make himself scarce.

But by noon the convoy was moving well, the infantrymen and light armor going in first, the heavy tanks rumbling through some time later in the morning. Units of the Fourth Armoured Brigade, which included such stylish army formations as the Household Cavalry, most usually photographed changing the guard outside Buckingham Palace, as well as the Irish Guards and the tanks of the King's Royal Hussars, were pouring in by lunchtime. The lead vehicles had soon cleared the crags and canyons of the defile and were then out in the hayfields and meadows of Kosovo proper, speeding along without interruption, except at two or three junctions where other units, who had come across the border later and from different places, joined the main northbound torrent.

The roadway, which by now had been marked by black-and-yellow tac-signs of a dagger and a Gurkha knife, the *kukri*, and with a thin orange wire on each side of it marking the swept and mine-free corridor, had now been given a formal designation, just as had the routes in Bosnia: whereas we had driven down to Sarajevo on Route CLOG, this one had been marginally more attractively christened: The Blace-to-Pristina route was known as Route HAWK. And the soldiers were fast fanning out from it now, to the villages that lay to the left and right of the highway, their populations, such as remained, supposedly waiting for this day of liberation, which they must have feared might never come.

Those few refugees who came along on the convoy with us, to be the first to see the villages from which they had been expelled, were taking a very considerable risk. Just before throwing them out, the Serbs on the frontiers had confiscated many thousands of Kosovo Albanians' identity papers and passports. All they had now were flimsy temporary documents, like the old Nansen passports, that had been issued by the Macedonian authorities. Now these same authorities had warned them that if they made the choice to go back into Kosovo they would not be able to come back, no matter what they found at home.

A young Kosovo Albanian woman named Aferodite, whom we had met in Tetovo, had earlier tried to seize the chance of coming with us. She brought her mother and father and brother, all refugees from the latest pogroms, to see her off. But once she realized that she might discover terrible things, and would not be able to come back to her parents so long as they remained in Macedonia, she suddenly balked. She drew us a map of where her house had been, and the names of some neighbors we might try to find. She wanted to know, especially, about a baby boy who had been born in her village, a boy named Trim. But she wouldn't come herself to find out, not until she knew she still had an escape route.

"There might be Serbs still there," she said, trembling. "I might find that what they have done to our place is just too much for me to bear. I might want to come back—and then I find the border closed. I will stay. For now I stay."

From what we could see on that haunting, memorably awful journey north, not a few of the Albanians who came on the convoy—and many of those others who, like Aferodite, decided to return some days or weeks later, when the situation calmed down—did find and see things that were too much to bear. We could see from the roadside scenes of the most appalling ruin. We passed villages—Kacanik itself, then Urosevac, then Gradimlje—where almost every house was gone, burned, wrecked, vandalized, covered with obscenities, the Serbian cross, Chetnik graffiti.

Such people as we could see were wandering around with a look of bedraggled bewilderment, gazing horrified at the devastation, as though for the first time. And then we spoke to them and found that this was in fact the case. They had been terrified by what had happened, frightened beyond belief when the mobs stormed in and began their long nights of pillage and force, of rapine and rape, and they had run away, vanishing into the shelter of the deep woods on the mountainsides. They had lived by their wits, eating leaves, trapping animals, drinking from streams. It was only today, and when they saw the long trails of armor glinting on the distant road, and saw that the cars flew British flags or the blue-and-white NATO burgees, and had the letters KFOR stenciled on their flanks, that they knew it was safe to come home. And so, muddy and ragged and weary, they staggered down into Kacanik and Urosevac and Gradimlje, and stared open mouthed in shock at what had happened while they had been away.

Before long they, and other soldiers, other examiners, were finding terrible, terrible things. Graves, newly dug, with scores of ominously long and spongy lumps in the soft and giving ground. Rooms in basements that—blood-spattered and with chairs and shackles and lengths of rusty chain, and with bullet holes in the plaster—had evidently been used as torture chambers or places of execution. Skeletons by the hundred. Detached bones, some with flesh and rags still adhering, which had been dragged away by dogs. The half-burned bodies of children. The bodies of old women raped and then hatefully mutilated. Men lying with their heads smashed in with sledgehammers, children cut in half with rusty scythes. And yet more graves, scores upon scores of crudely labeled memorials, fashioned not in one final moment of compassion and decency, but only to rid the area of the stench of death so that the killers could look more comfortably and without reminders for other ghastly deeds to perform. On all sides, almost everywhere you looked, there was evidence of the vandalism of the truly cruel, of the machinations of the appallingly vile.

The soldiers who went in to these first villages, gingerly wary of the booby traps and mines that the retreating soldiers and police had left behind, and who were advising in vain the villagers not to come until all was perfectly safe, were more stunned and shocked than most of them had ever been.

"Fifteen years I've been a para," said one sergeant, holding up a chain saw and a bloodstained hammer, and opening for view a box of crudely homemade knuckle-dusters, "and I've never seen anything as dreadful as this. How can people behave to one another like this? What kind of hatred makes a man behave so terribly?" I had known this soldier since Ireland days, and we both knew well that the hatreds of Ireland are deep and dire. "But never like this," said the soldier. "Never anything so bad."

A pattern soon became obvious: It was always the big houses, those of the wealthier Albanians, the merchants and the contractors and the successful farmers, that had borne the brunt of the destruction. Envy had clearly played a part in the victimization—the same envy that once made Nigerian Hausas turn on the Ibo, or makes some Gentiles turn on the Jews, an envy that is familiar around the world and has been forever, and which is born of economic discord, of imagined exploitation, a blind revenge on anyone who manages life better, who makes for himself and his family something that others in the community have never managed to do.

The reasons behind the murderous behavior of the Balkans are legion, and they are legendary. It is now thought quite improper to dismiss all that has happened and that will continue to happen as the consequence merely of "ancient ethnic hatreds." Economics, it is said, is in fact by far the more potent reason for the violence. And here, it seemed, was ample concrete evidence to back this theory up. Those who perpetrated the attacks in the villages we passed, where the big houses, the houses of the local squires and of what the Australians call the squatocracy, were fired first. The attacks were motivated, without a doubt, by an envy that came

from the economic disparities that coincidentally overlay the ethnic dissimilarities. It so happened that the Albanians here had evidently worked harder, had made more money, had managed to
succeed where their neighbor Serbian *Lumpenproletariat* had
not—and the Serbs had struck back at them, evening the economic score, demonstrating that equality was entirely possible,
provided that one reduced everyone else to a similar level of ruin.
The attacks and the atrocities were perpetrated not so much on
the Albanians as Albanians but as a people generally, who, unfairly
and in part *because* they were Albanians, had done so much better
than the local Serbs.

And yet. It was not so much the scale of the attacks—the raz-
ing of house after house after house after house—but the
vicious, venomous nature of the attacks that gave the lie to the
idea that economics was the sole or even the main motive. The
terrible things that were done—the deliberate maiming of children, the live evisceration of elderly women, the castrations with
razors, the battering with mallets, the sawing off of heads, the
use of blunt trowels to gouge out eyes, the rapes, the rapes, the
rapes—these were acts of inhumanity done out of hatred and
revenge, and that drew down on the appalling memories of generations and generations past.

It was the nature of these acts that had nothing to do with
money, or land, or territory, or with the manipulative cynicism
of politicians or criminals. It had to do instead with revenge,
pure and simple. For academics to remark dryly that ancient
ethnic loathings had little or nothing to do with what has been
happening in villages like those we saw that warm summer afternoon, were denying a simple and awful truth: that there can be
no imagining the horrors that can be born from the white heat
of pure and unalloyed hatred. The Serbs here in Kosovo were
getting back at the Albanians, as they saw it, for what the Turks
had done to them. History, at least as it had been taught to
them, should leave no Serbs in doubt that they, if as intolerant

and unforgiving as most in the Balkans so sadly are, had more than ample cause for doing so.*

A dozen miles before we came to Pristina there was a junction to a town called Lipljan on the left, and the column of soldiers, signposted by a man standing on top of a Challenger tank, all took the turn. There was a small crowd of Albanians here, and they cheering wildly as the column slowed and ponderously swung off the main road. Where the troops were going we weren't exactly sure; the three of us, however, decided we should go straight on. It seemed symbolically important that we first visit the capital of Kosovo. It would mean going without the comforting presence of the KFOR armor, true, but a city and its population would tend, I was sure, to offer some kind of protection, some kind of safety in numbers. It nearly turned out to have been a ghastly mistake.

The first sign that all was not well came just on the outskirts of town, when our way was blocked by a long line of tractors, piled high with people and their possessions, heading for the north. It took only a moment to reason that these were Serbs— peasant farmers who were themselves now frightened that the returning Albanians would wreak vengeance on them. So they were off toward Belgrade and Mother Serbia; and if the incoming NATO troops were trying to offer them sufficient reassurance to stay, these people were not listening. They were angry, terrified, hostile to all who had put them in this position. NATO was the villain, every bit much as were the Albanians and the guerrillas of the Kosovo Liberation Army (which we called the

---

*The most stomach-turning example of the kind of Turkish atrocity the Serbs might think they have cause to avenge appears in Ivo Andric's Nobel Prize–winning novel *The Bridge on the Drina*. It describes the torture and subsequent impalement of a peasant caught trying to wreck the Turkish bridge: It is an utterly haunting scene, a description that offers some insight into the depth and longevity of true Balkan hatred

KLA, but which people of all persuasions in the region called by the initials of the army's real name, the UCK).

All of a sudden our accreditation badges, for which we had lined up for six hours the day before, seemed more dangerous than protective. They had the acronyms NATO and KFOR emblazoned in blue on white: To anyone who might carry a grudge, they now bore the mark of Cain. We unclipped them, hid them in our jackets, hoping that no one had seen. A group of Yugoslav army soldiers were escorting the villagers to the main Belgrade road, and they came across and looked at our car with hostile curiosity—they must have suspected we were in the NATO van, and they looked for a moment distinctly as if they were having second thoughts about how to deal with us. But after a cursory look they grunted and moved back to their own refugees, scowling, pointing, looking back at us.

Pristina was an ugly town, by turns poor and pompous, grim and grandiloquent. It smelled of coal smoke, ash, and cabbage. There were huge and tottering brown tenements, an immense and gaudy marble university littered with broken glass and piles of smoldering garbage, a soccer stadium gifted by Tito as a demonstration of the benevolence of his regime toward all, Albanian and Serb alike. Its gates stood open, the field inside gray cracked mud. It was barely used, except that on Thursdays during the soccer season it was said to be ringed with Serbian riot police who would give the Albanian soccer fans a good crack on the head if they dared so much as to raise a finger.

The Grand Hotel, five stars beside the crooked neon letters of its name, rose from the center of town as a grisly beacon to Marxist realism. It was filled with angry Serbs, all smoking, most drinking heavily, all wondering what to do next, when the soldiers arrived. The lights were off, the elevators were stopped, the telephones were not working, and there were no rooms. But I had agreed to write a story of the NATO "liberation" of Kosovo for a Sunday newspaper in London, and the deadline was now ninety minutes away. For the following hour I hid myself behind a column at the back of a washroom, and typed frantically away, praying that the battery of my laptop would last. As to how I could transmit the copy, with no power and so no cell phone service, and the only satellite phone that I knew of still stuck with the convoy back at the turnoff—well, Write now! is the general rule in situations like this, and worry about transmitting the story later.

There was just one interruption. A pair of burly and unfriendly-looking Serb policemen, both with machine guns, were making a search of the hotel, found me lurking behind the column and asked me the Serbian equivalent of what the devil did I think I was doing, before going off in search of a manager, who they seemed not to be able to find. I wrote ever more furiously, well aware that they would be coming back. I managed, typing the last line with a flourish and then, presto! the power came back on, my cell phone came back to life, and I was able to telephone London and be put through to a copy-taking center nearby, and dictate those two thousand hurriedly written, ill-thought-out words. The first draft of history, as teachers have been known to call journalism, can be a sketchy thing indeed.

But then I found myself dictating the piece to a copy taker who, after taking down the first few paragraphs, confessed that he was more interested than usual, on that rainy English afternoon, to be hearing firsthand what was going on in the capital of Kosovo. The exchanges I had with that unknown man in a faraway town—the piece took perhaps twenty minutes to dictate, while I kept checking the hall for the two policemen, and my watch to make certain that I had met the deadline—added a rare moment of pleasure, I thought, to what had otherwise been a fairly wrenching day. Newspaper copy takers are a hard-bitten breed: men and women who, eternally unfazed, have quite literally heard it all, and from everywhere. They are infamous for uttering deep sighs, usually while the reporter is in the middle of dictating his or her purplest passages, and asking impatiently: "Is there much more of this?" But my man today was enthusiastic, eager to hear more; and when I told him that I had to go, as the two Serb policemen were now most certainly on their way back, cradling their machine guns in their arms, he said he was truly sorry, and I think I believed him.

"But you take good care," he added, and seemed to mean it. Moving as quickly as I dared, I cut the line, gathered up my computer, and fled back out into the open air. The day had been hot and oppressive, but now it was thundering, and within moments of my emerging, hailstones the size of cherries began clattering out of the sky. The policemen, who had followed me into the lobby, took a look up at the towering thunderheads, pointed at the carpet of mothballs gathering on the ground, shook their heads, and vanished back into the gloom. I got into the Fiat, pried it carefully out of its parking space and headed away. There were still no NATO soldiers in Pristina, and suddenly it seemed a jumpy, nervous, and rather less than welcoming place. And besides, the story of the afternoon, we gathered from our colleagues, was unfolding ten miles away, at the Pristina airport.

To the embarrassment and annoyance of the NATO planners, a small contingent of Russian troops had flown in to the airport the day before. No one in NATO wanted the Russians in Kosovo at all. The Kremlin had furiously opposed NATO's bombing campaign, not least because the Russians, as Slavs, had long been in broad sympathy with the aims and aspirations of their ethnically similar Serb cousins. Any Russian involvement in a Kosovo peace would, from the point of view of the West, and also of the Albanians, be highly suspect. They were bound to be, at least emotionally, rather less than wholly disinterested. In a firefight between the Serbian MUPs and the Albanian UCK, for example, at least some of a troop of Russian soldiers would be certain to take sides.

Diplomatically the situation was rather worse: The Kremlin made no secret at all of wanting to have Kosovo divided, with a

Russian zone policed by Russian soldiers, and a NATO zone policed by soldiers from beyond. But that, said NATO, would effectively mean the partition of Kosovo. And that, as well as further Balkanizing a region that had suffered from all too much Balkanization in the last decade—three thousand miles of extra frontiers since 1991, and endless outbreaks of warfare and bloodshed in consequence—would reward with land, with extra territory, those very Serbs who had indulged in the vile practice of ethnic purging in the first place.

No, said NATO very firmly, all soldiers sent to Kosovo to keep the peace should be under NATO control—answerable in the first instance to General Jackson, and then via an American general in Brussels to the NATO Political Council. Equally firmly the Russian government then told NATO it would do no such thing—and just twelve hours before Captain Rea and the thousands of men and heavy armor moved in across the Macedonian frontier, so two hundred Russian airborne troops and a handful of armored cars were flown in to Pristina airport, from which they refused to budge.

We drove over to see them. I first wanted to drive to the field by way of what one might call the usual route, through Kosovo Polje and past the famous battleground of the Blackbird Field where, more than six hundred years before, the Turks had defeated the Serbs—a defeat every Serb remembered still, and vowed to avenge. The hail had turned to rain, which was stopping as I crossed an overpass beside an old army base that had been bombed by NATO jets some days before and lay in still-smoldering ruins. A roadblock of MUP forces were waiting on top of the bridge, fingering their weapons. "Go away," is all they would say. "Turn around."

We decided to make the airport via the southern route, the way that the NATO forces appeared to have gone when they made the turn from the main road some hours earlier. We sped south, came to a turn and were confronted by a huge column of armor moving out of the area, back the way we had come. It was the Yugoslav army, beating a retreat as the Technical Agreement insisted it had to do, and its men were in no mood to let us pass. "Get out of the way," they cried, and pointed rifles and machine guns at us. "Go away."

I looked at the map, and tried another approach—passing through back streets of villages that displayed the dismaying contrasts of this strange and spiteful war. We could tell which were the Albanian villages—they were in ruins, charred and broken and deserted. And we could tell which were the Serbian towns— untouched, still alive with people—and angry, disaffected people at that, who shook their fists at us as we passed—where young men with guns moved toward us if we stopped.

I made the mistake of asking for directions in such a place, from a group of young men and soldiers manning a barricade of razor wire and burned-out cars. One of them—a tall and gangly youth with acne, his hand on the stock of his machine pistol—came toward us. He made the three-fingered gesture of Serb supremacy, and shouted with fury at us. "Get out! Get out! You have three minutes. Then your forces take over. Until then this is Serbia! Get out quickly! Three minutes—or else!"

It was uncomfortable, unsettling. At one stage we fell in behind a column of British armor, and a drunken, angry Serb, shouting at us incomprehensibly, tried to wrench my door open and made as if to pull us out. I shot forward, past the last Challenger tank, and asked its driver if I could sneak in between him and a Warrior armored car ahead. "Sure, mate!" he said, with a broad Cockney grin. "Anything for a fellow Brit. What are you mugs doing here anyway?"

The ensuing miles were anything but amusing, a worrying miasma of threats and mud, armor, and guns. But eventually we found ourselves at the airport main gate—among the very small number of civilians who had managed to get past what we were told were Serb checkpoints. What we found there was a scene of near-total farce. The Russian armored cars, eight-wheeled and noisy, were churning back and forth up the main runway, doing their best to provoke the British paratroopers, whose job, they had supposed, had been to take and secure the airport from the departing Serbs. The British soldiers stood in the rain looking perplexed, and every five minutes or so a loud voice would sound from a speaker mounted on a Russian vehicle: "Get out of way! Russians coming!" and the drivers would gun their engines and drive the massive machines almost directly at the waiting platoons, or at the gaggle of reporters waiting disconsolately, and equally puzzled, beside them.

General Jackson was by now supposed to be in Pristina, giving a triumphalist press conference in a suitably public building, telling the world that NATO had now officially liberated Kosovo, that freedom and democracy had triumphed over tyranny and violence, and that those forced out of their homes and their country would soon be free to come back and live in peace. But General Jackson is not a triumphalist figure, and he no doubt would have had some difficulty putting the right amount of sincerity in a statement of this kind—which is why I thought he was actually marginally more comfortable when we saw him, at a moment when the Russians briefly interrupted their own triumphal bluster and let him speak to the assembled microphones.

It was a dismally stage-managed affair, as it and everything to do with NATO's conduct of the propaganda war was bound to be. A press officer from No. 10 Downing Street, the official home of the British prime minister, was on hand to choreograph things. As that windswept and rain-soaked old warhorse, General Jackson, stepped briskly down from his helicopter she strode behind him, her army fatigues only barely disguising her and not fooling at all the Fleet Street men who knew her. Then, as the rain lanced down, so Mike Jackson, flanked by a phalanx of machine-gun-carrying sentries, offered the world NATO's prepared statement.

The Russians in the background promptly stepped on their accel-
erators, attempting as ordered to drown out his words with the
roar of their ill-tuned engines, and torrents of smoke lifted in the
background, as if half the field were suddenly on fire. The world
may have been watching the pictures, but on this occasion it most
certainly wasn't listening to the words.

And in any case the wind soon whipped the general's rain-
sodden papers into a porridge of papier-mâché, so that by the
time he reached the passage about the refugees soon being able
to return home, he had to dispense with it totally and rely on
memory and a few nudges and whispers from the woman behind
him. Then he strode away, the Russians quieting their engines.
Keith Graves, that most determined of television reporters,
shouted out the only question that the general deigned to answer.
"Was the presence of the Russians here an embarrassment?"

The general didn't miss a beat. "Not at all. We welcome them
as part of the KFOR. I look forward to discussing practical matters with them directly."

And off he strode—not knowing, perhaps, that so pleased
had President Yeltsin been with the execution of the Russians'
cheeky move that he had promoted the commander of the airport force. The man with whom Lieutenant General Sir Michael
Jackson was now off to parley had begun the day as a mere
major, commanding a force of a mere two hundred men. Now
he had been made into a lieutenant general, too, and Mike
Jackson would have to treat with him as a military equal.

Getting away from the airport was for us was even more difficult than finding it in the first place. Night was falling, and the
rain was helping to make what was sinister begin to look and
feel downright frightening. As soon as were past the airport
perimeter, and had left behind the friendly invigilation of the
British paratroopers, we felt very much on our own, very alone.

We took many wrong turns, and twice we came across gangs of
Serb youths, heavily armed, forming themselves into impromptu

roadblocks, menacing anyone trying to pass through. At one stage as I was speeding along a muddy track we passed two militiamen with rifles, and by accident I sprayed them with water as I crashed through a large pothole. They shouted, and raised their weapons and began to run—and then a hundred yards or so ahead I swore I saw the swinging red lantern of a roadblock, demanding that we stop. I assumed, for a brief moment, that our number was up. But the flashing light was simply a flag flapping in front of a lighted barn; there was no-one there to stop us, and the two running militiamen fell back and turned away, brushing the thick mud from their uniforms.

It took us a miserable hour to get back to the main road— our last direction given by a young soldier from Yorkshire, who came out from his tent and stood in the driving rain, showing us where to go on a laminated plastic map. The engine of the tank standing beside us throbbed warmly: I could, for a moment, feel something of the relief that many Albanians must be feeling right now, that at last they had some measure of security in their lives, that no one could take them away from their homes and torture and shoot them again. There was someone here to help.

But for how long? The question haunted us for the hours it then took us to drive back down the main highway to Macedonia. We weaved in and out of road blocks, watched yet more convoys churning past us, heading north where we were going south. One of the convoys was Dutch, and at nighttime its movement was even more impressive than the other convoys had been during the daytime. I was enthralled by the sight, and said so to a young woman who was standing by the road, taking pictures.

Oh yes, she said—an entire armored brigade, with light tanks and artillery pieces and self-propelled guns. Impressive, don't you think?

I remarked on her knowledge, with a fine display of patronizing clumsiness. Wasn't it odd, I said, that perhaps not even as lately as two days ago, phrases like "armored brigade" and "artillery pieces" and "self-propelled guns" had never even passed her pretty lips?

She grinned. "Oh yes they have," she replied. "This is all most familiar to me. Actually, I am a lieutenant in the Dutch Army. Do let me give you my card."

And with a broad smile she clambered up and onto a passing troop carrier, and waved farewell. Rose, proud feminist and scourge of old white males, had overheard it all. As she came toward me, I winced.

But yes, I continued as the Dutch faded from view—how long would soldiers such as these be detained here? And was all this, I wondered, indeed a real liberation? Was Operation Joint Guardian truly what General Jackson's speech suggested that it should and would be—an unarguably powerful means, under-written by the international community, of guaranteeing the safety and security of Kosovo, of helping to make it a place where all the ethnic groups who had been forced by history, accident and imperial fiat, to live together from now on, and to do so in peace?

I have to say that I doubted it. A military policy like this was just as unlikely to work here in the Balkans as it had been unlikely to work in Northern Ireland—another tiny province in which, in the aftermath of other more major decisions, the similarly ancient struggles for territory and power and influence, afflicted by simi-larly deep divisions of religion and culture, had set communities implacably and unforgivably at each others' throats, and seem-ingly so for ever. No, I felt certain—only if the foreign govern-ments could decree, as none of them could, that their soldiers would remain on the ground for years, decades even, only then might enough pressure be brought to bear so that some kind of apparent peace might take hold.

But if not, if the soldiers were there for only a short while, and if there was no certain foreign policy exerted over Kosovo other than the short-sighted aim of enforcing some kind of stability—

then a solution would probably never be found. If no solution was found then yet more trouble, and of a viciousness not even yet seen here, would break out again, somewhere, and soon. Perhaps it would erupt first in Macedonia, to where we were heading. Or perhaps in Montenegro, from where we had come some days before. Perhaps in Bulgaria. Or Greece. Or Turkey. Or even back up in Bosnia again.

Who knew? And when, and how? And what trigger? No one could know yet. But just one thing seemed to be clear, as the rain eased and the stars came out as we climbed back up the hills towards the Macedonian frontier. This had been no liberation, I thought—no matter how earnestly the press officer from London might have wanted it to be seen that way.

The foreign troops who were here and who would be coming in during the days and weeks to come, were becoming, as all outsiders were and have been for years, entrapped in the great swamp of the Balkans. This was for them indeed, more an entrapment that a liberation; and if there was any freedom in the air today, then it was, I rather thought, an illusory kind of freedom, a freedom that was ready to be whisked away with the slightest breath of the Balkan wind.

9

A City So Sublime

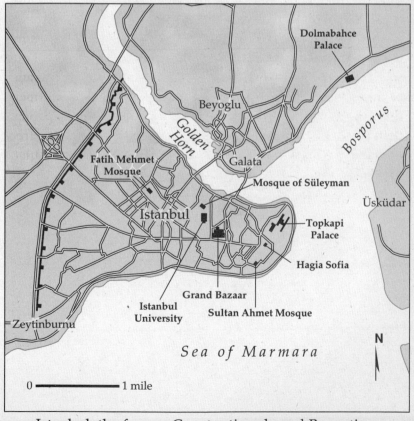

Istanbul, the former Constantinople and Byzantium

THE BULGARIA to which we drew up the next day in yet another black Mercedes, and into which were obliged to drive through yet another pool of muddy-water disinfectant and cleanse our wheels of accumulated Macedonian dirt, has long been a country in a state of difficult equipoise. Bulgaria is quite literally at a pivot point, a fulcrum—a buffer-state on a dividing line between Europe and Asia, between Eastern Orthodoxy and Islam, between the oppressions of the Russia lying across the Black Sea and the Turkey lying on its southern frontier, between the darkest kinds of Communism and the most rampant excesses of modern capitalism, between Ruritanian flamboyance and pretension and the high-tech modernity of the new Eurocracy.

What little it is known for more than amply illustrates the point. Bulgaria is famous on the one hand for being the world's great source of attar of roses (the volatile and fragrant essence that comes from flowers grown in one of its deepest fault lines, for it is on a geological and tectonic crossing point, too), for horseradish (which grows on its railway embankments and was at one time bought liberally by Messrs. Cooper of Oxford, condiment makers to the gentry) and for yogurt, which was first made in the Rhodope Mountains from a culture created out of a milk-curdling ur-germ known as *Bacillus bulgaricus*.

Its people are renowned for being among the most agreeable in Europe, famous for their courtesy, civility, and learning. So it was perhaps not surprising that when the Turks, in the terminal decrepitude of their empire, lashed out savagely at a timid Bulgarian uprising in the late 1870s, the world's intelligentsia rushed to the victims' side, much as was to happen in the Spanish civil war half a century later. So William Ewart Gladstone, Giuseppe Garibaldi, Oscar Wilde, Ivan Turgenev, and Victor Hugo all pledged their support for the eminently decent Bulgarians. Suddenly Bulgaria and its people became the cause célèbre of the more fashionable European salons—both because the Turks were so widely despised and because the poor Bulgarians the objects of such widespread affection.

And yet, and much more recently, it was a Bulgarian secret agency that tried to murder Pope John Paul II (using a Turk, Mehmet Ali Agca, to perform—and bungle—the deed). It was a Bulgarian agent for the Sigurnost who succeeded in murdering a BBC Bulgarian service employee and well-known dissident Georgi Markov, by stabbing him in the leg with an umbrella, its steel tip laced with ricin. It was Bulgarian secret police who used to force their way into the homes of the ethnic Turks who lived in villages in the south of the country and force them to sign papers changing their names—Mehmets becoming Mikhails, nearly a million such—on pain of torture or worse. And the word "bugger" also comes from here, from the word *Bulgar*, Bulgarian, and perhaps from Bogomil, and was first applied to a curious eleventh century sect that was born in what is now Bulgaria, and was infamous for its "abominable practices," which, if a Bogomil, included as well as buggery, the eccentric and short-lived belief that Christ and Satan were the twin sons of God.

So Bulgaria, a confused melange of attar of roses and abominable practices, seemed the perfect airlock, the crossroads, the pivot point, from which to pass from the insanity of the Balkans into the supposed serenity and sublimity of the city on the Bosporus that they once had called the Porte. We arrived on a sunny morning, with the grinding sound of the NATO tanks fading fast, and we left on a blistering afternoon three days later. We stayed in a hotel that was attached to the presidential palace, and so there were guards in high boots and shakos on sentry duty around by the back door and, in the courtyard, a churchly rotunda that had been built in the fourth century by the Romans and had frescoes a thousand years old. A presidential honor guard and a Roman rotunda attached to the back of our hotel! Sofia, it seemed to me, was a city with which it was easy to become enchanted and, in Rose's case, easy to become quite smitten.

For Rose had known a young Bulgarian man from some years back, when she lived in Venice, and here she had found him again. They had not been in contact since the time he drove all the way across to Croatia, and they had met for one sad last weekend in a village in Istria. It took some courage for Rose to look him up again when we arrived in Sofia, and for a while it took some ginger for him to breathe life back into a damaged friendship. But something did take place, and for all the while that I was in this quiet and dignified and flower-filled old city, I was left to my own devices, and I left them to theirs. In the end Rose decided that whatever had taken place was powerful enough that she would go back to Bulgaria from Turkey, and eventually she did. I would later receive letters telling of how she was sitting in a small apartment in a Sofia suburb, eating cherries and yogurt and drinking good Bulgarian red wines, and gazing silently into the middle distance with her Bulgarian beside her. He had the saddest eyes, she said, and she was smitten, and from what I could tell, quite happy too.

The American ambassador to Bulgaria was a friend of a friend: Avis Bohlen, daughter of the legendarily smooth American diplomat Chip Bohlen, a man who had been one of the great pundits on the more trying questions of the Cold War. She lived, as all American ambassadors of necessity must these days, amid conditions of great and irksome security. Once past the heavily armed gorillas in her street and at her door, however, she was a delight—knowledgeable, well read, and exuberantly pleased with her discovery of Bulgaria's joys. Her role as one of the more involved diplomats during the lately ended war had been fascinating and educational: She was only frustrated that some of the key diplomatic bargainings—on such questions as whether Bulgaria would permit NATO warplanes the right to pass through its airspace— had been conducted not by the individual national embassies, not by officials such as she, but by the NATO ambassadors themselves, and not in Sofia but in Brussels.

The ambassador's experience was somehow symbolic, I thought. For while Bulgaria is and always had been a country that looked as though it should be central to the doings of southern Europe, it never quite has been. One might think that centrality, at least to the Balkan problem, should have been hardwired into the Bulgarian nature: After all, no less than the Balkan Mountains, from which the Balkans get their name, are entirely in Bulgaria, for example; and nowadays the national airline is Balkan Airlines, suggesting a Bulgarian impress on all matters Balkan.* But this centrality has never been the case. In terms of the doings and undoings of southern Europe, Bulgaria has played only marginal roles: a base from which the Ottomans made their predatory excursions into Europe; the Russians' zone of protection, to keep the Turks at bay; a place for overflights, for transit, for permissions. But little or no influence of its own—beyond the dreamy scent of rose petals, and the needle-sharp little bacillus that lives on in every container of Yoplait or Dannon.

We drove away from Sofia with a young photographer named Boris, who wanted a lift to Turkey so that he might catch a plane from Istanbul and fly to see his parents, newly posted to Kazakhstan. He knew the best cafés en route, and we ended up among the cobbled streets of Philippopolis, now known rather less elegantly as Plovdiv, eating what was to become our favorite Balkan dish, a hotpot of cheese, eggs, and tomatoes baked in earthenware and known as *sirene po shopski*. He was also eager for us to try some

---

*The word is Turkish, and means "mountain." The Balkan Mountains are known in Bulgarian by their rightful name, Stara Planina.

of the scores of brands of plum and apricot brandies, or to choose from a list of wines so long that it suggested California, or Australia, or France (behind which come only Chile and Bulgaria, making up the leading five wine-exporting countries in the world). But I declined: The country road to the Turkish frontier was long and winding and dangerous, I had been told, and there were police with radar and breathalyzer kits behind every bush—just like Russia, and with penalties even more severe.

The first time I had come to Istanbul, in the spring of 1972, I had taken a stroll across a catwalk, a narrow ropeway, that stretched from Europe right into Asia. It was an extraordinary journey, and I believe I was the first person to do it—or maybe just the first Englishman. I duly wrote a piece about the venture, and in passing made a rather feeble feline joke, calling it a Persian Cat-Walk, since I fancied that from it one could eventually make it all the way to Tehran and Isfahan. But the joke was not to be: A mirthless subeditor declared the word *Persia* absent from the newspaper's then-current style book, and he changed the adjective to *Iranian* instead.

Nonetheless it had been a most impressive walk. I had come to Turkey from Paris aboard the Orient Express, and was staying at the Pera Palas, in a room that overlooked the Galata Bridge and the Golden Horn to all the minarets and domes of a perfectly imagined Istanbul. Earlier in the day I had walked down the hill to Karakoy and taken a ferry across to look at Haydarpasa railway station, in the event that I might take a train to Ankara.* On the way, looking out from the little boat's port-side

---

*Had I arrived a little earlier in the century I would have had to take scrupulous care with the timetables: Although all railway trains ran to European time, the Bosporus ferries ran to Ottoman time, on a clock that marked the start of the day not at midnight, but at sunset.

windows, I could see through the haze two towers, slender as minarets but glinting in the sun.

They were made not of stone, but of steel. They turned out to be not minarets but the twin support towers, one rising in Europe, the other in Asia, for the first of two suspension bridges that were being built across the Bosporus. An engineer I knew was in charge of the construction. I called him and he asked if I might like to walk across, along a cable than had been put up the day before. It would, he said, be a rather distinguished thing to do, rather Byronic: to be the first person to walk across the Bosporus, from one continent to another.

So, early the next morning, when it was still cool and when the mile-long steel cable was relatively tight and its catenary curve at its shallowest, I went up a rickety elevator to the top of the European tower. Down below me to the right was the long shoreside sprawl of the Dolmabahce Palace, built by the Ottomans in their waning years in the hope that the structure might kindle more faith and optimism in their rule than had the Topkapi Serai, which they would now abandon. It looked magnificent, its pink and yellow colonnades and spires and minarets glowing richly in the sun that was now rising from behind the Asian hills. And even when I was three hundred feet up, and among the mystified crows and seagulls gliding on the thermals, it looked unforgettably lovely, a symbol of something that had once been grand, even if at the time of its building the empire's once vast powers were crumbling into nothing.

And then, in a moment I prefer not to remember in detail, I stepped out and onto the wires—one pair of thick cables below my feet, two more slender ones to hold onto, safety ropes and snap links securing me. The wires bounced and shimmied ahead of me as I stood on the takeoff platform. It curved dizzyingly down toward the Bosporus, the shipping lanes busy with cargo vessels, and ferries sneaking across their paths, to and from Üsküdar.

I took a step, carefully, my foot slipping on the condensation that had not yet been burned away by the sun. The engineer was behind me, reassuring: "What could go wrong?" he asked. "The safety ropes will hold." And so off we marched, steadily, then more rapidly, the view unfolding before and behind as we made our way down toward the water, and to a central resting place made of planks that had been wired in place the day before. It took half an hour to get down; and only then could we stop, turn round, and admire a panorama of mosques and minarets and domes and palaces, the whole of what had once been the most awesome and powerful city in the world.

Here, laid out across the horizon, were the three promontories—Üsküdar on the left, the Asian side, and Beyoglü and Old Istanbul, separated by the Golden Horn, both on the European side on the right. The Black Sea was behind me, the Sea of Marmara ahead—and I remember vividly as we were standing there a dark gray Russian destroyer from Odessa passing by below, with sailors on the forepeak gazing up at the uncanny sight of two men suspended in the sky, and shouting to us in Russian exhortations that sounded very much like "Jump!"

The sight that unrolled before me—the domes and minarets of Old Stamboul, the universally recognizable silhouettes of the Hagia Sophia and the Blue Mosque, and the low palace in the green woods of Seraglio Point, the great Topkapi Serai itself—was barely believable, breathtaking in its beauty and a demonstration of such once-formidable power. A diamond between two emeralds, the city had been called. A jewel in the ring of the universal empire.

Gazing into the rising heat of that day, the images beginning to shimmer as the heat radiated up from the water, it was not too difficult to imagine what it must have been like when the Ottomans were in their ascendant days, when that immense tract of land from Budapest to Benghazi to Baghdad and the Caspian was helplessly under their rule and their administration, and the wealth of half the world flowed in and out of the sultans' dominions, through the gilded portals of Constantinople.

Dreamy, luxurious, abandoned, perfumed; tulips, carpets, marble, fountains; tobacco, coffee, opium, wine; divans, sofas, caftans, turbans; sultans, caliphs, viziers, muftis; idle, vicious, cruel, corrupt—the lexicon of the Ottomans is both very long and very specific. It is one that could apply to no other empire, for there has never been an empire like it. Nor any capital—for Constantinople, eclipsing all others for its jewel-like magnificence, was perhaps the only capital in the world as given up to pleasure as it was to ruling. The city over which I was gazing in rapture from the bridge-to-be that day had truly been, during the five centuries of the Ottoman dynasty, "the city of the world's desire."

We had arrived in the late afternoon, speeding into the maelstrom of modern Istanbul on the four-lane toll-road from Bulgaria, coming from a frontier that was still littered with the sagging remains of the old Iron Curtain watchtowers and rusted barbed-wire fences. Turks—even those who live in its European half—still talk of going to Europe, when they mean Bulgaria. The divide between the two neighbor countries is profound—but the more modern and sophisticated of the two is now Turkey, for when you leave the Bulgarian countryside you leave a place of narrow lanes and horse-drawn hay wagons; once into the flat plains of Turkey you emerge onto a four-lane highway with automatic toll-collection booths, and there is an atomic power station beside the road, steaming contentedly and providing all necessary power for the VCRs and cell phone networks of distant Istanbul.

The western sprawls of Istanbul, which we reached in little more than an hour, were vast, grubby, and vile. The pollution is dreadful, the noise terrific, the traffic as bad as in Bangkok, the dust as bad as in Cairo. But then we spotted a magical sign from the highway, TOPKAPI! as casually as if it had said PARADISE!, and we dropped off the road anyway, and into the anarchic Babel of the town, to spend the rest of the day exploring the nooks and crannies of this extraordinary palace—the storm center, some might say, of all that has happened in the Balkans for the last five hundred years.

Not all would agree with the phrase, of course—certainly not the sultan-caliphs themselves. They had a decided view on their vast empire, a self-satisfied assumption that what they had wrought was martial, tolerant, and civilized, and by and large and most happily Islamic. Those privileged—nay verily, *blessed*— to be living within its *laager* inhabited the Dar ul-Islam, the Abode of Peace; those beyond it suffered from having to inhabit the Dar ul-Harb, the Abode of War. The distortions of an imperial view are many, and are by no means the monopoly of the Ottomans—the British, the French, the Dutch even, all fancied their subjects to live in conditions of unalloyed bliss. But the Ottomans, they had a certain additional and manic detachment from reality: a detachment born in no small measure from their sultans' grand isolation in the vastness and comfort of Topkapi—a palace now viewable every day but Tuesdays on payment of five dollars, and two extra for the harem.

Thirty-one sultans ruled from Constantinople—the grandest of all being Süleyman I the Magnificent, who summarized his lofty position somewhat less than modestly as: "I who am Sultan of Sultans, the Sovereign of Sovereigns, the Distributor of Crowns to the Monarchs of the Globe, the Shadow of God upon the Earth, the Sultan and Padishah of the White Sea, the Black Sea, Rumelia, Anatolia, Karamania, Rum, Dulkadir, Diyarbekir, Kurdistan, Azerbaijan, Persia, Damascus, Aleppo, Cairo, Mekka, Medina, all Arabia, Yemen and those other countries which my noble ancestors— may God brighten their tombs!—conquered and my august majesty has likewise conquered with my flaming sword, Sultan Süleyman Khan, son of Sultan Selim, son of Sultan Bayezid." Court poets at Topkapi referred to the sultan as "the World Emperor and Messiah of the Last Age."

In their jeweled jungle of a palace the Ottoman sultans ruled from a position of absolute authority, a court arranged according to bewildering ziggurats of rank and with equally bewildering degrees of deference, all courtiers hemmed in by a system of unyielding and inflexible protocol—and in almost total silence. Officially the languages of the court were high-sounding Ottoman Turkish and, once so much of southern Europe had been bent to the Ottoman will, Serbo-Croat. But Süleyman the Magnificent cared little for talk, and decreed instead the use of a language of signs and signals, to be known as *ixarette*: It was taught to the court by mutes.

In many ways Topkapi is similar, in scale and complexity and secrecy, to the Forbidden City of Peking—though an atmosphere of luxury and fragrance still pervades these Ottoman structures, in sharp contrast to the air of intrigue and cruel decadence that hangs about the former court of China. There are in Istanbul, on the bluff overlooking the Bosporus, a cascading series of three courts, with hundreds of windows from which, it was said, the eyes of the empire would gaze out over all the citizenry and the subject peoples.

A visitor can stroll through all three courts today at will—although only the act of strolling through the sprawling garden of the outer court, the Court of the Janissaries, where there was a mint, a huge set of stables, and a kiosk where petitions might be presented, faithfully recreates the court as it always was—for anyone always could walk through the Court of Janissaries, even if one was foreign or a tourist. In those days one was halted only at the entrance to the second court—by janissary guards, or halberdiers—who would permit only the privileged or the cursed to pass beyond, and into the inner heart of the palace. (Much the same is true today: those who halt outsiders now do merely to take their tickets, obtained from a *guichet* beside the seraglio post office.)

The entrance into the second court was by way of the Gate of Salutation, through which only the sultan could ride a horse, and only a chosen few could follow on foot. The kitchens were

here—they could prepare food for twelve thousand diners at
once—as were the entrances into the harem, with its hundreds
of fresh-plucked and well-schooled odalisques,* and the sultan's
private quarters. The grand vizier had his office here as well,†
and such petitioners as might have been allowed through by
kindly or corrupt palace guards might present their papers
here, and thus assure even more direct access to those with the
power to help. When we arrived the court was filled with men
erecting bleachers and putting up klieg lights: Each summer
there is a performance of the Mozart opera *The Abduction from
the Seraglio*, staged in front of the very gate, beside the very
harem, from which the abduction supposedly took place.

This gate, which leads into the sanctum sanctorum of the third
court, was long known as the Bab-I-Aali, the High Gate. Now it is
called, rather more prettily, Babi-Sa'adet, the Gate of Felicity.
Beyond, guarded with sedulous care by the wily and protective
eunuchs, black or white, are the private rooms—the audience
chamber with the divan and the sofa at which foreign ambassadors might kneel and where the dragoman might drone, and
the treasury, the harem mosque, and the sultans' private libraries.

Here the occasional diplomats—who usually took the trouble
to learn Turkish, though some sultans made an equal effort to
learn French—came to kneel at the feet of the man who, throughout all Europe, was known by the initials as the one and only GS—

---

*The odalisques were divided into classes, and included the *ikbals*—
the sultan's favorites—and the *geuzdes*, those women to whom he had,
literally, "given the eye."

†And only a fair chance of surviving his occupation of it. Of the 178
grand viziers who worked from Topkapi, 1 in 5 died violently. There
were two traditional routes to the grave: Either the court executioner
bowstrung him (as with Kara Mustafa, whose severed head we saw in
Vienna), or the sultan knifed him personally.

the *grand signor.* They knelt, they said little, they then removed themselves by walking backwards—and if they had been fortunate they might have heard, or later claim to have heard, a single grunt of approval from the alcove in which the *signor* sat, silent and unmoving, but always listening, and all-powerful. "There is not one single thing," Rose declared late in the day, after we had wearied ourselves by wandering, entranced, from one hall to another, gazing at a thousand display cases, "that is not absolutely beautiful."

Everything is still preserved and guarded today—little has been plundered, so powerful were the Ottomans against all comers who might take from them. In one hall, where there is a cloak from the Prophet Muhammad, and a piece of the sacred black stone from the Kaaba in Mecca, we found an imam in a small glass cage. He was reading in sonorous tones, and unremittingly, from an ancient copy of the Koran. He was there, a palace official explained, to remind all visitors that this was a holy place as well, and not just a *serai* devoted to centuries of silent administration and bacchanalian abandon. The sultan, it must be recalled, was the Ottoman caliph too—he was the religious as well as the civil ruler, a man not only bound up in the business of war and conquest and the issuance of *firmans* and the acceptance of pleas but an interpreter of the words of the Prophet, and as a figure who might set an example to the faithful and the pious.

And then, finally, we came out onto the terrace overlooking the Bosporus, beside the privy gardens and above the Seraglio lighthouse, before which southbound Bosporus ships turn either left, to dock in the Golden Horn by the Galata Bridge, or right, to go through the Sea of Marmara and the Dardanelles past Gallipoli, and through to the Mediterranean. We stood in rapture in the late afternoon breeze, watching as the sun began to slide down, turning the Gulf of Marmara into a vast field of liquid gold, through which the ferries slid, in slow and measured curves, like the fins of distant carp.

And then the cell phone rang. Some weeks before, while I

was in Vienna, I had given the number to a scholar named
Erwin Lucius, the head of the Austrian Cultural Center in Istanbul. Since I had seen what influence the Ottoman Turks had
had on Viennese life—a cannonball in the cathedral tower, a
taste for coffee, the croissant, and the infrequent possibility of
viewing the preserved head of a long-dead grand vizier—I wondered if the Hapsburgs had had any lasting influence at all on
the lives of the Turks of Constantinople. I imagined that Dr.
Lucius would know.

He was calling to say he would be happy to see us the following morning, if that was convenient. It was, and I blessed the
efficiency of the loaf-haired secretary back in Austria, who had
remembered the date of our arrival here rather more accurately
than I had. And so Rose and I left for a taxi back across the
Golden Horn and to the Pera Palas Hotel—where we discovered two things: that the hotel was much costlier and consider-
ably seedier than when I had been there twenty years before;
and the famous elevator, the first ever made, was now not working. But that night there was a dance of Turkish schoolchildren
in the main dining room, and had it been working they would
no doubt be playing around in its cage of fretted ironwork and
keeping the guests—including the two of us, weary now that we
were so close to journey's end—from sleeping.

On the way home, as we walked back through the squares and
gardens and mosques and museums and the Hippodrome of Sultanahmet, I stopped before one place of pilgrimage—a high marble gate that was topped with a curving fan-shaped porte cochère.
It was an undistinguished-looking gate now, merely an entrance-
way to some obscure departments of the Istanbul city government, a place where trams would stop, and where policemen
would lounge and smoke their richly aromatic cigarettes.

But until 1923, when the last sultan abdicated, left by the Orient Express, and went to live and die in Switzerland (and be
buried in Damascus), this was the gate that had taken over the

name Bab-I-Aali, the High Gate, from the one that separated the first from the second court of Topkapi. This was the gate that led into the main offices of the Ottoman grand vizier—the gate through which passed all the official administrative business of the empire. For three centuries this gate was known to all by the name that came to stand for the entirety and grandeur of the Ottoman Empire itself—the Sublime Porte. Whatever business was done by the king or doge or mameluke or czar or Hapsburg emperor and even, in later years, by the American president, was conducted with *the Porte*. That was all that needed to be said. The Porte *was* the Empire, as one might later say the White House was the United States, the Elysée France, or, more prosaically, that Downing Street was Great Britain.

And a prosaic comparison is perhaps not inappropriate. For no one who passes sees this gateway now as anything much more than an entrance to a series of buildings where a citizen of Istanbul might get his driving license or his library card. As the greatest indignity of all, these days it has a blue-and-white enamel plate attached to it, bearing a number. It has and is, of all things, an address: The Sublime Porte is now 15, Alemdar Caddesi, Istanbul. The mighty here have fallen quickly, and they have fallen far.

Once the tide of empire had visibly begun to ebb—once the siege of Vienna had been overwhelmed, and the Ottomans started to be chased back to their lairs—so the Austrians themselves began to cast a covetous eye on the possibility of spoils. Within three years of the failure of the siege, the Austrians had taken Budapest (or Buda as it was then) and two years later, Belgrade (though in a sick convulsion the Ottomans recovered it half a century later). Back in Constantinople people began to fear that a Christian army would suddenly appear at the gates. House prices fell. There was a mass migration across the Bosporus to Asia. There were veiled mutterings against the indifference and pomposity of the sultan and his court, the luxury and abandon, the absurdities of his ram fights and of camel wrestling, and of the cruel caprices of the courtiers' whims.

At its zenith the empire was truly vast—Morocco to Mesopotamia, Poland to Yemen—and when it began to totter, Russia and Austria discussed dividing it between them. In Moscow, especially, there was a move to reestablish Byzantium in Constantinople, and with a Russian prince to rule as emperor. In 1908 the Austrians formally annexed Bosnia and Herzegovina, still then technically Ottoman territory. The whole of the tottering Empire was then available for plunder, and the Austrians above all wanted to have the larger share for themselves. But it was not to be: Their own follies saw to it that it was the Russians who gained the ascendancy, and took the greater part of the Ottomans' northern dominions. Vienna was left with almost nothing.

The Russians were eventually to turn the Black Sea from a Turkish lake into a Russian, to possess the old Ottoman lands from the Crimea to the Caucasus. The Hapsburgs were on the other hand fated to retreat themselves, to withdraw from the northern Balkans just as fast as the Ottomans were withdrawing from the southern. And today, after all of that defeat and humiliation and withdrawal, all that the Austrians have left is Austria—and in the Istanbul that had caused them so much vexation and anxiety, one impressive *yali*, a mighty waterfront house beside the Bosporus.

The *yalis* of Constantinople, for many still stand down by the sea near the Dolmabahce Palace and by the hotel that was once the Ciragan, offer some remembrance of what was once called "the Ottoman way." Their setting, for a start, was magnificent. The light down by the strait was always so intense, the water of the seaway was so vividly blue, the wooden walls of the *yalis* were so high, and the houses and gardens within so magnificent and so lush—everything on the coast spoke of luxury and indolence, wealth and disdain. There were marble cascades and fountains and highly colored oil paintings; there were kiosks and cupolas; lattices of carved marble, jewels, and fragrant olive-wood; and jungles of roses, jasmine, and honeysuckle.

This was where the sultans' obsession with tulips began. More than eight hundred varieties were listed in an Ottoman flower book, and one grand vizier who bred the flowers created forty-four new varieties. This is where the house cooks made dishes of eccentric specificity—stuffed fish in which not single lesion could appear on even a single scale, and confections that used only the left legs of animals, the sultanly chefs believing that since the animals invariably favored use of the right, these limbs would prove indelicately tougher, the left ones tenderer.

On the terrace of a *yali* you could sit and watch the boats go by, or the young giggling children diving endlessly into the cool and deep waters, and while doing so you could sip tamarind juice, or dip your fingers in grape treacle, and one tale had it that you could order a particular red jam containing, along with the rose petals and Circassian strawberries and cherries from Giresun,* tiny amounts of finely crushed rubies.

It is in such a wooden house, on the fashionable spur of Yenikoy, that Dr. Lucius now has his office, and from where he can ruminate on past events, if he cares to, and in an atmosphere of great imagined charm. The mansion, white and cool and sprawling in a broad seaside meadow, was built for an Armenian banker and then handed in 1884 as a personal gift to the old boiled-beef eater, Franz Josef, by the Sultan Abdülhamīd II. (It cannot be demolished: The few wooden *yali* left in today's Istanbul are preserved by government fiat, and can only be moved, never torn down.)

When I first met Dr. Lucius I was struck by the odd symmetry

---

* The town in northern Anatolia after which the cherry is named. The Greeks called it *Kerasos*. It was the Romans who first found the fruit and named it after the town.

of the occasion: It was droll, I thought, that at the end of the journey I would be meeting an Austrian with tweeds and spectacles and a dryly sardonic academic manner and who was in interests and demeanor just like Dr. Düriegl, the director of the Historical Museum of the City of Vienna, where I had begun this journey. And like Dr. Düriegl, he too was fascinated by the tale of Kara Mustafa Pasha, the grand vizier at the time of Sultan Mehmet IV. When I mentioned the name he drew in a rapid breath. "Ah, yes—that difficult old devil!"

The diplomatic fuss over the remains of Kara Mustafa continues. The head is in Vienna, the body in a village called Merzifon, northeast of Ankara, close to the southern shore of the Black Sea. Dr. Lucius had only that morning been helping to organize a symposium, due to be staged in Merzifon itself, on the life and times of Kara Mustafa, and he was helping to arrange for Austrian speakers to come and talk about the strategy behind the unhappy siege. No doubt, he said, given the passions felt by so many Turks, the incoming Austrian academics would have a trying time. No doubt there would once again be pleas, demands, perhaps even diplomatic insistence, that the head be sent back, to be buried next to the body to which it belonged. (Or was *thought* to belong. When I suggested DNA testing of the two sets of remains, to see if a match was likely, all the scholars involved in the debate showed themselves to be happily detached from reality by confessing they had never even considered the idea. "It would certainly end all the confusion," said one of them, chortling.)

But there were many happier and less controversial links between Vienna and Istanbul, Dr. Lucius added. The first medical school in Constantinople had been opened by an Austrian. A Viennese doctor—a man named Hammerschmidt, who had his name changed to Abdullah Bey—had inaugurated the Turkish Red Crescent. The greatest of all the many histories of the Ottomans is that known familiarly as *The Hammer*—written by the Austrian imperial embassy's late-eighteenth-century dragoman Josef von Hammer-Purgstall, who dressed in Ottoman style and toured for years through every corner of the Empire. In more modern times Austrian foresters helped set up the Turkish reforestation schemes; Austrian pharmacists helped establish the chemical industry; Austrian generals trained the modern Turkish army; Austrian architects designed the Turkish parliament in Ankara, as well as several of the capital's ministries and the current President's house; and the first monument erected in the memory of the maker of modern Turkey, Kemal Atatürk, was sculpted in 1926, by an Austrian.

"Is that enough, perhaps?" asked Dr. Lucius, "to show how much better matters are today, than when Kara Mustafa was just outside the Ringstrasse?"

And what other Balkan harmonies might there be, I wondered, here beside the Golden Horn? I knew from Anja, the young woman with whom we had spent time back in Sarajevo, that there was a sizable Serbian community in Istanbul. Most of them were Muslims from the Sanjak of Novi Pazar, that fingerlike extension of Ottoman rule that intruded between southwestern Serbia, Kosovo, and Montenegro. They huddle close together in the old part of the city, off the Divan Yolu, close to the sprawling covered market. There are Sanjak communities in Izmir and Erzerum, all tucked away in the inner cities, all doing deals, involved at the shadier end of the economic spectrum. In Istanbul they have gathered in the shadow of a small hotel, the Balkan, which is always full of newcomers, usually migrants who have wearied of the fighting or the troubles they all foresee.

It was easy to find Anja's old boyfriend, Daut. Everyone from the Sanjak in Istanbul seems to know everyone else. There is a hugger-mugger camaraderie among the traders and businessmen and otherwise amiable rogues who lurk in the tiny stalls and basement rooms clustered around the hotel. Daut was at the family jewelry shop; he had a dozen thin gold chains sus-

pended from the fingers of one hand and a bottle of beer in the
other hand, and he was idly watching a soccer match on television. He jumped with delight at his girlfriend's name, and
within minutes became positively sentimental about Sarajevo.
He had been there for much of the war, dealing, making
money, involved in goodness knows what.

And when we told him we had been in Kosovo, he called all
his friends from the street, and we soon had an excited audience, eager for news of the bombing and of the situation that
day. They knew that NATO had bombed towns in Novi Pazar; I
told them that I only wished we had been able to get there—but
technically the Sanjak was Serbia still, and the Yugoslav authorities had cracked down hard and wouldn't let anyone in.

"This is why we're here," said Daut, and his friends nodded
approvingly. "There's no freedom in the Sanjak—the VJ and the
MUP are giving us trouble all the time. The difference is—we're
better dealers, better traders than the Kosovo Albanians, or the
Bosniaks. The Serbs need us—we make their system work."

Daut did not suppose there would be trouble in the Sanjak—
he did not expect the Belgrade government to order a program of
repression of the Muslims there, as they had, to their cost, in
Kosovo. "The next trouble won't be in the Sanjak—it will be in
Montenegro, there's no doubt about it," he said. "And as we and
Montenegro have a common border—I guess we could feel the
effects. But Milosevic, or whoever succeeds him there, is going to
crack a few heads in Montenegro. You mark my words. There'll be
a lot more of us here in Turkey before this business is done with."

They liked the Turks, and the cosmopolitan character of a
city which has been a crossroads for all of its existence. Daut
spoke a formidable array of languages—Russian, Bulgarian,
Turkish, Polish, Italian, English—and of course Serbian. He
could get along perfectly well and might stay for years.

"But of course what we all really want to do is to go home. We
have so much in common with the Serbs, apart from our religion

of course—we get on with them. And the Serbs need us—we are their Jews, their Chinese. We're nothing for the Serbs to feel afraid of. We'll make money, they'll make money, everyone will get along.

"But for now—it is too dangerous. And besides, business is too slow. We can make more money down here. It's just that I—we, all of us—miss the old place. I telephone, when the circuits are working, and I hear their voices, and I feel so sad. The people of the Sanjak are the best there are. We sing, we dance, we drink. We are the very heart of the Balkan people. So what are we doing in Turkey?"

A small indication of Daut's attitude—and the attitude of the Sanjak people more generally—came later in the evening. We had gone to a bar, to hear a *gusla* player singing sentimental songs that made the Sanjak boys look soulful, homesick. The television was burbling away in the corner, when pictures came on the screen of Abdullah Ocalan, the Kurdish leader who was on trial on a tiny prison-island in the Sea of Marmara. Daut called for quiet and had the volume turned up. Ocalan had been found guilty, the announcer said. He would be sentenced in two weeks' time.

Daut cheered loudly. "That bastard, Ocalan. Of course he's guilty. Compared with him, Milosevic is an angel. An angel. I tell you, Ocalan has killed fifty thousand people, at the very least. He's guilty all right—and he should hang for it. And people should know that, compared with him, Milosevic is really not all that bad. There are worse men in the world. And far worse people than the Serbs."

I had one final mission in Istanbul, a task that also involved looking back along this journey, toward the Balkans. Specifically I had one question left—about the fate of poor old Montenegro, where there had been the argument—one that will be bound to assume greater importance if, as the Sanjak boys were warning, there is trouble brewing—between the two old Orthodox patriarchs. Which of the pair, I had been wondering ever since, was in the right?

Which of the churches of Montenegro deserved the loyalty of the people? Was it the Serbian Orthodox Church, which from its ancient monastery and been offering spiritual leadership for centuries, and most decidedly since the end of the Montenegrin royal family after the end of the Great War? Or should the people now rightly turn, as good and patriotic Montenegrins, to this new Montenegrin Church, which was being run by the Metropolitan Mihailo from its small suburban house on the outskirts of that tiny capital in the mountains, Cetinje? It would be in Istanbul, I suspected, that I would be able to find the answer.

Because Istanbul was far more than what it appeared to be today—this bustling, polyglot, polytheistic crossroads city that stands on the cusps of both Europe and Asia and is eagerly planning a future for itself as a world capital enjoying the benefits of both the continents on which it lies. And it was much more than its predecessor Constantinople had been, too—far more than the exotic headquarters for the mighty but always dreamily expiring empire of the Ottomans. It had long also been Byzantium—ever since the schism that had split the Roman church in two it had been the spiritual center of the Orthodox Church.

For a thousand years, from the three hundreds until the Ottomans stormed the Hagia Sofia church in 1453, Byzantium had been the anchor to a Christian empire that stretched from Ravenna in the west to Mesopotamia in the east, from the Sava River in the north to Tripolitania in North Africa. The emperors ruled in Greek, as Christians; they employed Roman law and the basked in and spread the best of Hellenistic culture. The nearly ninety Byzantine emperors, from Zeno to Constantine XI, at their best ran a tolerant, prosperous, and enlightened empire. The most powerful architect of its fortunes, the great Emperor Justinian, who ruled for thirty-eight years in the sixth century, was born near what is now the great railway-junction city of Nis, in Yugoslavia. When NATO planes were bombing Nis, their pilots likely thought they were exerting enormous power over the land. Probably most were unaware that one of the very greatest forces ever to have shaped Balkan history came from directly below, deep within their target zone.

The rules of the Orthodox Church, worldwide, give all of the member churches—the Russians, the Greeks, the Serbs, the Cypriots—total autonomy and authority. Except in one small sense, a somewhat indistinct sense of external authority that hovers somewhere between sentiment and tradition, and that is vested in a figure known as the ecumenical patriarch, and who always lives in Istanbul. (Or Constantinople, as his business card defiantly proclaims.)

The patriarch—officially addressed as "Your Beatitude"—is always drawn from Istanbul's dwindling Greek community and is regarded officially by the government as simply the Greek patriarch. To the church worldwide, however, he is its still center—a symbol, not of authority, but of, let us say, Orthodox good manners. He will raise an eyebrow or look askance—and a whole canon of behavior in a distant patriarchate will subtly change. He is not there to order or to be obeyed: He is there to counsel, and to warn.

The current ecumenical patriarch, Bartholomew, was appointed in 1991, and like his predecessors for two thousand years, lives in the district of old Istanbul called the Fener, from the word *Phanar*, the Greek word for the lighthouse that once stood there to warn of a shoal in the Golden Horn. His achdeacon, a supreme authority on ecclesiastical questions, is an American named Peter Anton from San Antonio, Texas, and whose formal priestly name is Archdeacon Tarasios. He is a learned, fussy, bustling man, who when he had our audience was constantly on the telephone, handing out books and press releases and his E-mail address, all the time shooing in and out of his study supplicants and mendicants and aspirant priests, and those new members of the church who wished to be blessed by a brief audience with the patriarch himself.

His papers and utterances contain all manner of words utterly unfamiliar to the layman, suggesting Orthodoxy to be a most complicated faith: I saw on his desk, or noted him to have used the words *autocephalous, vicariate, exarch, pharmakolytria, eparchial, patristic,* and *stauropegial.* Not surprisingly, given such a vocabulary, it was difficult to pin him down to so simple a matter as whether the Montenegrin Church had the proper authority, or whether the people of Cetinje and Podgorica and Kotor should regard the priests of the Serbian Church as their spiritual leaders

But eventually he did offer an answer, though he did not wish to be quoted formally as saying anything at all. In ecclesiastical matters, it appeared, the Office of the Ecumenical Patriarchate of Constantinople holds the line. It has no direct power over the churches, except for a very small number of the less well known branches. But in matters of doctrine and discipline and one might say, taste, the patriarch attempts to exert what influence he can, and in a subtle, gentle manner. It might have been recently noticed, for instance, that the patriarch of Serbia made a sermon in Belgrade that was critical of Mr. Milosevic? Well, it was no secret that Bartholomew had spoken with him some while before—privately, quietly, and about what was not known. But a conversation had been held. A statement had been made. An American might say simply: Do the math.

In the specific matter of Montenegro, the matter was abundantly clear. The new Montenegrin Church was a wholly spurious invention. The man who calls himself Father Mihailo had held a post in Rome and was no longer doing so. It was not within the authority of the ecumenical patriarch to say why. But the properly constituted ecclesiastical authority in Montenegro is the Serbian Orthodox Church—and while that may not always be the case, it is very much the case now. The new one was merely spurious.

So that was it. The boys from the Sanjak had prophesied trouble in Montenegro. The people whom we had encountered while we were there had all warned of trouble in Montenegro. And now here was yet another reason, one might suppose, for why in time some Montenegrin people at least might have cause to feel slighted, or dismayed, or angry.

I felt gloomily apprehensive as we left the dusty confines of the Fener, with the chanting of monks echoing faintly from an upstairs room. It was remarkable, I thought, that here in old Istanbul, even now, there was a residual power and a relict influence that could manage still to stir the Balkan pot, to fan the Balkan flames, and to be the ultimate cause of distant havoc yet to come, in the lands that these people, Byzantine and Ottomans both, had each directed for so long.

We went down to Sultanahmet for our last dinner and sat outside at the Rumeli Café, drinking good Turkish beer and Anatolian red wine, and eating lamb and eggplant and almond *lokum* and coffee. We argued gently, as to whether what we had seen in the hundreds of miles that lay behind us had been anyone's *fault*—whether any one person, or place, or cultural or religious influence, could have been said to have led directly to the kind of troubles that we had seen and read about today and yesterday and for so very long before. Had it been the Turks, for instance—had it been their brutality, their corruption, the savage complications of their administrative formulae—that left such a residue of bitterness and hatred that only vengeance could assuage.

I was still haunted by George Higgins Moses, and the words in that old copy I had of a once-wise magazine. "It is at Constantinople," he wrote, and it seems well worth repeating,

that the problems of the Near East have always centered in their acutest form. There, where teeming thousands throng the Bridge of Galata; where twenty races meet and clash with differences of blood and faith never yet cloaked beneath even a pretense of friendliness; where fanaticism and intrigue play constantly beneath the sur-

face of oriental phlegmatism and sporadically break forth
in eddies of barbaric reaction; where all the Great Powers
of Europe have for generations practiced the art of a devi-
ous diplomacy—there, I say, has always been found the
real storm-center of the danger zone of Europe.

So could we perhaps agree with the old Serb proverb: "Grass
never grows where the Turkish hoof has trod"? Did those Serbs
who butchered Albanians in the weeks and months before ever
look into their victims' eyes and say to themselves, This, you
know—this is for the Turks?

Or do we think quite otherwise—and blame the Serbs as a
race? Or do we find fault with the southern Slavs as a people? Or
with the Illyrians, who claim so much of the now-Slavic Balkans as
their own? Or does the heart of the Eastern Question, as it was
known, lie within the Great Schism? Or is the fault with those dignified and duplicitous Viennese in general, or with that master
mechanician and geopolitical cynic, Prince Metternich, in particular? Was it all the result of the meddlesome dealings of the Great
Powers, the Triple Alliance of then, the United States today?

Or is it all to do with Islam—or is it the fault of all the gods,
conjoining Allah with the pantheons of Orthodoxy and the
Church of Rome as well? Or is it, more fundamentally, the geology, or the tectonics—for this is a place of earthquakes still,
even here in Istanbul—and earthquakes produce, do they not,
an unstable and fractious people?

Or perhaps do we blame no one and just shrug our shoulders and relegate the region to the backwaters as somewhere
incomprehensible, intractable, and, one is tempted to splutter
with exasperation, impossible?

But then it was a little before eight o'clock, and the sun had set
over the Sea of Marmara, and unseen, from one of the slender
minarets above the Blue Mosque, a *muezzin* began to call. His
voice, amplified by electronics, echoed and boomed around the

square, and for a moment all at the café tables, and all the people passing by outside, were stilled, enchanted and respectful of this ancient and poetic cry. I picked up my telephone as quietly as I could, and dialed the number of a woman I knew (and had once loved) in New York, where it was still the middle of the afternoon. She answered, and I held the telephone up into the soft air, and let her listen to a sound she knew well, and that I knew well that she would like to hear.

And as I played the sound of the Ottoman call to her all those thousands of miles away I gazed up into the purple of the Turkish evening sky, and I watched the seagulls circling, illuminated by the floodlights like tiny ghosts, as they glided endlessly around the very tips of the four minarets, and over the huge dome under which, even now, scores of the faithful were kneeling to their God in Mecca. The force of Islam, unchanging and unchanged, seemed then of a power and majesty like no other.

Silence fell, suddenly and thunderously. I put the telephone back to my ear, and in the distance I could hear the thin siren of a police car making its way up Madison Avenue. The ancient and the modern, the eternal and the fleeting, briefly connected in a flicker of electronics.

"That was enchanting," said the voice at the distant end. And then, "So—you've finished?"

"Yes," I replied. "I've arrived."

Epilogue

THREE DAYS LATER I was in Bulgaria again, buying an airline ticket for the journey back home. The airline office was almost empty but for the two ticket agents, both of whom were young women. I asked them where they were from.

One, it turned out, was an ethnic Turk from southern Bulgaria. The other had come down from Belgrade: She was a Serb. Her office had been closed because of the NATO bombing, and the company had temporarily transferred her to the office in Sofia.

I remarked with some surprise that this was rather unusual, having a Muslim and a member of the Serbian Orthodox Church working side by side. "Surely," I ventured, "and particularly now during the war, you must find working together very difficult indeed?

The women laughed, as if they had been asked this question once too often already.

"No, don't be absurd," one of them said. "We get along just fine."

And then they did something they had clearly rehearsed before, and had rehearsed well. Each of them raised her left arm and held it out straight, for me to see.

On each there was a gold wristwatch, by Cartier.

And that, of course—that they had money, that they could buy things, that they could escape the rigors of Balkan poverty—was the reason. And maybe, in time, and for everyone, it would be the answer.

Glossary and Dramatis Personae

AFOR   Acronym for NATO's Albania-based security force.

Aga   Turkish tribal leader.

Albanians   Non-Slavic Indo-European people, descendants of the ancient Illyrians, who inhabit Albania itself as well as much of the Serbian province of Kosovo and western Macedonia.

Andric, Ivo   1892–1975. The Nobel Prize–winning author (1961) of *The Bridge on the Drina* and other works, Andric was a Croatian-born Yugoslavian diplomat

Apache   American attack helicopter, formally the McDonnell Douglas AH-64, designed for day or night all-weather combat. Its reputation suffered somewhat in 1999 after the Apache was deployed in Albania and proved to be somewhat less than invaluable.

Attar of roses   A fragrant, volatile essence distilled from roses, used as a perfume base.

Bailey bridge   Prefabricated steel lattice bridge, designed by the British engineer Sir Donald Bailey and meant for rapid assembly on battlefields.

Balkans   The word *Balkans*, which comes from the Bulgarian word for mountain, loosely defines the peninsular region of southeastern Europe that is bounded by the Danube River, the Adriatic and Black Seas, and the border of Greece. But the word has also come to stand, in ways both sad and pejorative, for the intractability of the regions social and political problems and, more generally—and with the use of the words *Balkanize* and *Balkanization*—for the numerous attempts, usually failing, to alleviate the problems of mutually warring states by redrawing their boundaries to make them ever smaller and more ethnically exclusive.

Baklava   A Turkish dessert, made from pastry, honey, and nuts.

Berlin, Treaty of   An agreement among the European powers, forged during the summer of 1878, that essentially laid the foundations for the Balkan crises that have erupted with grim regularity ever since.

Bey   Turkish prince or governor.

Bogomil   A member of a heretical tenth-century Bulgarian dualist sect, believing that Satan and Christ were both sons of God.

Bosniak   Current colloquial name for a Bosnian Muslim; in Turkey the term is used for any Yugoslavian Muslim—Serb or Montenegrin, too—who chose to emigrate.

Byzantium   Former name of the city that was to become Constantinople and eventually modern Istanbul: the capital of the Eastern portion of the Roman Empire, which, with its Hellenistic religious traditions, survived for more than a thousand years after the collapse of Imperial Rome.

Caftan   A long, loose-flowing Turkish robe, favored briefly by young Westerners of indolent habits.

Caliph   The chief civil and religious ruler in Muslim society. In the Ottoman Empire the sultan was also caliph, but when the sultanate and the caliphate were dissociated in 1922, the last ruler was reduced to being a caliph only.

Chetnik   Serbian guerrilla fighter, often now used as a term of Muslim or Croat abuse. The word means "Yugoslav Army of the Fatherland." *See also* Partisans.

Chinook   Twin-rotor helicopter, the CH-47, made by Boeing and used for transporting troops (it can carry up to forty) and heavy matériel, including underslung vehicles.

Chokidar   Hindi word for "night watchman."

Constantinople   Ottoman capital of Turkey, 1453–1923: formerly Byzantium, now Istanbul. The Orthodox Church headquarters still regards it as the city's proper name.

Convertible marks   Currency now used in Bosnia, on a par with the deutsche mark.

Cook's Continental   Former and now colloquial name for monthly European railway and ferry timetable published by Thos. Cook, carried by all seasoned travelers and homebound dreamers. The rest of the world is covered in Cook's equally legendary *Overseas Timetable.*

Crna Gora   The local name for Montenegro.

Czarigrad   The name Russia planned to give to Constantinople in the event of their successful occupation of the city in 1878.

Dayton   Generally accepted name for Bosnian peace-and-partition agreement secured at Wright-Patterson Air Force Base near Dayton, Ohio, in November 1995.

Didicoi   The Romany word for Gypsy, or Roma.

Dinaric Alps   Range of steep limestone mountains defining the Adriatic coast of the former Yugoslavia.

Dinkel   A wheatlike grain, grown in southern Europe, also known as spelt.

Divan   The Turkish council, which, under the chairmanship of the grand vizier, essentially ran the Ottoman Empire; also the long, low seat where audiences were held or judgments given.

Djukanovic, Milo   The young (b. 1962) prime minister of the Yugoslav Federation's Republic of Montenegro.

Doge   The duke or chief magistrate of the Republics of Venice and Genoa.

Dragoman   A guide-interpreter in, generally, a Near Eastern or Islamic country.

Eastern Question   The former term, often used with a sense of weary exasperation, for the political problems of the Balkans and Southeastern Europe.

Egnatian Way   The Roman road connecting the Adriatic with the Bosporus, running from what is now Albania through Greece to Turkey.

Effendi   Sir, Master.

Emir   A prince, a Turkish military commander.

Eothen   Meaning "from the East," the title of and only difficult word in Alexander Kinglake's magnificent book of travels in the Near East, published in 1844 and never since out of print.

Fener   The old Greek quarter of Istanbul, and headquarters of the Orthodox Church—the only surviving relic of old Byzantium.

FYROM   Acronym for the Former Yugoslav Republic of Macedonia, used in some quarters to soothe Greek anger at what they consider Skopje's illegal expropriation of the name of their eastern province.

Gheg   A northern Albanian people and language, in constant rivalry with their southern neighbors, the Tost (*q.v.*).

Grand vizier   The Chief Imperial Minister of the Ottoman Empire, the hugely powerful right-hand man of the Sultan.

Gurkha   Diminutive Nepalese soldiers of fierce reputation, hundreds of whom have been assigned since Indian independence to both the British and Indian armies, and claiming to be mercenaries in neither force. Their loyalty to the British crown is legendary, and they have won many battle honors in wars and skirmishes from Burma to the Falkland Islands. A Gurkha battalion assigned to NATO was the first regular unit into Kosovo in June 1999.

Gusla   A single-stringed bowed instrument of mournful sound used by Slavs to accompany the reciting of epic poems.

Halal   Food prepared according to Islamic law and tradition.

Halvah   A Turkish sweet made of honey and sesame flour.

Hammam   The Turkish bath: communal, steamy, and dreamily erotic.

Hammer film   Low-budget horror movie, after the somewhat-less-than-Oscar-standard sex-and-gore films made at the London-based Hammer Film Studios.

Hapsburg   Great European sovereign dynasty, originating at Castle Hapsburg in Aargau, Switzerland, and ruling, through its Spanish and Austro-Hungarian branches, immense swaths of territory from Holland to the Balkans.

Harem   The family quarters or, more commonly, the female quarters of a substantial Turkish or Arab house or palace.

Herzegovina   The hot and dry southern portion—named for a German duke, or *herzog*—of the Bosnian Federation.

Hofburg   Vienna's vast imperial palace, from which the Hapsburgs ruled for six centuries, until 1918.

Hoxha, Enver   Albanian leader and principal architect of the state's fiercely isolationist, rigidly xenophobic, and diehard communist policies. He died in 1985 and is little missed.

Humvee   U.S. Army–made High Mobility Vehicle, with distinctive wide-track appearance. A civilian version, the Hummer, has found some limited appeal among the American rich.

IFOR   In Bosnia, NATO's Dayton-agreement Implementation Force.

Illyria   Country north and east of the Adriatic, roughly congruent with the Dinaric Alps (*q.v.*), and subsumed into the former Yugoslavia.

Imam   The officiating leader of prayer in a Muslim mosque.

Istria   A large peninsula on the eastern Adriatic coast, south of Trieste.

Ixarette   Sign language, introduced for reasons of serenity and dignity to the Ottoman court by Süleyman the Magnificent (*q.v.*), and initially taught by a pair of mute brothers.

Janissary The Ottoman Empire's crack infantry soldiers, and Sultan's guard: often, and until their abolition in 1826, they were Slavs, tributary children from Balkan Christian families.

Jasenovac Notorious Croatian concentration camp near Zagreb, where thousands of Serbs and Jews were butchered, often following forcible conversion to Catholicism.

Juche North Korea's rigid policy, invented by Kim Il Sung, of socialist self-sufficiency.

Kaaba The black dolerite cube at the center of the Great Mosque in Mecca, and thus the spiritual heart of the Islamic faith.

Kapia The wider central part of a Turkish-built bridge, where merchants might set up stalls, sentries might stand, and passersby might rest or stop to gossip.

Karst Porous limestone and the unusually dramatic topography that it and the erosive effect of rain- and stream-waters help create.

Kastrioti, Gjerg The former name of the great Albanian warrior-hero, Skanderbeg (*q.v.*).

KFOR NATO's Kosovo Force.

Kismet The Turkish word for fate.

KLA Kosovo Liberation Army, a guerrilla group bent on securing an independent Kosovar state. *See also* UCK.

Krajina The old military frontier between the Austro-Hungarian and Ottoman Empires, populated on Hapsburg initiative by Serbian refugees, creating Serbian Orthodox enclaves in what later became Catholic Croatia.

Kukri The sharp curved knife traditionally carried by all Gurkhas (*q.v.*). The legendary sharpness of the weapons is such that, during the Falklands War, Argentine soldiers were led to believe they could have their heads cut off during the night and not know it. It briefly became part of the wake-up drill for some less intelligent conscripts to shake their heads to make sure this had not happened.

Lazar, Prince Heroic Serb leader, subject of countless epic poems, who was defeated by the Ottomans—choosing death rather than dishonor at Turkish hands—at the Battle of Kosovo Polje in 1389.

Lokum From the Turkish phrase for "comfortable morsel," the soft, gummy, and sweetly fragrant substance that came to be known as "Turkish delight."

Konditorei An elegant, mirrored Viennese coffeehouse, often frequented by middle-aged women.

Mamelukes Egyptian rulers, originally Caucasian slaves, who ruled from Cairo under the authority of an Ottoman viceroy.

Marmite A dark and viscous yeasty delight much loved by Britons, and fervently missed by all expatriates; not to be confused with the similarly colored but feeble Australian imitator known as Vegemite.

Metternich, Prince Clemens von Austrian statesman, one of the great geopoliticians of all time, architect of nineteenth-century European stability and conservatism.

Metropolitan A senior Orthodox cleric, senior in rank to an archbishop but inferior to a patriarch: addressed as "Your Beatitude."

Milosevic, Slobodan The almost universally reviled bogeyman of the Balkan conflict since 1989, he remains indicted by the Hague War Crimes tribunal, though simultaneously remaining president of his country. Milosevic was born of a Montenegrin father and mother, both of whom killed themselves; he married and remains married to his childhood sweetheart, Mirjana, who, as is so often the case, appears to be the power behind this particular throne. Milosevic, a former official in the Yugoslav gas monopoly and an exceptionally skillful Communist Party boss, has managed to outflank almost all foreigners with whom he has had to deal, giving him a

reputation as one of the craftiest and most difficult nationalist figures in postwar Europe. There is a belief abroad, almost
certainly erroneous, that his removal from office would solve
the Balkan problems for all time; most nations' foreign policies include his removal high on their global wish lists.

Muezzin   The public crier who calls the Islamic faithful to
prayer from the minaret of a mosque.

Mullah   An Islamic scholar and divine.

MUP   The Serbian special police, dark of uniform and, it is
said, of intent.

Nansen passport   Identification papers issued to stateless per-
sons following the massive European refugee movements of
World War I; named for Fridtjof Nansen (1861–1930), the
Arctic explorer who championed the cause of the displaced.

Novi Pazar   A fingerlike extension of onetime Ottoman rule
between Serbia, Bosnia, and Montenegro, which housed
many sacred Orthodox relics and churches. The people
from this so-called sanjak (*q.v.*) are invariably Slavic Muslim
converts, reputed for their trading abilities and commercial
cunning.

Ocalan, Abdullah   Kurdish guerrilla leader and terrorist
fighter; Serb militants like to point to his violent predilec-
tions as an indication that, in the region, Milosevic and his
allies do not have a monopoly on making mayhem.

Oslobodenje   Sarajevo daily newspaper, published continuously
during the city's three-year siege, 1992–95.

Osmanlee   Alternative spelling for the name of the Ottoman
(*q.v.*) dynasty.

Ottoman   The dynasty founded by Osman (or Othman) I, in
or around 1300, whose forces swept through western Turkey
to capture Byzantium in 1453 and thereafter conquered a
vast region from Central Europe to Africa and the Middle
East, which was known as the Ottoman Empire. Following
the unsuccessful siege of Vienna in 1683, a long period of

decay ensued, the empire eventually becoming known as "the sick man of Europe." The final sultan was forced to abdicate in 1922, ending the Ottomans' immense influence on world history.

Partisans   Antifascist liberation guerrilla fighters in wartime Yugoslavia, led by Josip Broz Tito (*q.v.*). *See also* their Serbian counterparts, the Chetniks.

Pasha   A Turkish military commander, his rank noted by the number of horsetails—three being the highest—displayed as a symbol in war.

Pavelic, Ante   Croatian fascist leader during World War II, whose irregular Ustashi (*q.v.*) troops committed a series of particularly dreadful atrocities against Serbs, Jews, and others, largely at the behest of the occupying Nazis. Pavelic died in Madrid in 1959.

Porte, The Sublime   Used allusively to mean the Ottoman Empire—in fact the gateway into the grand vizier's offices, and to the Ottoman divan.

Portmeirion   Holiday village in North Wales, designed in Mediterranean-fantasy style by the eccentrically brilliant architect Sir Clough Williams-Ellis. The village was made famous as the setting for the 1960s television series *The Prisoner*, starring Patrick McGoohan.

Princip, Gavrilo   Serb nationalist assassin of the Archduke Franz Ferdinand, heir to the Hapsburg throne, in Sarajevo, on June 28, 1914—the event that essentially triggered World War I. His blow against the Austro-Hungarian Empire was regarded as heroic until the mid-1990s, when Sarajevo's understandably altered mood toward all Serbs resulted in the plaque and his footprints, memorials to the event, being removed.

Rasputin   Siberian mystic, healer, and philanderer who was introduced to the imperial Russian court by Militsa, daughter of the Montenegrin king.

Raznatovic, Zeljko Serbian paramilitary leader also known by his *nom de guerre* Arkan: viciously nationalistic, leader of a group of irregulars, the Tigers, and perpetrator of appalling atrocities.

Ricin Poison derived from the castor bean, used in the murder of the Bulgarian dissident Georgi Markov.

Sanjak (in Turkish, *sancàk*) An Ottoman military district.

SAS Special Air Services, a British army unit often detailed for small-scale, undercover, deniable military operations.

Seselj, Vojislav Serbian ultranationalist paramilitary leader, associate of Milosevic (*q.v.*), though later imprisoned by him.

SFOR NATO's Stabilization Force based in Bosnia, successor to IFOR (*q.v.*).

Shqiperi Albania.

Sigurimi Albanian secret police.

Sigurnost Bulgarian secret police.

Skanderbeg Albania's best-beloved martial hero, 1405–68, given his name and title—*Iskander-bey*, Prince Alexander—by the Turks who raised him; he later embraced Christianity, returned to Albania, and successfully repelled thirteen attempted Turkish invasions. *See also* Kastrioti, Gjerg.

Slav An enormous eastern and southern European racial grouping that embraces, among others, Russians, Bulgarians, Serbs, Croats, Bosnians, Montenegrins, Slovenes, Poles, Czechs, and Slovaks.(But notably not Albanians, however.) The country known as Yugoslavia (*q.v.*) was a loose union of the southern (*Jugo*) Slavs.

Sofa An elevated platform on which supplicants were permitted to sit during an audience with a high official of the Ottoman court. Sometimes the hall of audience itself.

Srpska, Republika The Serbian-dominated "entity" within Bosnia, created in the wake of Dayton (*q.v.*), and effectively ruled as a separate semiautonomous province, distinct from the Bosnian-Croat Federation that rules the remainder of the country.

Stari Most   The exquisite Turkish-built bridge (1566) over the Neretva river in Mostar (which derives its name from the Turkish word for bridge), destroyed by Croatian artillery in November 1993—ironically on the anniversary of the tearing down of the Berlin Wall. Its four centuries of existence stood as a symbol of the ethnic cohesion of Bosnia; its destruction showed that same cohesion's vulnerability and fragility.

Stari Planina   The Bulgarian name for the Balkan Mountains, which have given their name—the word *Balkan* means simply "mountains"—to the entire region.

Stepinac, Alojzije   1898–1960. The Roman Catholic archbishop of Zagreb reputed in some quarters to have given tacit ecclesiastical support to Ante Pavelic (*q.v.*) and his notorious Ustashi fighters during World War II; imprisoned for alleged war crimes. Catholic supporters claim he was a victim of Communist propaganda. Elevated to the status of Cardinal in 1952 by Pope Pius XII, and beatified by Pope John Paul in 1996. Jews and Serbs in particular, who suffered horribly at the hands of the Ustashi, find the Vatican's unyielding respect for Stepinac somewhat unseemly, and controversy about his wartime role—which, in the absence of several mysteriously missing records, is uncertain—continues.

Süleyman the Magnificent   1495–1566, ruled the Ottoman Empire as Sultan Süleyman I, from 1520 to 1566. It is generally recognized that during his reign, the Ottomans achieved the zenith of their administrative, military, and architectural genius. Istanbul's largest and grandest mosque, Süleymaniye, is a breathtaking reminder of his achievements.

Sultan   The Turkish sovereign.

Tito, Josip Broz   1892–1980, the anti-Soviet Communist leader of Yugoslavia, whose skills in holding the fractious ethnic groups together in a single country are now regarded with nostalgia as a mark of rare political genius. Tito's father was a Croat, his mother a Slovene; and the young Josip Broz (the name *Tito* was added when he was forty-two) was apprenticed as a locksmith. His rise to power began when, as an antifascist communist leader, he led his Partisan (*q.v.*) fighters to harass the occupying Germans. He ruled Yugoslavia as president from 1953 until his death, and remained a figure much respected by all sides in the later conflicts.

Tost (or Tosk)   Albanian tribal group, composed of peoples living generally south of the Shkumbi River, most often landless and subsistence-level peasants. *See also* Gheg.

UCK   Initials of the vernacular name of the Kosovo Liberation Army.

Ustashi   Irregular Croat nationalist army, closely allied with the Nazis in World War II, which committed appalling bestialities against Serbs, Jews and other minorities. *See also* Pavelic, Ante.

Vizier   An Ottoman minister-administrator.

VJ   Vojska Jugoslavije—the rump Yugoslav army, generally now Serbian, with a number of pressed Montenegrin recruits.

Vlach   The name for those Christian herdsmen who, along with the Serbs, originally populated much of the region between the Danube and the northern Adriatic.

Wehrmacht   The World War II name for the German army, and which after the defeat fell out of favor. It is now returning to more common usage, as for the German units recently attached to NATO in the Balkans.

Yali   An elegant waterside residence, often made of wood and with a formal tulip garden, on the shores of the Bosporus in Constantinople (*q.v.*).

Yugoslavia   A relatively short-lived and inherently unstable federation of southern Slavic peoples that was born after World War I as the Kingdom of the Serbs, Croats, and Slovenes, and which began to disintegrate after little more than seventy years, following the death of President Tito (*q.v.*). The name is currently retained for the Federation of Serbia and Montenegro, but the name *Yugoslavia*—which means, literally, "the union of southern Slavs"—has very little semantic validity.

Zupan   Leader of a *zupa*, a confederation of Serbian villages.

Suggestions for Further Reading

T O ANYONE WRITING about the Balkans swiftly comes the sobering and humbling realization that there are already an immense number of books on the region—the shelves at the library of the Royal Geographical Society in London, where I always go first when embarking on a foreign trip, positively groan with tomes, but tomes that are, by and large, almost as unreadable as they are apparently indigestible. From the beginning of the nineteenth century every historian, every writer of letters to *The Times*—every motorist, even—seemed to wanted to play a part in a debate on the Eastern Question, to have his say at great length, and then for posterity place his say between covers of red morocco. And the tradition continues to this day: Few regions of the world can have exerted—and continue to exert— such a magnetic pull on the world's literary drabs, and works of terrible dullness and labyrinthine sobriety continue to thunder from the presses, destined to win a few respectful and uncomprehending reviews and then to molder and gather eternal dust. Most deserve to go unread; and if this book suffers the same fate, then I can't say that I wasn't warned.

But assuming that some readers remain engaged, as I surely am, by the infuriating enticements of the Balkans, I would direct their attention to just three books that stand out, head and shoulders, from all the rest. The familiar but little-read 1943 classic by Rebecca West, *Black Lamb and Grey Falcon*, though far too long and far too full of amusing invention to impress purists and pedants, remains wonderfully readable and hugely wise. Robert Kaplan has done a splendid job with his *Balkan Ghosts*, written in 1993, even though he deals more rigorously with Greece and Bulgaria than with the Balkans in the strictest sense, and even though his writing has been so lucid as to influence heavily President Clinton's policy caprices in the region. And finally, and most important of all, there is Ivo Andric, who won the Nobel Prize for Literature in 1961 in part for having written, in 1945, *The Bridge on the Drina*, a work that captures the beguiling insanity of the Balkans like no other, and that will make even the sternest of historians weep at the madness of it all.

All three volumes are still in print (in paperback, from Penguin, Vintage, and the University of Chicago Press, respectively), and should be devoured by anyone who wishes to take a further interest in what is, it has to be remembered, an unending story—a saga that will go on, I suppose, until the waters of the deluge finally submerge every last spire and minaret and steeple between the Danube and the Peloponnese.

For Help Along the Way

F IRST, AND WITHOUT THE SLIGHTEST DOUBT, I want to
thank quite unreservedly my good friend and helpmeet
Rose George, who kindly took time off from a holiday in India
to accompany me through a long spring and summer in the
Balkans, and to apply her crucial linguistic and critical faculties
to the successful completion of the adventure. We make in the
best of circumstances a most unlikely couple: separated by more
than two decades and living three thousand miles apart, we are
perpetually and fundamentally at odds with one another on
almost every level—we disagree on everything from politics to
diet (she, an ardent vegetarian, facing something of a problem
among the Slavic carnivores), from music to motor cars—and
we spend much of our time fighting like furies. But we are
somehow addicted to one another's company, and we remain at
heart the best of friends. She is for me the ideal traveling companion, and I find it difficult to contemplate any journey to the
faraway—as recently to the Corryvreckan whirlpool in Scotland,
or to Manila, or the back streets of Osaka—without hoping that
she comes along. She was of invaluable assistance on this occasion, and I doubt if I could have written the book without her.

Before and during the journey we met a wide variety of helpful people (though occasionally, and especially in Kosovo, some who were very unhelpful indeed). Among those whom I wish to thank most particularly are Peter Anton, Patrick Bishop, Avis Bohlen, Daut Bozokurt, Robin Clifford, Guy Crofton, Zlatko Dizdarevic, Shaun Going, Peter Hunt, Danica Jankovic, Günter Düriegl, Jorgen Grunnet, Pyotr Gwozdz, Sybilla Hamann, David Harrison, Mike Jackson, Peter January, Christian Jorgensen, Doris Knecht, Lejla Komarica, Lena Kovalenko, Dieter Lorraine, Jelka Lowne, Erwin Lucius, Sylvie Mattl, Simon Mann, Jean Meisel, Sarah Miller, Fritz Molden, Janet Rogan, Don Branco Sbutega, Mike Scanlon, Vesna Stamenkovic, Milena Stantcheva, Daliborka Uljarevic, Tom Wallace, and, as always, my friend Juliet Walker.

Larry Ashmead of HarperCollins was kind enough to suggest this book, after I had first visited Macedonia on assignment for the genial and generous Con Coughlin, foreign editor of the *Sunday Telegraph*, and to whom I thus owe an immense debt. Juliet Annan of Viking Penguin in London was similarly enthusiastic about asking me to attempt the formidable task of making some sense out of the chaos of the Balkans. I did at first wonder if I was being handed the most poisoned of chalices; if there are errors of judgment, fact, or interpretation, they are very much my own and should in no way reflect on the eagerness of others that I attempt this book.

I wish to thank my agents, Peter Matson in New York and Bill Hamilton in London, as well as Agnes Krup and her tireless and adorable assistant at the time, Jenny Meyer. The tireless invigilations of Allison McCabe and Anya Waddington, my editors in New York and London, respectively, helped turned my unorganized scribblings into something approaching a coherent narrative—as did Sue Llewellyn's assiduous copyediting—and for this I thank them wholeheartedly.

The editorial staff at *Condé Nast Traveler* in New York—Tom Wallace, Gully Wells, Lisa Hughes, Gerry Rizzo—were splendidly supportive, as they always manage to be when I absent myself for long periods of time. They were especially tolerant on this occasion, considering that I was writing about a part of the planet that currently, and for understandable reasons, attracts precious few tourists and hardly any people who wander the world for pleasure and enlightenment. My fondest hope, in the aftermath of this terrible little war, is that the Balkans may quieten themselves now, a quiet that will in time perhaps allow visitors to find their way into some of the loveliest countryside imaginable, and to encounter a people whose pride, history, and passion render them, in more peaceful times, the most endearing, most fascinating, and most unforgettable Europeans of all.

The Balkans in 1999

Listen to

The Professor and the Madman

As read by the author

Simon Winchester

ISBN 0-694-52243-0 • $29.95/$43.50 (Can.)
6 1/2 hours • 6 cassettes; Unabridged

"Winchester's reading is perfectly suited
to the material. Highly recommended."
— *Austin American Statesman*

"Kudos go to Winchester, a born reader who narrates
with great style, sucking you into this tale of two
dissimilar men working toward a shared goal."
—*San Antonio Express-News*

"One of the best of the year."
— *Library Journal*

Praise for the abridged version, read by Simon Jones

ISBN 0-694-452066-4 • $18.00/$26.50 (Can.);
3 hours • 2 cassettes; Abridged

"The drama and twists of turns of life are highlighted by the
author's words and the elegant reading by Simon Jones."
—*The Chapel Hill News*

Available at your local bookstore, or call 1-800-331-3761 to order.

 HarperAudio
A Division of HarperCollinsPublishers
www.harpercollins.com